D0792950

Studio Thinking 2

THE REAL BENEFITS OF VISUAL ARTS EDUCATION

Second Edition

LOIS HETLAND,
ELLEN WINNER, SHIRLEY VEENEMA,
AND KIMBERLY M. SHERIDAN

Foreword to the Second Edition by Louise Music
Foreword to the First Edition by David N. Perkins

Teachers College, Columbia University
New York and London

National Art Education Association
Reston, Virginia

For Elliot Eisner, who blazed the trail,

and for Maestro Mateo Hazelwood, 1954–2012,
who championed the translation of Studio Habits to music education.

Published simultaneously by Teachers College Press, 1234 Amsterdam Avenue, New York, NY 10027
and the National Art Education Association, 1806 Robert Fulton Drive, Suite 300, Reston, VA 20191

All photos are by Shirley Veenema, with the following exceptions: page 5, Figure 1.1, Exhibition photo by
David Ardito; in the color insert: top 2 photos for "Sam's Transformation Over 4 Years" by Kim Sheridan; all
photos for "A Feast for Your A-MUSE-ment" by Mónika Aldarondo

Library of Congress Cataloging-in-Publication Data

Hetland, Lois, 1953–
    Studio thinking 2 : the real benefits of visual arts education / Lois Hetland, Ellen Winner,
        Shirley Veenema, and Kimberly M. Sheridan ; foreword to the second edition by Louise Music ;
        foreword to the first edition by David N. Perkins. — Second Edition.
            pages cm
    Includes bibliographical references and index.
    ISBN 978-0-8077-5435-1 (pbk. : alk. paper)
        1. Art—Study and teaching—United States. 2. Team learning approach in education—United States.
    I. Title. II. Title: Studio thinking two.
    N353.S78 2013
    707.1—dc23   2012048854

ISBN 978-0-8077-5435-1 (paper)

Printed on acid-free paper
Manufactured in the United States of America

20 19 18 17 16 15 14 13   8 7 6 5 4 3 2 1

Contents

Foreword to the Second Edition

In 2003, the Alameda County Office of Education made a commitment to bring more arts into the 18 school districts of Alameda County. Our schools were under-resourced and had an unacceptable racial achievement gap and drop-out rate—30% for Hispanic students and 40% for African American students. And at that time, No Child Left Behind policies compelled most educators to place a disproportionate amount of attention on preparing for high-stakes measures that judged educational success narrowly on test scores in mathematics and English language arts and squeezed out time for history, social studies, science, and the visual and performing arts. It was no easy task to make a case for arts in education under these circumstances.

As a strategy, the Alameda County Office of Education (ACOE) developed a partnership, funded by the U.S. Department of Education, the J. Paul Getty Trust, and the Ahmanson Foundation, with researchers from Project Zero at the Harvard Graduate School of Education, faculty from the Center for Art and Public Life at the California College of the Arts, and teachers and administrators in public schools in Oakland, Berkeley, and Emery school districts. Our goal was to pilot the newly minted and not-yet-published Studio Thinking Framework. Teachers found that using the Studio Habits of Mind deepened student and teacher engagement and continuously informed decisions about art-making and program improvement. The Studio Habits became a foundation for discovering powerful intersections across subjects that then served as starting points for the purposeful and reflective practice of arts integration. Over time, we formalized what had been learned from Studio-Thinking-in-practice into a certificate program of courses that builds the capacity of K–12 teachers and teaching artists as leaders of professional learning communities for arts integration in schools and districts.

Now, 10 years later, the second edition of *Studio Thinking* emerges at an historic and urgent moment in public education. National, state, and regional leaders across the country are preparing for the 2014–2015 school year when multiple-choice standardized tests will be replaced with a new generation of performance assessments aligned to Common Core State Standards. Two national Race to the Top initiatives, SMARTER Balanced Assessment Consortium (SBAC) and Performance Assessment Partnership for Readiness for College and Careers (PARCC), have involved 46 states in a conversation about how educators can best prepare our nation's children to embrace and successfully engage with the daunting challenges of the future. The tide is turning toward thinking and learning!

The new CCSS represent a grand and necessary departure from the fragmented bits of knowledge and skills of previous state content standards. The previous standards were long lists that often broke up rich and connected learning opportunities into narrow bites that required "teaching to" mastery of particular facts and skills. In contrast, the new CCSS provide opportunities for applying English language arts and mathematical practices in authentic contexts. For example, students might be asked to make persuasive arguments about issues of civil rights in history or social studies, or to apply mathematical skills of modeling and mental reasoning to developing an understanding of environmental degradation in science. In other words, the new approach initiated by the CCSS asks teachers to support students in *using* what they know to achieve something important.

That approach parallels how we in Alameda County have used Studio Thinking in arts integration—to bring artful thought and attitudes to bear on real-world problems and projects, both in arts classrooms and across the curriculum. The Studio Habits of Mind name what is core in the arts. They are the verbs of thought, action, and attitude in the arts, just as the English language arts and mathematics Common Core State Standards (CCSS) are for those content areas. Our decade of using the Studio Thinking Framework in California's schools positions us for success in this new era because of the foundation of reflective, creative, and critical thinking developed in our schools and districts.

Practitioners in Alameda County, throughout California, and across the country who have been using the Studio Habits of Mind to plan instruction and assess student learning hold a rich archive of examples from practice that can illuminate the transition in all disciplines to new performance assessments aligned to CCSS. In September 2012, we began to share and extend our ongoing learning through discussions within a virtual network of teachers, teaching artists, and school administrators in Illinois, Massachusetts, New York, Minnesota, Colorado, Utah, Missouri, and elsewhere. Once a month we gather online for much-needed collegial conversations, hosted by the Chicago Teachers' Center at Northeastern Illinois University, about how the Studio Habits of Mind connect to good professional practice, to planning and assessment in the arts, and to making visible the essential role of the arts in a complete education for every student.

As we learn again and again in these and other professional conversations, there is much good experience to build on as the education community seeks to re-create professional practice, re-imagine issues of learning and teaching, and hold itself to new standards of shared accountability through an emerging generation of improved performance assessments aligned to CCSS. A lot has been learned already about the power of the arts to infuse and animate learning and teaching in the other content areas, in ways that bring those subjects to life and that fully engage young people and teachers alike. Now we have the chance to apply that learning broadly.

Education is in a new moment of both opportunity and urgency. Our ability as educators to make needed improvements in public education has everything to do with whether our society will be able to address the critical and pressing issues of democracy, economy, environment, interdependence, and diplomacy that we face as a global community. As educators, policymakers, and citizens, the Studio Thinking Framework helps us confront the issues of our time with a renewed appreciation not only for the essential role of the arts in transforming education, but also with useful strategies for communicating across differences, engaging and persisting in spite of frustration and difficulty, and envisioning and creating innovative solutions to the challenges of our shared future.

A Chinese proverb says that luck occurs at the intersection of opportunity and effort. We in Alameda County were, by that definition, very lucky in 2003 when we took the opportunity to work with and benefit from the research of Lois Hetland, Ellen Winner, Shirley Veenema, and Kimberly Sheridan. Embracing this new research-based analytical framework and inserting it into a stressful educational environment required the commitment and mutual support of dedicated teachers, teaching artists, school administrators, and project personnel. That investment paid off from the start, and now the national implementation of Studio Thinking across disciplines provides a strong base of knowledge and practitioner research to build into the true promise of the CCSS. For us, Studio Thinking has been the key that unlocks both self and community visions that tap into human motivation, ability, and wisdom so that, together, educators can partner with youth and create a better future for everyone.

—Louise Music,
Executive Director of Integrated Learning,
Alameda County Office of Education,
Hayward, CA, September 2012

Foreword to the First Edition

You do not have to read very far into *Studio Thinking* to feel that, like Lewis Carroll's Alice, you have stepped through the looking glass into a fantasy world where the colors are brighter, the scenes richer, and the adventure altogether more engaging than what you recall about school. You are likely to find rather drab not only many of your memories of studying mathematics or history, but also many of your school arts experiences. Certainly I do. It's not that my arts teachers lacked the knack; I actually think they were rather good. It's just that not enough time was staked out for the patterns of learning we read about here.

So, having stepped through the looking glass into this strange world of studio learning, how do we make sense of it all? Here the pathways branch. Maybe the visual arts are a special sort of undertaking, some might say. Or maybe these are very special teachers and very special students. Or maybe this is the sort of messing around we can afford when we're not dealing with high-stakes core subject matters.

But what if none of these answers leads anywhere worthwhile? What if, far from a fantasy world, studio learning turns out to be much more realistic regarding the way learning really works than most typical classroom settings?

Toward vetting these possibilities, let's get a little clearer about that studio world on the other side of the looking glass. Exactly what is so very exotic about it, compared to typical patterns of educational practice? My longtime colleagues Lois Hetland, Ellen Winner, Shirley Veenema, and Kim Sheridan do a fine job of portraying the world they have studied, the rhythm and the drama and sometimes the comedy of the studio classroom. For one thing, as the name studio thinking suggests, students spend most of their time developing works of art, instead of reading books or listening to ideas from their arts instructors or doing highly targeted technical exercises. We discover that all these traditional elements have a presence, but with distinctive proportion and placement. We learn that receiving information in the form of Demonstration–Lectures is a strong part of the pattern, but information is immediately applied as the studio work proceeds. It's not just for next week or the year after, it's for today—this canvas, this pot, this sculpture. We also learn that the studio work is spiced with a surprising amount of reflection. The studio teachers we meet are constantly circulating among the learners, prodding them to think about what they are doing and why they are doing it, as well as conducting critical reflective sessions where the group stands back and contemplates the enterprise, its significance, its progress, its shortfalls, and its lessons for the future.

This quick picture of events on the other side of the looking glass leads toward a big generalization. Most educational practice reflects what might be called an *export paradigm*. What learners do today focuses on exporting knowledge for use in a range of envisioned futures. The math in the textbook is for application somewhere, sometime, in some supermarket or on some income tax form or during possible careers in business, engineering, or science. The history acquired might someday help to make sense of an election and to cast a vote more wisely. The specific activities—problem sets for honing skills, answering questions toward understanding principles, memorizing information toward quizzes—are blatantly exercises that target much later payoffs.

What is so very odd about studio learning is its *import paradigm*. It's about using knowledge right now in a serious way for a complex and significant endeavor. Learners deploy what their instructors explain and demonstrate to produce meaningful and engaging works of art. Of course, it's not just about now, it's about later too. The world of later is well served by the kinds of projects addressed and the reflective discourse around them.

Studio learning is not the only pattern of pedagogy that attempts this import paradigm. Many teachers of the core disciplines find ways to engage learners in problem-based learning, project-based learning, case study approaches to learning, and community participation activities, to mention a few. Although such endeavors (like studio learning) can vary enormously in their quality, they display a common deep structure: Students learn for later by importing knowledge into rich undertakings now.

Back to the looking glass question: Where is the fantasy and where is the reality for learning? Well, speaking of looking glasses, it's worth remembering that the whole point of education is to function as a mirror of the future—not a flat mirror, presenting to the learner an anticipated future in all its messy, complicated, and upsetting details, but a convex mirror that renders the future in a substantially reduced and more tractable but still multidimensional form. Learning is likely to be successful to the extent that what learners do today mirrors the future. So the basic point here is pretty simple: An import paradigm in general is a better mirror of the future than an export paradigm, even though, paradoxically, the export paradigm seems to shoot for the future more directly.

Why is the import paradigm a better mirror? Turning to studio thinking specifically, studio activities are fully developed junior versions of what we would like learners to get better at and do more of later. Good studio activities capture the full motivational, technical, and creative dynamic of creating works of art as a professional artist or a serious amateur might do later in life. There are challenges of craft and of expression. There are experiments, failures, and successes. There are demands for reflection and self-discipline. Without the authors' sensitive profile, one might imagine studio work as mostly a matter of developing technical skills. Nothing of the sort. While this is part of the game, the learners' struggles with their challenges cultivate a number of studio habits of mind, for example: persistence, envisioning possibilities, expressing, observing, reflecting, and stretching beyond the immediate and familiar.

The export paradigm does not score so well as a mirror of the future. For one thing, the mirror is often broken into a hundred shards, reflecting only bits and pieces of what will come. The export paradigm suffers from what I like to call "elementitis." We teach the elements now, with the idea that they will coalesce later. We teach component skills, vocabulary, principles, theories, core examples, and when a student asks, "But what is it all for?" the answer promises that it will all come together next year, or in high school, or in college. Mind you, this is not a caution against spending some serious time on technical elements that need targeted development.

We see plenty of that in studio work. It's a caution against the endless deferral of large-scale meaningful undertakings.

The export paradigm also tends to suffer from "aboutitis." The export paradigm tries to approach future complexities by talking about them rather than engaging in them. Thus, students typically learn information *about* history—often rather intricate stories about what happened and how others interpreted it—rather than engaging in historical reasoning or interpreting current events through an historical lens. The analogy in the world of art would be learning a lot about artistic creative processes without actually doing much of it. Aboutitis, like elementitis, makes education less of a mirror of the future.

There is a natural reservation about all this. However stimulating our journey through the looking glass of studio learning, perhaps like Lewis Carroll's fantasy worlds it speaks to real life only indirectly and suggestively. Perhaps bits and pieces of studio thinking and other import approaches might fruitfully come into the teaching of the core disciplines, but that's about it. Perhaps those disciplines do not for the most part accommodate so well the rich full-scale endeavors of the studio.

Such a reservation is, I fear, more a failure of ingenuity and imagination than anything else. Indeed, one does not even have to imagine. What amount to studio learning versions of study in the core disciplines already exist in thousands of classrooms, facilitated by thousands of dedicated teachers—various incarnations of strategies mentioned before, such as problem-based learning, project-based learning, case study approaches, community participation, and so on. No fantasies, these are realities today.

And it's no fantasy that, for both logical and psychological reasons, the import paradigm is a better bet. Importing knowledge into complex meaningful endeavors now, with the future in view, is a stronger model of learning than warehousing knowledge for the future. It's the Humpty Dumpty of the export model that's the fragile one. And that's not Jabberwocky! So let's step through the looking glass into *Studio Thinking* and join Lois, Ellen, Shirley, Kim, and a number of art teachers and students for a vision not only of learning in the arts but what could be learning most anywhere.

—David N. Perkins,
Carl H. Pforzheimer Jr.
Research Professor of Teaching and Learning,
Harvard Graduate School of Education

Preface to the Second Edition

It's 10:32 AM, and your art students have just left for their next class. You race into the faculty room for coffee before your next group arrives, only to find visitors from another school who've been looking for you. They want to hear about your classes. How do you teach art, they want to know.

You try to collect your thoughts while attempting to look composed. How can you adequately describe your responsive, intense, multifaceted classroom? There are the students, of course—each one of them is different. And there's the curriculum—you're teaching drawing right now, and painting comes at the end of the term. There's your current project, and the schedule, and how you keep records. There are materials, how you acquire them, store them, maintain them, set up access to them—that's a conversation all by itself. Not to mention dealing with your students' families (it's report time, naturally), the administrators ("Are you covering the standards?"), your fellow art teachers, the partner organizations, the resource room, the social workers, and the school psychologist. Then there's the school principal, always wondering whether time dedicated to the arts might be better used for math or reading. There's what you do about assessment and reporting, and how you deal with teachers in other subjects, and field trips, and homework, and absences. . . .

You ask your visitors, "How much time did you say you had?"

When we began our study of rigorous teaching of visual arts at the high school level, we knew we were entering a complex landscape, and we meant to find language to help teachers and researchers describe it. We were not looking for a prescription that dictated what *should* be done and what was *best*. Rather, we wanted to map visual arts teaching in ways that would allow teachers and researchers to

see that territory more clearly, to convey more easily what they knew about classrooms and teaching, to ponder alternate routes they might take, and to learn more readily from other experienced travelers. From the start, we were quite sure that visual arts teaching involves more than instruction in merely art techniques, and we sought to uncover the full spectrum of what really is taught and how that's accomplished. Our goal was to understand the kinds of thinking that teachers help students develop in visual arts classes and the supports they use to do that.

We have written this book to introduce that descriptive language and to offer practical examples of these two types of concepts—*how* teachers plan and carry out instruction, which we call the *Studio Structures* (see Part I) and *what* is taught in visual arts classes, which we call the *Studio Habits of Mind* (see Part II). The many examples given of art projects are taken from the teachers who graciously invited us into their classes to observe them and their students in action. We provide photographic images, quotations, and anecdotes to ground the concepts in real classrooms within the real opportunities and limits of schools.

We have chosen not to follow the development of each particular art project from start to finish. Rather we draw on parts of a project pertinent to our discussion. The projects are labeled with numbers indicating their chapter and location within a chapter, and for readers who may want to focus on the development of particular projects, we have provided cross references throughout our discussions. In Appendix A we include a table listing all the projects referred to in the book and their locations in the chapters.

Our focus in this book is primarily on the decisions teachers make, but in several places we also show how students respond to these decisions in their work, talk, and behavior. As you read, pay attention to the many different ways teachers describe what they intend students to learn, and the many adaptations each teacher uses of the four organizational Studio Structures (see Part III). Our aim is to provide strong evidence that the real curriculum in the visual arts extends far beyond the teaching of technique, and to demonstrate that such teaching engenders the development of serious thinking dispositions that are valued both within and beyond the arts.

NEW IN THE SECOND EDITION

Our second edition, *Studio Thinking 2*, capitalizes on what we have learned since publication of our first edition in 2007. Through observation and conversations with educators in diverse contexts, and through reflections on our own research and practice, we have deepened and broadened our understanding of what studio thinking is and how it can be used.

Studio Thinking 2 is expanded in the following ways.

Exhibition: A New Studio Structure for Learning (Part I, Chapter 4; Part III, Chapter 16)

We have added Exhibition as a fourth Studio Structure for learning (in addition to Demonstration–Lecture, Students-at-Work, and Critique). This is an overarching structure containing all three of the other structures. Our new Chapter 4 describes this structure, and our new Chapter 16 discusses how the Exhibition structure fosters each Studio Habit of Mind.

Studio Habits of Mind Chapters Revised (Part II, Chapters 5–12)

We have revised the Studio Habits of Mind chapters in Part II as follows.

- We begin each chapter with an expanded definition of the habit based on what we have learned from teachers who are putting the framework into practice.
- Each habit is presented as a disposition that includes not only skill, but also alertness (noticing appropriate times to put the skills to use) and inclination (the drive or motivation to employ skills).
- We consider the ways in which each habit interacts generatively with others.
- We discuss how each habit is a general way of approaching thinking that can be seen in all art forms, not only the visual arts, as well as in non-arts disciplines. The identification of ways in which habits cross disciplinary boundaries can lead to new and motivated research on transfer of learning from the arts.

How the Framework Has Been Used (New Chapter 17)

The concluding chapter is entirely new. It describes how the Studio Thinking framework has been used in curriculum planning (sometimes in conjunction with Common Core State Standards), teaching, and assessment across art forms and in non-arts disciplines. We also present how the framework has been used outside of schools—in community centers, preservice education programs, museums, research, and policy. We hope to hear from anyone who is using the framework. Please write to us at lois.hetland@gmail.com

Acknowledgments

This research was funded by the J. Paul Getty Trust. We thank Barry Munitz, former President and Chief Executive Officer of the J. Paul Getty Trust, for believing in this project; Jack Meyers, former Deputy Director of the J. Paul Getty Grants program, and Sir Kenneth Robinson, former Senior Advisor to the President of the J. Paul Getty Trust, who served as our program officers; and Deborah Marrow, Director, The Getty Foundation. Patricia Palmer, a researcher at Harvard Project Zero, deserves special thanks for helping with the filming, interviewing, coding, data analysis, and project coordination.

We thank Dr. Linda Nathan, former head of the Boston Arts Academy, and Dr. Stephanie Perrin, retired head of the Walnut Hill School, for generously allowing us to conduct our research in their schools. This research would not have been possible without the collaboration of five inspiring visual arts teachers, Beth Balliro, Kathleen Marsh, and Guy Michel Telemaque from the Boston Arts Academy, and Jason Green and Jim Woodside from the Walnut Hill school. Mónika Aldarondo, Creative Director and Senior Project Coordinator, Boston Arts Academy, contributed to this Second Edition. We also thank the students who allowed us to video them as they worked through the long afternoons in the art studio.

We thank Carol Fromboluti, our program officer at the U.S. Department of Education, which funded an extension of this work in Alameda County, California; Louise Music, Executive Director of Integrated Learning at the Alameda County Office of Education; Ann Wettrich, Executive Director of the Museum of Children's Art, Oakland, California; and all the teachers and artists who have worked with us in Alameda County, California.

We also thank the many educators and artists listed here who have contributed to our thinking and/or used the Studio Thinking Framework since the 2007 publication of the first edition of *Studio Thinking*. We know that there are many others whose names we do not know. We thank you all and are eager to hear news at anytime from those who put our framework to use. Please write to us at lois.hetland@gmail.com

David Alexander, Advisor to the Boston Ballet's Center for Dance Education

David Ardito, Director of Arts, Arlington, MA

Mark Borchelt, Associate Professor of Dance, Utah Valley University, Orem, UT

Candace Brooks, Education Development Center, Waltham, MA

Ray Cagan, Arts Learning Coordinator, Alameda County Offices of Education, Hayward, CA

Sharron Cajolet, Exhibiting Artist, Director of Arts Integration, Head of Arts Department, Gloucester Community Arts Charter School, Gloucester, MA

India Clark, Curator of Education, Massachusetts College of Art and Design, Boston, MA

Kevin Clark, Professor and Director for Digital Media, Innovation and Diversity, George Mason University, Fairfax, VA

Guy Claxton, Co-Director, Centre for Real-World Learning; Professor, University of Winchester, Winchester, UK

Judith Contrucci, former Coordinator of Visual and Performing Arts for the Cambridge Public Schools, MA

Kitty Condon, Art Teacher, Chicago Public Schools, and all the teachers working with the Chicago Teachers' Center Studio Thinking and American Art Project

Barbara Cox, Arts Education Partnership Coordinator, Perpich Center for Arts Education, Golden Valley, MN

Mark Cross, Director of Interchange, Center of Creative Arts (COCA), St. Louis, IL

John Crowe, Associate Professor of Art Education, Massachusetts College of Art and Design, Boston

Lucinda Daily, Exhibiting Artist, Photography Teacher, Berkeley High School, Berkeley, CA

Matt Dealy, Program Manager, Arts at the Center, Chicago Teachers' Center at Northeastern Illinois University

David Donahue, Associate Provost and Professor of Education, Mills College, Oakland, CA

Todd Elkin, Visual Arts Teacher and Consultant in Arts Education, Washington High School, Fremont, CA

Shawna Flanigan, Director of Education, Center of Creative Arts (COCA), St. Louis, MO

Joe Fusaro, Exhibiting Artist, Senior Education Advisor, Art21 Inc., NYC; Visual Arts Chair, Nyack High School, Nyack, NY

Karol Gates, Content Specialist for the Arts, Colorado Department of Education, Denver

Elise Gallinot, Program Director, KID smART, New Orleans, LA

Lynn Goldsmith, Principal Research Scientist, Learning and Teaching Division, Education Development Center, Waltham, MA

Jessica Hamlin, Director, Art21 Educators' Program, New York, NY

Evan Hastings, Consulting Theater Teacher, Bangalore, India

Matthew Hazelwood, former Conductor, National Youth Orchestra of Colombia; Music Advisor, Colombia's Batuta Youth Program (deceased)

Lois Hetland's colleagues and students at the Massachusetts College of Art and Design, Boston

Aline Hill-Ries, Director of Programs and Professional Development, Studio in a School, NYC

Jim Jer-don, Spanish Teacher, Winsor School, Boston

Faith Johnson, Exhibiting Artist, Student, Massachusetts College of Art and Design, Boston

Tana Johnston, Art Curriculum Consultant and Coach, Alameda County Office of Education Alliance for Arts Learning Leadership, Hayward, CA

Gunta Kaza, Professor, Graphic Design, Massachusetts College of Art and Design, Boston

Jaime Knight, Exhibiting Artist, Visual Arts Teacher, Berkeley High School, Berkeley, CA

Cleopatra Knight-Wilkins, Senior Project Director for the Arts, Boston Public Schools (retired)

Robert Leyen, Art Education Graduate of Massachusetts College of Art and Design; Art Teacher, Boston Arts Academy

Chris Lim, former Superintendent, San Leandro Public Schools, San Leandro, CA

Steve Locke, Associate Professor of Art Education, Massachusetts College of Art and Design, Boston

Bill Lucas, Co-Director, Centre for Real-World Learning; Professor, University of Winchester, Winchester, UK

Peter Lutkoski, Assistant Principal of the Middle School, American School of London, UK

Alison Marshall, Founder, Throughlines Dance and Theater, Phoenix, AZ; National Faculty of Dance, Lesley University, Cambridge, MA

Julia Marshall, Professor of Art Education, San Francisco State University

Camilla McComb, Art Teacher, Hayes Intermediate School, Grove City, OH

Arzu Mistry, Exhibiting Artist, Designing Education Center for Education, Research, Training and Development and Research Associate, Project Vision, Srishti School of Art, Design, and Technology, Bangalore, India

Louise Music, Executive Director, Integrated Learning, Alameda County Office of Education, Hayward, CA

Trena Noval, Consulting Arts Educator, Peralta Elementary School, Oakland, CA

Kimberly Powell, Assistant Professor of Education and Art Education, Pennsylvania State University

Stephanie Riven, former Executive Director, Center of Creative Arts (COCA), St. Louis, MO

Renee Sandell, Professor of Art Education, George Mason University, Fairfax, VA

Ricco Siosocco, Adjunct Faculty, Massachusetts College of Art and Design, Boston

Marie Smith, Exhibiting Artist, Art Education Graduate of Massachusetts College of Art and Design, Boston

Ellen Spencer, Senior Researcher, Centre for Real-World Learning, University of Winchester, UK

Mary Ann Stankiewicz, Professor-in-Charge of the Art Education Program, Pennsylvania State University

Miriam Stahl, Visual Arts Teacher, Arts and Humanities Academy (AHA) at Berkeley High School, Berkeley, CA

Connie Stewart, Associate Professor of Visual Arts and Executive Director of The Center for Integrated Arts Education, University of Northern Colorado, Greeley

Sara Stillman, Art Teacher, Emeryville High School, Emeryville, CA

Jennifer Stuart, Art Teacher, San Francisco Friends School

Kate Thomas, Director, Arts at the Center of Teaching and Learning, Chicago Teachers' Center, Northeastern Illinois University

Mary Jo Thompson, Art Teacher, Coach, Professional Development Facilitator, Arts for Academic Achievement, Minneapolis Public Schools

Dale Zalmstra, Art Teacher, Village East Elementary School, Denver

ONE

Making the Case for the Arts

WHY ARTS EDUCATION IS NOT JUST A LUXURY

Arts education has always been in a tenuous position in the United States. All too often the arts have been considered a luxury in our schools—an arena for self-expression, perhaps, but not a necessary part of education. This attitude was exacerbated by the federal No Child Left Behind legislation that was passed in 2001 to improve school performance by setting standards of accountability. With mandated, standardized tests in mathematics, reading, and language arts administered each year, the focus of schools shifted to raising test scores in these areas, since negative consequences resulted for schools if scores did not achieve specified levels. Because No Child Left Behind emphasized accountability in literacy and numeracy and not the arts, even though the arts were included as a mandated subject area, the result is even less support now for the arts in many of our schools than there had been in the past.

In reaction to the increasingly weakened position of the arts in our schools, arts advocates have tried to make the case that the arts are important because they improve students' performance in traditional academic subjects that "really count," such as reading and mathematics. Believing that educational decision makers won't accept arguments based on the inherent value of arts learning, arts advocates have skirted the fundamental question of the core benefits of studying the arts and fallen back on instrumental justifications for arts education—what we see as possible "bonus" effects of arts education. Few seem to care that these instrumental arguments are often made with little empirical or even theoretically plausible basis.

Our position is that before we can make the case for the importance of arts education, we need to find out what the arts actually teach and what art students actually learn. In this book we describe what students are meant to learn when they study the visual arts seriously. We chose the visual arts as our laboratory, but we could as well have chosen music, dance, or drama. It is our hope that others will extend this kind of study to the other art forms. We present the case here that the visual arts teach students not only dispositions that are specific to the visual arts—the craft of the visual arts and an understanding of the art worlds within and outside of the classroom (Efland, 1976, 1983)—but also at least six additional dispositions that appear to us to be very general kinds of habits of mind, with the potential to transfer to other areas of learning. The word *disposition* is one we have taken from the work of David Perkins and his colleagues (Perkins, Jay, & Tishman, 1993; Tishman, Jay, & Perkins, 1993; Tishman, Perkins, & Jay, 1995). It refers to a trio of qualities—*skills*, *alertness* to opportunities to use these skills, and the *inclination* to use them—that comprise high-quality thinking. Our Studio Habits of Mind are dispositions that we saw being taught in the studio classrooms; we believe these dispositions are central to artistic thinking and behavior.

Based on our work to date, we cannot yet say whether the dispositions we identified in arts teaching and learning do or do not transfer to other fields, although we present the preliminary results of a new study in Chapter 17 suggesting that envisioning may transfer from visual arts to geometry.

The work described here lays the groundwork for examining whether learning in the arts transfers to learning in non-arts disciplines. Only when we have established the kinds of dispositions that the arts teach can we address the questions of whether, to what degree, and in what ways these dispositions are learned and whether they transfer to other areas of the curriculum, including ones considered by some to be more "basic" than the arts.

THE FAILURE OF INSTRUMENTAL ARGUMENTS

Let's take a look at a few of the most prominent instrumental claims for arts education that have circulated in recent years. A 1995 report by the President's Committee on the Arts and Humanities claimed that "teaching the arts has a significant effect on overall success in school," and noted that both verbal and quantitative SAT scores are higher for high school students who take arts courses than for those who take none (Murfee, 1995, p. 3). In the first few pages of *Champions of Change: The Impact of the Arts on Learning*, an influential publication from the Arts Education Partnership and the President's Committee on the Arts and Humanities, we read that "learners can attain higher levels of achievement through their engagement with the arts" (Fiske, 1999, p. viii). And former Georgia Governor Zell Miller handed out classical music tapes to all parents of newborns, arguing that music improves spatial reasoning and would therefore improve math and engineering skills (cited on "All Things Considered," National Public Radio, January 13, 1998). These are strong claims, and we wondered whether the research evidence supported them.

In a project called REAP (Reviewing Education and the Arts Project), we examined these instrumental justifications for arts education (Winner & Hetland, 2000). We conducted 10 meta-analytic reviews. A meta-analysis combines and averages the results of similar studies to yield a general result. It also compares groups of studies matched by variables that may influence results (e.g., who teaches, the duration of instruction, parental involvement, study design). We combined groups of studies appearing since 1950 that tested the claim that specific forms of arts education result in learning that transfers to specified forms of non-arts learning (e.g., reading, mathematics, verbal/mathematics test scores, spatial reasoning).

Our findings were controversial. They revealed that in most cases there was no demonstrated causal relationship between studying one or more art forms and non-arts cognition. We did, however, find three areas where a causal relationship was conclusively demonstrated:

1. Classroom drama improves reading readiness and reading achievement scores, oral language skills, and story understanding (Podlozny, 2000).
2. Listening to classical music improves performance on some spatial tests in adults. However, since the effect is transitory, lasting only 10–15 minutes, this finding has no direct implications for education (Hetland, 2000a). Unfortunately, people like Zell Miller jumped from this finding to the conclusion that if babies listen to classical music, their SAT scores will show lasting positive effects 18 years later!
3. Classroom music programs in which children experiment with instruments, improvise, and move to music improve performance on some paper and pencil spatial tests (Hetland, 2000b). However, little is known about how long the effect lasts or its relationship to performance in school subjects.

We also reported a number of areas for which no clear causal implications can yet be drawn. We found inconclusive evidence that music improves mathematics learning (Vaughn, 2000) and that dance improves spatial learning (Keinanen, Hetland, & Winner, 2000). We found no evidence that studying visual arts, dance, or music improves reading (Burger & Winner, 2000; Butzlaff, 2000; Keinanen et al., 2000).

That leaves our most controversial finding. We amassed no evidence that studying the arts, either as separate disciplines or infused into the academic curriculum, raises grades in academic subjects or improves performance on standardized verbal and mathematics tests (Winner & Cooper, 2000). This finding was based on an analysis of experimental studies—ones that measured children's academic performance before and after arts training and compared their growth with control groups that did not get as much arts training. Given the studies available in the research literature, our analysis showed that children who studied the arts did no better on achievement tests and earned no higher grades than those who did not study the arts.

This finding has confused many people because there is in fact a correlation in the United States between how much arts students have studied and the level of success they demonstrate on the SAT: SAT scores increase steadily as students take one, two, and three years of arts courses in high school, and they rise more sharply with four years of arts courses (Vaughn & Winner, 2000). But we cannot conclude from this that the arts courses *cause* the scores to rise. The first lesson in any statistics class is not to confuse correlation with causality. There are various other possible explanations for this arts–SAT correlation besides the possibility that studying the arts causes SATs to rise. For example, academically strong students may choose to take more arts courses than academically weak students, because they know that profiles for college admissions are enhanced by demonstrating a wide breadth of interests (here, arts are not causing SAT improvement). Or, parents who value academic achievement in their children may also value the arts and thereby encourage their children to work hard and take arts courses. In this scenario, *parents* are causing both arts involvement and SAT improvement, but the arts play no causal role in SAT scores.

A study in Britain underscores the problems in jumping to a causal conclusion based on this correlational evidence. The British study found just the opposite of what has been reported in the United States—in Britain, the more arts courses students took in secondary school, the *worse* they performed on their national exams (Harland, Kinder, Haynes, & Schagen, 1998)! Of course, researchers in the United Kingdom did not use this as evidence that studying arts *causes* low achievement, because this was not part of their ideology. They realized that in their nation, academically weak students are counseled into the arts, and this is a likely explanation for the negative correlation between arts study and exam scores. The situation is different in the United States: Here we advise weak students to take lower level classes or remedial academic classes, but not to take the arts.

We concluded that the instrumental claims about the effects of arts education on learning in other subjects go far beyond the evidence, a point supported by the Rand report, *Gifts of the Muse: Reframing the Debate About the Benefits of the Arts* (McCarthy, Ondaatje, Zakaras, & Brooks, 2004), and also made in Britain by Adrian Ellis (2003). Anger greeted our report. Some characterized us as enemies of the arts, arguing that publishing our research would destroy quality arts education for children in the United States. One scholar told us that we should never have asked the question, but having done so, we should have buried our findings.

We were shaken. Our goal had been to find the truth behind the claims, and to change the conversation from glib and superficial arguments for transfer, that in the long run may weaken the case for arts education, to a more thoughtful consideration of what the arts really offer. Arts advocates told us to give up—they called our approach an "arts for arts sake" argument, a tack they insisted was both elitist and doomed to fail. Advocates, they told us, must do what works—and that meant arguing for the arts as a vehicle for strengthening the kinds of basic skills stressed by No Child Left Behind and making this case *whether or not* there was evidence to support it.

Our response? First, justifying the arts only on instrumental grounds will in the end fail, because instrumental claims for the arts are a double-edged sword. If the arts are given a role in our schools because people believe that arts cause academic improvement, then the arts will quickly lose ground if academic improvement does not result, or if the arts prove less effective in improving literacy and numeracy than high-quality, direct instruction in these subjects. When we justify the arts by their secondary, utilitarian value, the arts may prove to have fewer payoffs than academic subjects. Arts educators cannot allow the arts to be justified wholly or primarily in terms of what the arts can do for mathematics or reading. The arts must stand on what they teach directly. If along the way we find that the arts also facilitate academic learning in other subjects, then we have a wonderful side effect. But in justifying arts programs on an instrumental basis, we devalue the arts and fall prey to the anti-arts or arts-as-frills strain that accompanies the back-to-basics movement in the United States.

Second, we have never said that studying the arts does *not* transfer to academic learning. Arts learning may or may not transfer, depending on what is taught and how (Salomon & Perkins, 1989). But the research on transfer to date does not allow us to conclude that transfer of learning occurs. In the words of David Perkins (2001) commenting on the REAP meta-analyses, "it is important to stand back from their findings [about lack of transfer] and ask whether the game is essentially over. . . . Some would say that it had never really begun" (p. 117). We agree with Michael Timpane, former university president and former federal education office policy director, who was paraphrased as follows:

Arts education research today is at an early stage of its development. . . . [in the future, it may become clear that it is similar to] research on reading [a generation ago], where the accumulation of studies over time gradually honed the understanding of educators and policymakers as to the best policies and practices. (Deasy & Fulbright, 2001, p. 34)

The most glaring oversight in the studies conducted thus far on arts transfer is that researchers have failed to document the kinds of thinking that are developed through study of the arts. If the arts are to retain a place within public education, arts educators must answer the questions of what the arts can teach and what students can learn from the arts. Only when we have determined and can document levels of what students actually learn when they study an art form does it make sense to look for transfer of that learning to other subjects. Many of the studies we meta-analyzed did not carefully report what and how teachers were teaching in the arts compared with control classrooms or programs, nor did they assess what students learned. Without knowing how teaching in arts classes differs from teaching in control conditions, nor the level of learning achieved by that arts instruction, one cannot responsibly predict why, what, or how learning in the arts might transfer outside of the arts.

The field of arts education, while passionate, is vague about these questions. So also is the public's understanding of what is learned in the arts. Just ask someone what students learn in art classes, and you are likely to hear that they learn how to paint, or draw, or throw a pot. That's true, but it only tells us what they do, not how they learn to think. This reply is analogous to saying that students learn writing skills in writing class. Of course students learn artistic craft in arts classes. But we must ask what else they learn. Does experience in the arts change students' minds so that they can approach the world as an artist would? Students must be given the opportunity to think like artists, just as they should also be given the opportunity to approach the world mathematically, scientifically, historically, and linguistically. The arts are another way of knowing the world—as important as the other disciplines to our societal health.

THE FRAMEWORK OF STUDIO THINKING

In the study described in this book, we set out to discover what excellent visual art teachers teach, how they teach, and what students learn in their classes. We looked closely at what goes on in five excellent, but very different, arts classrooms. (The five teachers we studied and the methods we used to conduct our research are described in Appendix B.) Despite the debates and the rhetoric about the importance of the arts in education, surprisingly, no other formal studies had, to our knowledge, directly examined the kinds of teaching and learning that actually occur inside the visual arts classroom. A few pioneering studies have investigated in careful detail what goes on in non-arts classrooms (e.g., Lampert's *Teaching Problems and the Problems of Teaching*, 2003; Stigler & Hiebert's *The Teaching Gap*, 1999; and Stevenson's *The Learning Gap*, 1994), and we have followed in the traditions set by these three books.

Based on what we found in our study, we developed the framework we call *Studio Thinking*. This framework describes two aspects of studio art teaching: (1) four *Studio Structures* (how learning experiences are organized), and (2) eight *Studio Habits of Mind.*

Studio Structures for Learning

The visual art teachers we studied organized their instruction by using many variations on a few basic patterns of time, space, and interactions. Four of these patterns focus on learning: Demonstration–Lecture, Students-at-Work, Critique, and Exhibition. A fifth focuses on management: Studio Transitions, when students move from one structure to another, or prepare to start or end art class. When poorly executed, transitions eat up valuable learning time, and when well-run, they may also provide a few more moments for focused, one-on-one interactions between teacher and students. An overview of the four learning structures is presented in Figure 1.1, and they are discussed in more detail in Chapters 3, 4, 13, 14, 15, and 16.

Studio Habits of Mind

We also observed a "hidden curriculum" in visual arts classes, and we argue that this is their real curriculum. We came to the conclusion that, in addition to two basic arenas of learning—teaching the craft of the visual arts (e.g., techniques, tool use, organizing and maintaining studio spaces), and teaching about the art worlds beyond the classroom (e.g., in art history, visual culture, galleries, curators, critics, collaborations, teams, mentorship)—at least six other important kinds of general cognitive and

Figure 1.1. Four Studio Structures for Learning

Demonstration–Lecture

- Teachers (and others) deliver information about processes and products and set assignments
- Information is immediately useful to students for class work or homework
- Information is conveyed quickly and efficiently to reserve time for work and reflection
- Visual examples are frequent and sometimes extended
- Interaction occurs to varying degrees

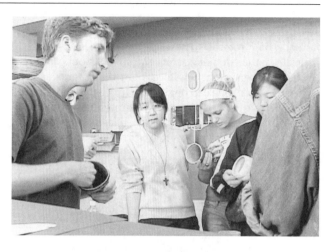

Critique

- Central structure for discussion and reflection
- A pause to focus on observation, conversation, and reflection
- Focus on student works
- Works are completed or in progress
- Display is temporary and informal

Students-at-Work

- Students make artworks based on teachers' assignments
- Assignments specify materials, tools, and/or challenges
- Teachers observe and consult with individuals or small groups
- Teachers sometimes talk briefly to the whole class

Exhibition

- Selects, organizes, and publicly displays works and/or images and related text
- Can involve any or all of the other three structures
- Takes many forms, whether physical or virtual, installed or performed, ephemeral or permanent, sanctioned or guerrilla, informal or formal, or curated gallery style
- Often occurs outside of class space and time, including in virtual spaces
- Develops in phases: Planning, Installation, Exhibition, and Aftermath

Figure 1.2. Eight Studio Habits of Mind

We present the Habits of Mind in an oval because they are non-hierarchical, so none logically comes first or last. The habits do not operate and should not be taught in a set sequence that privileges one or another over the others. Instead, one can begin with any habit and follow its generative energy through dynamic, interacting habit clusters that animate studio experiences as they unfold.

Develop Craft

Technique: Learning to use tools (e.g., viewfinders, brushes), materials (e.g., charcoal, paint); learning artistic conventions (e.g., perspective, color mixing)
Studio Practice: Learning to care for tools, materials, and space

Understand Art Worlds

Domain: Learning about art history and current practice
Communities: Learning to interact as an artist with other artists (i.e., in classrooms, in local arts organizations, and across the art field) and within the broader society

Engage and Persist

Learning to embrace problems of relevance within the art world and/or of personal importance, to develop focus and other mental states conducive to working and persevering at art tasks

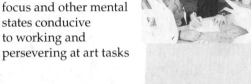

Stretch and Explore

Learning to reach beyond one's capacities, to explore playfully without a preconceived plan, and to embrace the opportunity to learn from mistakes and accidents

Envision

Learning to picture mentally what cannot be directly observed and imagine possible next steps in making a piece

Reflect

Question and Explain: Learning to think and talk with others about an aspect of one's work or working process
Evaluate: Learning to judge one's own work and working process, and the work of others in relation to standards of the field

Express

Learning to create works that convey an idea, a feeling, or a personal meaning

Observe

Learning to attend to visual contexts more closely than ordinary "looking" requires, and thereby to see things that otherwise might not be seen

attitudinal dispositions are developed in serious visual arts classes. These dispositions are central to learning in many subjects, and they may well transfer to academic subjects.

The dispositions that emerged from our study bear some striking similarities to those that Elliot Eisner, in his book *The Arts and the Creation of Mind* (2002a), has argued that the arts teach (e.g., learning to attend to relationships, flexibility, and the ability to shift direction, expression, and imagination). Our research sets the stage for informed studies of the transfer of arts learning. However, whether or not transfer of learning occurs from arts instruction, the kinds of thinking developed by the arts ware important in and of themselves, as important as the thinking developed in more traditionally academic subjects.

In our study we witnessed teachers striving to instill all eight "Studio Habits of Mind" (or dispositions). We observed that whenever teachers were helping students develop technical skills (part of the habit of mind we refer to as Develop Craft: Technique and Studio Practice), they were also inculcating one or more of the other seven habits of mind. These habits of mind are dispositions that are used in many academic arenas and in daily life: the dispositions of *Observing, Envisioning, Reflecting, Expressing, Exploring, Engaging and Persisting,* and *Understanding Art Worlds*. Once taught in the arts studio, these dispositions might transfer to other contexts of learning.

These habits of mind are important not only for the visual arts but for all the arts disciplines, as well as for many other kinds of study. Similar mental habits are deployed in the serious study of dance, music, theater, science, mathematics, history, literature, and writing. For example, students must learn a great deal about tools and materials in a science lab, and this kind of learning is analogous to the art studio habit we call *Develop Craft*. The disposition to *Engage and Persist* is clearly important in any serious endeavor: Students need to learn to find problems of interest and work with them deeply over sustained periods of time. The disposition *Envision* is important in the sciences (e.g., generating hypotheses), in history (e.g., developing historical imagination), and in mathematics (e.g., imagining how to represent space and time algorithmically). *Express* is important in any kind of writing that one does, even in analytical nonfiction and historical narratives. *Observe*, or its corollaries, listen and attend, is required across all disciplines. The disposition to *Reflect*

(becoming aware of one's decisions and working style, becoming able to assess one's work and that of others) is also important in any discipline. Similarly, *Stretch and Explore* emphasizes the need to experiment and take risks, regardless of the domain of focus. *Understand Art Worlds* has its parallels in other disciplines, when students are asked to identify links between what they do as *students* in a particular domain and what *professionals* in that domain do, have done, and are doing. Good science, history, English, and mathematics teachers (as well as teachers of any other subject) propose problems to think about that are currently being grappled with by contemporary practitioners and engage their students in understanding how the work, patterns of interaction, and thinking taught in classes operate in the world beyond the classroom.

However, we urge our readers to be cautious in interpreting these comments. Even if a habit learned in the arts is also used in other disciplines, it does not follow that learning one of these habits in the arts classroom actually strengthens that habit when the student enters a science, mathematics, history, literature, or writing classroom. It may work the other way around, with habits learned in academic subjects transferring to learning in the arts. Alternatively, the same habits could be learned separately in each kind of classroom. Explicit efforts to link subjects must be made regularly if transfer is to occur reliably (Salomon & Perkins, 1989). The transfer from arts to academics hypothesis remains just that—a hypothesis to be tested. But with these studio habits identified, we can now test plausible hypotheses.

For example, it seems reasonable to suggest that the habits of both observing and envisioning may transfer to a science class. If students were explicitly taught to think about habits of mind that they had acquired in arts class and to try to use them in biology class, for example, these dispositions might indeed transfer. In short, for each of the habits identified as learned in the arts, we can now think carefully about how and where this habit might be deployed outside of the arts and then test for such transfer. The first step is to assess how well each habit has been learned in a parent domain (art is the "parent" if learning transfers from art to another subject); the second step is to determine whether the strength with which a habit in the arts is learned predicts how well the habit is used in a target domain, outside of the arts (e.g., mathematics or reading). This is a logical way to go about testing for transfer.

The model we present here of visual arts learning is consistent with, but does not replace, the National Standards for Arts Education (from the Consortium of National Art Education Associations) or the many state standards that have been developed for learning in the arts. The standards specify a particular group's stance (e.g., a state or a national arts association) about particular levels and types of student achievement in the visual arts. In contrast, our Studio Habits of Mind identify more general cognitive and attitudinal dispositions that allow students to meet these standards. Thus our findings complement the standards and allow us to unify learning in the visual arts from the earliest to the most advanced levels of education, and across national and local contexts.

In September, 2007, at the same time as the first edition of this book appeared, the *Boston Globe* published our thoughts about the importance of arts education in the Ideas section. That short piece was widely circulated in the arts education community, and republished in the *NAEA Newsletter* (2007) and the *Arts Education Policy Review* (Winner & Hetland, 2007). In this piece we argued that "We don't need the arts in our schools to raise mathematical and verbal skills—we already target these in math and language arts. We need the arts because in addition to introducing students to aesthetic appreciation, they teach other modes of thinking we value." It is our hope that research will go on to put this claim to the test and demonstrate that the habits of mind we saw being taught in the arts classroom do indeed become instilled in learners and do generalize beyond the art studio. We reprint the full piece from the *Globe* starting on page 9.

CONCLUSION

There are promising signs emerging today in arts education that the role of arts learning in and out of schools may be growing stronger. In 2006, California reinstituted state-wide support for arts in public schools with $105 million in funds intended to be reallocated annually, along with a $500-million, one-time allocation to build infrastructure for the arts and physical education (e.g., buying kilns, presses, computer arts equipment). Parents want their children to be inspired and not just memorize facts, and they are coming to realize that the arts play a critical role in inspiring children (Bostrom, 2003). The Wallace Foundation funded the Rand Corporation's report that argues against instrumental claims for the arts (McCarthy et al., 2004) and commissioned a study by Harvard Project Zero on what counts as quality in arts education today (Seidel, Tishman, Winner, Hetland, & Palmer, 2009). There is renewed interest among private funders in improving arts education. And the U.S. Department of Education and the White House Domestic Policy Council developed the Turnaround Arts initiative, with funding from the National Endowment for the Arts as well as a number of private foundations, in which eight schools are receiving funding for arts education. Major artists, including Chuck Close, Yo-Yo Ma, Damien Woetzel, and Sarah Jessica Parker, have each adopted one of the schools and help to lead master classes.

We hope that this book provides arts educators, advocates, and researchers with the arguments they need to lobby for strengthening the arts in our schools. Arts teachers, those who prepare arts teachers for licensure, and principals and curriculum directors can use our findings in conversation with one another, with beginning teachers, and with teachers of other disciplines, so that the understanding of arts' role in teaching disciplinary thinking becomes clearer to all educators. Our findings should help arts teachers refine their teaching practices, help arts advocates explain arts education to decisionmakers, and help researchers explain proposed studies to funders. Non-arts teachers have much to learn from how excellent arts teachers personalize instruction, engage in just-in-time interventions as they circle the room while students work, and stimulate students' critical and self-reflective skills during regular critique sessions. Finally, as mentioned, the Studio Thinking Framework lays the foundation for more precisely targeted and plausible transfer studies.

ART FOR OUR SAKE: SCHOOL ARTS CLASSES MATTER MORE THAN EVER—BUT NOT FOR THE REASONS YOU THINK

Reprinted from Winner, E., & Hetland, L. (2007. September 2). Art for Our Sake. *Boston Globe*.

Why do we teach the arts in schools?

In an educational system strapped for money and increasingly ruled by standardized tests, arts courses can seem almost a needless extravagance, and the arts are being cut back at schools across the country.

One justification for keeping the arts has now become almost a mantra for parents, arts teachers, and even politicians: arts make you smarter. The notion that arts classes improve children's scores on the SAT, the MCAS, and other tests is practically gospel among arts-advocacy groups. A Gallup poll last year found that 80% of Americans believed that learning a musical instrument would improve math and science skills.

But that claim turns out to be unfounded. It's true that students involved in the arts do better in school and on their SATs than those who are not involved. However, correlation isn't causation, and an analysis we did several years ago showed no evidence that arts training actually causes scores to rise.

There is, however, a very good reason to teach arts in schools, and it's not the one that arts supporters tend to fall back on. In a recent study of several art classes in Boston-area schools, we found that arts programs teach a specific set of thinking skills rarely addressed elsewhere in the curriculum—and that far from being irrelevant in a test-driven education system, arts education is becoming even more important as standardized tests like the MCAS exert a narrowing influence over what schools teach.

The implications are broad, not just for schools but for society. As schools cut time for the arts, they may be losing their ability to produce not just the artistic creators of the future, but innovative leaders who improve the world they inherit. And by continuing to focus on the arts' dubious links to improved test scores, arts advocates are losing their most powerful weapon: a real grasp of what arts bring to education.

It is well established that intelligence and thinking ability are far more complex than what we choose to measure on standardized tests. The high-stakes exams we use in our schools, almost exclusively focused on verbal and quantitative skills, reward children who have a knack for language and math and who can absorb and regurgitate information. They reveal little about a student's intellectual depth or desire to learn, and are poor predictors of eventual success and satisfaction in life.

As schools increasingly shape their classes to produce high test scores, many life skills not measured by tests just don't get taught. It seems plausible to imagine that art classes might help fill the gap by encouraging different kinds of thinking, but there has been remarkably little careful study of what skills and modes of thinking the arts actually teach.

To determine what happens inside arts classes, we spent an academic year studying five visual-arts classrooms in two local Boston-area schools, videotaping and photographing classes, analyzing what we saw, and interviewing teachers and their students.

What we found in our analysis should worry parents and teachers facing cutbacks in school arts programs. While students in art classes learn techniques specific to art, such as how to draw, how to mix paint, or how to center a pot, they're also taught a remarkable array of mental habits not emphasized elsewhere in school.

Such skills include visual-spatial abilities, reflection, self-criticism, and the willingness to experiment and learn from mistakes. All are important to numerous careers, but are widely ignored by today's standardized tests.

In our study, funded by the J. Paul Getty Trust, we worked with classes at the Boston Arts Academy, a public school in the Fenway, and the private Walnut Hill School for the arts in Natick. Students at each school concentrate on visual arts, music, drama, or dance, and spend at least three hours a day working on their art. Their teachers are practicing artists. We restricted ourselves to a small sample of high-quality programs to evaluate what the visual arts could achieve given adequate time and resources.

Although the approach is necessarily subjective, we tried to set the study up to be as evidence-based as possible. We videotaped classes and watched student-teacher interactions repeatedly, identifying specific habits and skills, and coding the segments to count the times each was taught. We compared our provisional analysis with those the teachers gave when we showed them clips of their classes. We also interviewed students and analyzed samples of their work.

In our analysis, we identified eight "studio habits of mind" that arts classes taught, including the development of artistic craft. Each of these stood out from testable skills taught elsewhere in school.

One of these habits was persistence: Students worked on projects over sustained periods of time and were expected to find meaningful problems and persevere through frustration. Another was expression: Students were urged to move beyond technical skill to create works rich in emotion, atmosphere, and their own personal voice or vision. A third was making clear connections between schoolwork and the world outside the classroom: Students were taught to see their projects as part of the larger art world, past and present. In one drawing class at Walnut Hill, Jim Woodside showed students how Edward Hopper captured the drama of light; at the Boston Arts Academy, students studied invitations to contemporary art exhibitions before designing their own. In this way students could see the parallels between their art and professional work.

Each of these habits clearly has a role in life and learning, but we were particularly struck by the potentially broad value of four other kinds of thinking being taught in the art classes we documented: observing, envisioning, innovating through exploration, and reflective self-evaluation. Though far more difficult to quantify on a test than reading comprehension or math computation, each has a high value as a learning tool, both in school and elsewhere in life.

The first thing we noticed was that visual arts students are trained to look, a task far more complex than one might think. Seeing is framed by expectation, and expectation often gets in the way of perceiving the world accurately. To take a simple example: When asked to draw a human face, most people will set the eyes near the top of the head. But this isn't how a face is really proportioned, as students learn: our eyes divide the head nearly at the center line. If asked to draw a whole person, people tend to draw the hands much smaller than the face—again an inaccurate perception. The power of our expectations explains why beginners draw eyes too high and hands too small. Observational drawing requires breaking away from stereotypes and seeing accurately and directly.

We saw students pushed to notice what they might not have seen before. For instance, in Guy Michel Telemaque's first design class of the term at the Boston Arts Academy, 9th-graders practice looking with one eye through a cardboard frame called a viewfinder. "Forget that you're looking at somebody's arm or a table," Telemaque tells his students. "Just think about the shapes, the colors, the lines, and the textures." Over and over we listened to teachers telling their students to look more closely at the model and see it in terms of its essential geometry.

Seeing clearly by looking past one's preconceptions is central to a variety of professions, from medicine to law. Naturalists must be able to tell one species from another; climatologists need to see atmospheric patterns in data as well as in clouds. Writers need keen observational skills too, as do doctors.

Another pattern of thought we saw being cultivated in art classes is envisioning—forming mental images internally and using them to guide actions and solve problems. "How much white space will you be leaving in your self-portrait?" asked Kathleen Marsh at the Boston Arts Academy. "How many other kinds of orange can you imagine?" asked Beth Balliro, also at the Boston Arts Academy, as she nudged her student to move beyond one shade. We noticed art teachers giving students a great deal of practice in this area: What would that look like if you got rid of this form, changed that line, or altered the background? All were questions we heard repeatedly, prompting students to imagine what was not there.

Like observing, envisioning is a skill with payoffs far beyond the art world. Einstein said that he thought in images. The historian has to imagine events and motivations from the past, the novelist an entire setting. Chemists need to envision molecular structures and rotate them. The inventor—the envisioner par excellence—must dream up ideas to be turned into real solutions. Envisioning is important in everyday life as well, whether for remembering faces as they change over time, or for finding our way around a new city, or for assembling children's toys. Visualization is recognized as important in other school subjects: The National Council of Teachers of Mathematics and the National Science Education Standards both see it as essential to problem-solving, but art classes are where this skill is most directly and intensively taught.

We also found innovation to be a central skill in art classes. Art classes place a high value on breaking the mold. Teachers encourage students to innovate through exploration—to experiment, take risks, and just muck around and see what can be learned. In ceramics, for example, capitalizing on error is a major consideration, says Balliro at the Boston Arts Academy. To a student struggling to stick clay together, she says, "There are specific ways to do it, but I want you guys to play around in this first project. Just go with that and see what happens and maybe you'll learn a new technique." Teachers in our study told students not to worry about mistakes, but instead to let mistakes lead to unexpected discoveries.

Finally, many people don't think of art class as a place where reflection is central, but instead as a place where students take a break from thinking. But art-making is nonverbal thinking, and verbal thinking (often public and spoken) is a focal activity of arts classes. We repeatedly saw art teachers push their students to engage in reflective self-evaluation. They were asked to step back, analyze, judge, and sometimes reconceive their projects entirely.

During class critiques, and one-to-one as students worked, teachers asked students to reflect: Is that working? Is this what I intended to do? Can I make this better? What's next? At Walnut Hill School, Jason Green questioned individual students almost relentlessly as they began a new clay sculpture: "What about this form? Do you want to make the whole thing? Which part of it?" In group critiques, students also learned to evaluate the work of their peers. Making such judgments "in the absence of rule" is a highly sophisticated mental endeavor, says Elliot Eisner, a noted art-education specialist at Stanford University.

Though we both have a long history in arts education, we were startled to find such systematic emphasis on thinking and perception in the art classes we studied. In contrast to the reputation of the arts as mainly about expressive craft, we found that teachers talked about decisions, choices, and understanding far more than they talked about feelings.

By unveiling a powerful thinking culture in the art room, our study suggests ways that we can move beyond the debate over the value of arts, and start using the arts to restore balance and depth to an education system increasingly skewed toward readily testable skills and information.

While arts teachers rightly resist making their classes like "academic" classes, teachers of academic subjects might well benefit from making their classes more like arts classes. Math students, for instance, could post their in-process solutions regularly and discuss them together. If students worked on long-term projects using primary sources in history class, they would learn to work like real historians and their teachers could offer personalized and "just in time" guidance.

Despite the pressures to prepare students for high-stakes tests, some teachers and schools continue to use methods similar to those in the art studio. Ron Berger, a former 5th-grade classroom teacher in a public school in Shutesbury, Mass., provides an inspiring example. He adopted an arts-like approach to all subjects, including math, language arts, science, and social studies. His students engage in long-term investigations rather than one-shot assignments or memorization. Their work is continually assessed publicly in critiques so students develop the ability to reflect and improve. Projects are "real work," not "school work"—work that is original and makes a contribution to knowledge.

For example, students investigated the purity of drinking water in their town wells, working in collaboration with a local college and learning how to analyze the water in a college lab. No one in the town knew whether the well waters were safe, and the students discovered and reported that they were. Deborah Meier, a leading American school reformer and founding principal of the Mission Hill School in Boston, praises Berger's teaching. She worries that "Top-down mandates may actually hinder this kind of culture of high standards."

We don't need the arts in our schools to raise mathematical and verbal skills—we already target these in math and language arts. We need the arts because, in addition to introducing students to aesthetic appreciation, they teach other modes of thinking we value.

For students living in a rapidly changing world, the arts teach vital modes of seeing, imagining, inventing, and thinking. If our primary demand of students is that they recall established facts, the children we educate today will find themselves ill-equipped to deal with problems like global warming, terrorism, and pandemics.

Those who have learned the lessons of the arts, however—how to see new patterns, how to learn from mistakes, and how to envision solutions—are the ones likely to come up with the novel answers needed most for the future.

Part I

STUDIO CLASSROOMS: THE *HOW* OF STUDIO TEACHING

Walk into a studio art class, and you may feel you have left school. The students look relaxed; sometimes they sit on the floor or music plays softly. After materials are set up students dig in, not concerned about getting clay on their hands or paint on their jeans. You see the teacher introducing concepts and demonstrating, and then you watch as students become engrossed in their projects. Often their work is part of a much longer project, already begun, extending for weeks. Sometimes a work of art by an established artist is displayed and discussed because something the artist did relates to today's work. Today we are working on light. Let's see how Edward Hopper used light. Today we are working on portraits. Let's look at Cubist portraits and compare them with more realistic ones to get a feel for the many ways there are to represent the world. Our next unit is about power. Let's look at Kara Walker, Carrie Mae Weems, and Layla Ali.

Students talk among themselves quietly as they begin to work, and the teacher circles around, watching for teachable moments and zeroing in on individual students with a comment, suggestion, question, or critique. At a midpoint or the end of class there are often critiques in which students are gathered to share and discuss their work, sessions in which critical judgment and metacognition are nurtured.

A studio classroom is much more complicated than it looks at first impression. The students who originally appeared so casual are actually working hard—they are thinking visually, analytically, critically, creatively.

In Chapter 2 we discuss how teachers develop a studio culture—how they design the physical environment and how they create projects that are engaging and focused on developing students' thinking. In Chapter 3 we delve into the three structures of a studio art classroom through which teachers guide student learning: Demonstration–Lecture, Students-at-Work, and Critique. In Chapter 4 we describe the structure that we call Exhibition, an overarching structure that includes the other three Studio Structures for learning.

TWO

Elements of
Studio Classrooms

On the surface, a studio classroom might appear to require little teacher planning. Teachers usually talk briefly and often quite informally. While students are making art, teachers might appear, to casual observation, to be milling about aimlessly. And when the group looks at students' work and talks about it together, teachers respond in an impromptu way and encourage students to do much of the reflecting. Getting students to clean everything up might appear to be the toughest part of art teaching!

However, this informality belies the careful thinking and artfulness required to make a studio class work. As we observed art teachers, we saw three areas of focus that teachers used to make their art classrooms into places in which students engage rigorously in learning:

- Creating a studio culture
- Focusing thinking with studio assignments
- Teaching through artworks

In what follows, we describe the elements we observed in each of these areas of focus.

CREATING A STUDIO CULTURE

Studio classrooms have a different "feel" than classrooms in many other disciplines. The space is set up to promote work-flow, there is sometimes music playing to create a mood and to sustain and/or modulate students' energy, and students are usually absorbed by handling (often messy and sometimes complex and even dangerous) materials and tools.

The teachers we observed were attentive to a range of elements (e.g., space, time, language, music, and routines) that contributed to creating a studio culture to support the learning they intended.

Designing the Physical Space

The arrangement of space is a powerful factor in helping to accomplish instructional goals. A primary consideration is getting materials and tools into students' hands efficiently. When teachers have the space, they often set up materials stations that students can access from several directions to avoid waiting, and then ask students to collect what they need. Other times, when materials must be put away because space is shared, teachers use student assistants to pass out materials from a central materials center. Teachers sometimes choose to set up the classroom just enough to get students started, and then, throughout the class, bring students new materials for later phases of work.

Wall space is also a potential teaching tool. At the Boston Arts Academy, Kathleen Marsh, Beth Balliro, and Guy Michel Telemaque organized wall spaces, for example, to express disciplinary, school, and personal values; models of work; and intentions for learning. Even though the rooms at the Academy are shared, teachers still use the walls to display a rich array of professional and student artworks and texts of various types, including instructions for routines, goals, quotations, announcements, and humorous and personal reminders. Similarly, at Walnut Hill, Jason Green and Jim Woodside also use the walls to teach. One wall in Jason's ceramic studio features a large matrix of tiles that reveals how systematic mixing and layering of glazes produce different effects after firing. Jim's classroom walls are usually lined with students' works in progress, both from students in the current class and from students in other classes.

The organization and labeling of space to house materials and tools is also an important consideration. Jason has clear plastic drawers labeled and filled with ceramic tools, and he labels shelves with students' names as personal storage areas for works in progress. Jim labels spaces for student portfolios, again, so all student work is accessible to both students and teacher for review and reflection.

Configurations of furniture also have a great impact on how classes function. Beth sets up the studio in a totally different arrangement when she starts a unit on clay, and she switches it again when she starts a painting unit. These adjustments accommodate different social groupings as well as different uses of materials. Jason also reconfigures the classroom space between units, removing the pottery wheels when the class begins to focus on sculpture. As sculpture begins, he sets up a central table and individual sculpture stools so students can choose how to position themselves relative to their work and their peers. Jim keeps his studio quite open, often with a central object of focus (e.g., a 10-foot diameter still-life of variously sized boxes, a splay of crumpled black paper hanging from the ceiling). This spatial choice unifies the class and also encourages students to explore several vantage points before committing to a position for drawing. In addition, Jim uses three different "seating" options to promote students' taking varied perspectives on their work. Students can observe from a low level (sitting on the floor with a drawing board propped on a brick), from a mid-level (sitting astride drawing horses), or from above (standing at easels). All of these space considerations build in flexibility that reminds and encourages students to think about the effects of other people, materials, and processes on the concepts being addressed. Teachers use space to support their learning intentions.

Designing Classroom Light and Sound

Teachers also create atmospheres with light and sound to help students persist in their work. In several of the classes we observed, teachers used music as background to help students develop a flow in their work, whether to energize or calm them. For example, both Kathleen and Guy Michel sometimes held "Open Studio," in which students harness their energy with popular music and a social buzz. In these classes, students joke, talk, and move around a lot as they work. Jim often plays more upbeat music in the late afternoons, to lift the energy during the late hours of long afternoon classes when students are tired. And for clean-up, some teachers use popular music to provide an energetic, upbeat atmosphere and to manage the routine—when the song is over, the class assesses what's left to be cleaned and starts in again as necessary.

Conversely, for projects that require quiet concentration, Kathleen sometimes declares a "Closed Studio." In these sessions, students work silently while calming music plays in the background as an aid to concentration for those who are easily distracted. Jim often used more complex jazz playing quietly in the early hours of classes, when students are making decisions about composition and focusing on new skills. Again, teachers make the choice of music intentionally so that it supports students' learning for particular challenges.

Light is another tool teachers use to set atmospheres conducive to learning. In Kathleen's portrait assignment, students each set an individual light source to create the strong values they were emphasizing in their charcoal drawings. Jim frequently changes the lighting for particular challenges and even during a single class. He pulls the shades, uses spotlights, turns overhead lights on or off, and occasionally lines the window shades with strings of small white lights. In addition to creating aesthetic interest, such variation emphasizes the strong influence of light on mood and encourages students to use it as an element in their artworks to express different attitudes and meanings with values.

Designing the Social Climate

Teachers not only design the physical space, they also design informal and sometimes more formal ways that students interact with one another and with teachers to create a social climate that nurtures learning.

Teacher–Student Interactions. As students make artworks, teachers observe and intervene. Such observation and responsive teaching is critical to student learning. Teachers are also aware and thoughtful, however, of students' needs for privacy at times to develop a relationship with materials, tools, and their own work. For instance, Jim often spends the first 10 or so minutes of a Students-at-Work session tidying up and organizing the classroom. That is not just an efficient use of time for managing materials. It also gives the students a chance to enter into their work in personally meaningful ways. Similarly, we noticed Jason working on his own coil sculpture during a Coil Project. He used his sculpture stool as a perch from which to observe students when they needed time without being distracted. By stepping back, these teachers set an atmosphere of unobserved independence for the students, while remaining close enough to see what is going on and being ready to intervene with questions, suggestions, or demonstrations as the need and opportunity arise.

Studio teachers' use of language models artful talk for students that helps them think about their work in more sophisticated ways. The language also conveys important messages about what is valued and possible in that classroom. The teachers we observed often used such words and phrases as *decisions, planning, think about, what if, you might consider, I wonder if, experiment, it might be because, you could try (x or y or z)*, and so forth, all of which are utterances intended to encourage approaching work or ideas thoughtfully. This kind of talk encourages the studio habits of Reflection ("tell me how you're deciding"), Envision ("see it in your mind"), and Stretch and Explore ("play around"). Students internalize the vocabularies for thinking about art that teachers model. In our observations of classes and our later interviews with students, we frequently heard students use the same language as their teachers when talking about their work.

Peer Interactions. Teachers also need to ensure that students feel safe and respected by each other. For instance, teachers at the Boston Arts Academy explicitly instruct students in how to make constructive criticism rather than hurtful comments in critiques. For the beginning students, they taught peer critique methods such as making a positive comment first and then phrasing suggestions for improvement in neutral terms (e.g., "I wonder what would happen if you . . . ," "Have you thought about trying . . . ," "That makes me think about . . . ," and "I had trouble with that . . . and I tried . . . and it worked pretty well.").

Teachers also want to create a climate where students are engaged with each other, collaborating and learning to participate in a community of artists. While Jim acknowledges that students are not always as clear and helpful to each other in their advice during critiques as he might be, he encourages them to talk so that they learn to learn from one another:

> If I had them never talking to each other . . . it could be a sort of a flat atmosphere where not much exchange goes on. At worst, it could be a competitive, threatening atmosphere . . . you're going to have an atmosphere. . . . Something's going to happen, so you may as well take control of it and make it serve your needs, serve the class.

FOCUSING THINKING WITH STUDIO ASSIGNMENTS

Assignments are one of the main ways that teachers guide and nurture students' learning. By constraining a few directions of thinking and emphasizing others, assignments can shape the direction students aim their investigations with materials, tools, and processes.

What Are Studio Assignments?

Assignments guide particular kinds of learning. They specify or suggest the range of materials and tools to be used, and they pose one or more challenges that are open-ended and result in varied solutions. Assignments vary in length (from a few minutes to several weeks), can be done in class or as homework, and promote growth for students at a wide range of levels. Most centrally, assignments focus students on particular intentions teachers have for their learning. Studio assignments can support the development of dispositions.

TEACHING THROUGH ARTWORKS

In many high school classes in non-arts disciplines, connections between work made by professionals and by students are often left to chance. Professional work seems more a source of "true facts" than of evidence for how disciplinary experts think and express that thinking. Nor is student work exploited as a way to foster thinking, or as a way to show the thinking that students have already developed. Instead, work is completed in private, graded in private, and privately stowed (or thrown) away.

In contrast, in the studio classes we observed, work by both professionals and students has a prominent place as evidence of thinking and understanding. Whether as an introduction to an assignment, a quick example while students are making art, or when teachers and students are talking about work in progress or completed, studio teachers seize frequent opportunities to use works of art as sources of information. Because "making" is at the center of the studio experience, what is made also has an important place. Artwork, both finished and in progress, is made by professionals and made by students, and we saw teachers employ a number of strategies to make the artwork into effective teaching tools.

Among the best strategies are those that engage students in thinking about artists' processes. Video clips produced by several organizations can be used to reveal artists' processes and thinking in their own words. For example, Art21 (http://www.pbs.org/art21/artists) offers videos of contemporary artists speaking about their work from their studios, as does Spark (http://www.kqed.org/arts/programs/spark/), an educational outreach program from KQED public television, which presents artists and arts organizations from the San Francisco Bay area in Northern California. The Tate Channel (http://www.tate.org.uk/context-comment/audio-video) features artists and works shown at the Tate Modern in London.

Student work is public, and teachers use it as a central tool for learning and reflection. Often, student work from various classes is casually hung or stored in sight around the room. Sometimes, the work is merely a background, and other times it becomes a focal example of a problem or solution. Students also see each others' work as it is created, hear teachers' comments to peers, and participate directly in commenting on their peers' work in critiques. Student work is ubiquitous in studio classes, and although obvious, its importance in creating an atmosphere of collaboration, peer critique and support, and revision could easily be overlooked.

Professional work is also used as a teaching tool. It models possibilities for artistic problems and solutions, and teachers use it in a wide variety of ways. For example, at Walnut Hill, Jason and Jim set up a show of their own work as the year began. The show introduced the students to their teachers' aesthetic values, attitudes, and skills and sent a clear message to students: Your teachers are working artists.

Such modeling continued throughout the year. Jason brought in collections of pottery made by his potter friends, as well as invitations from their shows, both of which revealed a wide range of variations to consider in the current assignment. Similarly, he set up a computer in a corner of the clay studio and burned CDs that students could borrow of pictorial sequences of clay-making processes and images of work related to the assignment from other places and eras. Jim brought in stacks of art books and reproductions for his Cubism class, showing individual students examples as they worked on particular problems, and which provided ready material for profitable browsing. He also used works by professional artists to help students visualize problems, as he did by showing pieces by Hopper and Diebenkorn when introducing the assignment to express relationships between figures.

At the Boston Arts Academy, Guy Michel frequently used art magazines to illustrate design principles and challenges. Beth made copies of images of traditional African vessel types. Kathleen gave a slide show as she introduced the assignment to make self-portraits in hats and vests. In addition, teachers set up contacts with practicing artists and other members of the art world, such as curators, restorers, and designers. Students visited museums and studios and reported back to the class. And artists visited classes and worked with students—e.g., artists from the Institute of Contemporary Art worked with students at Boston Arts Academy on a sculpture project.

Reflecting on Work at Different Stages of Completion

Artwork, and particularly student artwork, is not just looked at and talked about when it is "done." The teachers we observed held critiques on sketches, on works in mid-process, on completed works, and on bodies of work from a semester, year, or from all 4 years of high school. Critiques at different stages have different functions: Critiques of works in progress can help students hold their initial plans more loosely and consider different ways of completing their work. Critiques of finished works or bodies of work can help students think and talk about what they have accomplished and imagine the next challenges they might face.

Keeping Talk About Artwork Grounded

The teachers we observed worked to keep talk about artworks firmly grounded on specific pieces. As they commented on a piece, they gestured toward aspects of the work that illustrated their words. Jason, for example, often held and encouraged students to touch, rub, hold, and use the ceramic objects in the studio—and also those that students had previously made and taken home already. During critiques, students are encouraged to point out parts of the work that interest them or connect to a point they wish to make. As words are connected to visuals, ideas become more clear and concrete.

Selecting and Arranging Work Intentionally

Teachers select and arrange works to encourage students to draw thoughtful comparisons among them. For example, at the start of the assignment in which students built sculptures from repeating elements ("unit" sculptures), Jason asked students to examine structures that repeated units, such as stacks of plaster molded bottles, a brick wall, and a fired mud-wasp's nest. As conversations about works progress, teachers focus on works that illustrate a point particularly well, often by physically moving a piece to the center of the temporary display. Every work need not be discussed in every critique. Sometimes the point is to compare and contrast approaches across works; at other times, central ideas can be discussed more cogently and vividly by looking at single works. Of course, it is important for all

students to receive regular response to their work, but setting up the expectation that not all pieces will be discussed in *every* conversation is helpful in making looking at artwork a more flexible part of the studio routine.

Using the Work to Illustrate Key Concepts

When teachers give an assignment, not all students may understand key concepts. Looking at artwork allows a chance to revisit and illustrate the central ideas. For instance, Jason describes how examining finished student work helps students realize the importance of attending to small details of ceramic craft.

> Things do become, I think, a lot clearer when the work is finished. . . . I may have been talking about how not to leave a sharp edge on a trimmed foot. And after the pot is fired and it comes out, . . . you can almost cut your hand if they didn't smooth something out. So things like that become amplified. . . . and hopefully [they] recall . . . information that I gave them earlier . . . it was in the back of their mind—but now . . . it solidifies. And their example's right there in front of them.

Now, with these elements of studio classrooms in mind, we turn our attention to describing the three basic Studio Structures for learning that studio teachers use to organize time, space, and interactions with and among students in efforts to facilitate their learning.

THREE

Studio Structures for Learning

THREE FLEXIBLE CLASSROOM FORMATS

Over the course of a semester, class time can be organized in many different ways to support (or obstruct) student learning. Different goals and projects require their own instructional shapes. The studio arts teachers we studied organized space, time, and interactions in their classes by using variations on three basic Studio Structures: *Demonstration–Lectures*, *Students-at-Work*, and *Critiques*.

These three Studio Structures foster an apprentice/master-craftsman relationship between student and teacher: These structures help create an atmosphere in which student artists work as artists with other artists (teachers and peers). Each structure supports specific aspects of student learning. Demonstration–Lectures convey information, so they forecast whatever the assignment is meant to teach (e.g., *Expression* for an assignment focusing on the emotionally evocative space between figures; *Envisioning* for an assignment focused on imagining a vessel that would suit a particular ritual purpose). The Students-at-Work structure emphasizes the growth and development of individual students, because it keeps the *making* of art at the center of the learning experience and allows teachers to shift attention flexibly from student to student and to carefully observe students and evidence of their learning as they work. Thus, we see the Students-at-Work structure as the one that most helps teachers attend to an individual student's "zone of proximal development" (Vygotsky, 1978, 1984)—the range within which an individual can learn when supported by a more competent other.

And Critiques support a dynamic flow of thinking among teachers and students that connects the *intended* learning in particular assignments with the ongoing *enacted* learning of individual students.

In addition to these three *learning* structures, we defined a *management* structure, *Studio Transitions*. Classes always began and ended with Studio Transitions, and sometimes mid-class transitions also occurred (e.g., breaks). The teachers found different ways to minimize the time spent in transitions (e.g., set-up and clean-up), which, unless carefully managed, can use up a lot of time that could be spent on learning. For example, since getting started and cleaning up can impinge profoundly on time for learning, the teachers we observed spent a good deal of time in the beginning of the year establishing management routines to keep transitions from unduly interfering with time for art-making. Teachers showed students where and how materials and tools are stored, assigned roles for cleaning up the studio, and created individual spaces for students to store their work and materials.

Teachers varied and sequenced these structures in a host of ways, depending on their goals and projects. The simplest way is to begin with a Demonstration–Lecture, followed by a Students-at-Work segment, and concluding with a Critique. Typically, however, these structures were ordered differently, lasted for varying lengths of time, and were repeated within a single class. Teachers also made many modifications within each type of structure; for example, within Critiques, they might use written or oral forms, employ them in mid-process or to synthesize learning around finished works, or to focus talk differently (e.g., on "what bugs you," or "what works"). But all the teaching we observed could be categorized into combinations of these structures.

THE DEMONSTRATION–LECTURE

I'll do demonstrations in throwing—I mean, I try to do it pretty quickly. . . . just so they can have a chance to work. Because I mean, that's really why they are there.

—Jason Green

The *Demonstration–Lecture* is a brief, visually rich lecture by the teacher to the class (or to a small group) that conveys information that students will use immediately. Students see authentic art being made, tools being used, or images of work made by others. Demonstration–Lectures, therefore, offer inspiring models. Here are the basic ingredients:

- *Group Focus.* Demonstration–Lectures have a group focus for efficiency. The teacher demonstrates to the whole group, either to give an overview of a project or of several materials, tools, and/or processes students will use that may require further one-on-one or small group follow-up, or to focus on a single, specific technique that can be employed in the assignment.
- *Visual Emphasis.* Information is presented visually so it engages and informs students. Teachers frequently use images and model processes in Demonstration–Lectures.
- *Immediate Relevance.* Demonstration–Lectures relate to work students will be doing soon.
- *Brevity.* Demonstration–Lectures are brief so as to allow enough class time for students to make and reflect on their work.
- *Connection.* Demonstration–Lectures connect ideas. They relate skills, attitudes, and concepts already introduced to those that will be explored and developed in Students-at-Work and Critique structures of current and future classes. Sometimes, teachers use the informal apprentice–master quality of these class segments to build students' appreciation for the ways that they can serve as resources to each other, suggesting that students who have more experience consult with others.

A Contrast to Traditional Lectures

Art students (as well as students of other disciplines) are often visual thinkers. Visual demonstration captures the attention of such students. In addition, it illuminates for all students complex, multistep thinking that might otherwise be difficult to understand and remember, and it shows students what artistic expertise looks like. The essential difference between Demonstration–Lectures and traditional lectures is the frequent and often extended use that teachers make of visual examples, including objects (e.g., artworks, still-life objects, tools), images (e.g., books, slides, photographs, posters or cards, electronic media), and processes (e.g., modeling step-by-step how to use materials or tools to accomplish particular intentions). In Demonstration–Lectures, teachers rarely talk for long without referring to something that can be seen.

A second way in which the Demonstration–Lecture diverges from traditional lectures is that the information presented is intended to be immediately useful for carrying out class work and homework. This motivates students to pay attention and helps them maintain focus. Because of the emphasis on brevity in Demonstration–Lectures, interaction among students and teachers may be brief, although teachers do interact with students to varying degrees during these class structures. Occasionally, Demonstration–Lectures even become general class discussions.

Finally, through Demonstration–Lectures, teachers present a wide variety of models for ways to meet and solve visual arts challenges. Through modeling, students learn about the relationships among the materials and tools of a medium, what artists have done in the past with these materials and tools, and what they themselves might do with them. The information presented is not for the purpose of memorization, but for starting students off in working creatively to make art. Generally, teachers show several approaches or images, so that students use examples as inspiration rather than something to copy. Through modeling, teachers exemplify their beliefs about art and working as artists. In addition to the specific processes and multiple examples introduced in Demonstration–Lectures, the structure exposes students regularly to their teacher as an artist, who is thinking and experimenting purposefully, playfully, autonomously, and collaboratively. The teacher models the methods through which art students as well as mature artists develop artistry.

The Role of Demonstration–Lectures

Through Demonstration–Lectures, teachers introduce what they want students to learn in three general ways:

- Setting tasks (assignments)
- Illustrating concepts
- Modeling processes, approaches, and attitudes

The three examples that follow show how three teachers adapt the Demonstration–Lecture structure to their particular needs.

SETTING TASKS:
AFRICAN POTTERY PROJECT   (EXAMPLE 3.1)

While introducing ceramics to the 9th grade at Boston Arts Academy, Beth Balliro leads an interactive Demonstration–Lecture to set up a project in which students are to make pottery in pan-African styles using coil-building and surface-patterning (see also Example 12.2). She uses the Demonstration–Lecture to introduce the new project and show how it relates to research on Africa that the students are conducting in their humanities course. Later, Beth demonstrates coil-building as a technique. In the part of the Demonstration–Lecture described here, Beth sets a practical, theoretical, and cultural/historical background for the work the students are about to undertake.

As is typical in Demonstration–Lectures, Beth addresses the class as a whole about a project they will start on right away. "We're going to start looking at some context, I guess you could say. Some sort of ideas surrounding the artwork we're about to start making." The Demonstration–Lecture is brief, to give students time to explore these ideas in their own artwork. "We're going to fly through this. So don't fall behind. Stay on top of things," Beth tells her students.

Beth starts out by providing some background on African ceramics. She makes it accessible through a story about John Biggers, a contemporary African American artist, and his visual impressions of West African art from a visit to Ghana. Many of her students read below grade level, so Beth structures a shared, oral reading from a short text that students would have had difficulty understanding on their own. The reading is supported by reference to many visual images of ceramic vessels, and these ground the interactive Demonstration–Lecture in the concepts she wants her students to understand (i.e., style, definitions of "art," coil-built pottery, and pattern).

The two-page reading is in a packet dominated by eight pages of images of richly patterned African ceramic vessels made by a coil technique. Through these pictures, Beth engages her students conceptually in identifying and comparing elements of the "style" she wants them to interpret in the creation of their own vessels. "OK, we're going to spend some time during this first part of the class talking, reading, and listening. So get your minds ready to do that. . . . I'm also going to be pointing out a couple of things in your packet." She emphasizes the importance of the concept of *pattern* by pointing to the drawings in the packet and to objects in the room, such as a student's shirt. Then, she asks her students to select three images that would inspire the design of their own vessels. The images allow the students to think about "style" and "pattern," and to envision what they could begin to do with those concepts in their own creations.

Finally, the Demonstration–Lecture serves as the vehicle for connecting the skills and concepts required for this project (coil technique, patterned surfaces on ceramic vessels), the context of African culture (i.e., the focus of their humanities course), and the further skills students will explore later in Students-at-Work and Critique sessions (style, form, other hand-building techniques, and the question of what counts as art within different cultural contexts—a recurring theme in Boston Arts Academy art classes). Thus, the atypical features of this Demonstration–Lecture (e.g., we rarely saw as much interaction or reading as is illustrated here, and we often saw examination of actual objects rather than pictures of objects) illustrate how flexible the structure can be in accommodating the goals of the teacher, the constraints of the context, and the needs of the students.

ILLUSTRATING CONCEPTS:
TILE PROJECT   (EXAMPLE 3.2)

At Walnut Hill, Jason Green uses Demonstration–Lectures extensively to introduce assignments, illustrate concepts, and model use of techniques and tools. In the following example, we see him introducing a project that will involve creating tiles as a way to think about texture on the "skin" of a ceramic sculpture (see also Examples 10.2 and 12.5). Conceptually, Jason wants students to understand the "states of the clay"—that is, states like slip, slurry, plastic, leather-hard, bone-dry, bisque-fired, glaze-fired, and all the intermediate "states" that ceramicists use as their raw material for making art with clay. In addition, he wants students to develop the habits of (1) imagining many possible processes and outcomes and adapting their visions as they work with the material, and (2) pushing themselves to create many possibilities by playing purposefully with the material before they commit to a technique for a finished piece.

The students are in the spring term of their year-long course in ceramics when Jason calls them over to introduce the new assignment:

> The next part of the project after we get your form built, the 3D part built, we're going to put some texture on the outside, . . . So before you do that, you're going to make . . . two flat tiles. One of those tiles is going to use all the states of the clay.

Jason quickly shows the students images of tiles from different cultures and eras, in various styles and shapes, all from photos in a stack of art books he has borrowed from the library. He then demonstrates using a slab roller and a template for sizing the tiles. To help students imagine possibilities, Jason shows them various processes using hands and hand-tools, including smearing, scratching, cutting against a template, and experimenting with surface textures. As he talks and demonstrates, Jason shows or passes around pieces of clay in different "states": bone-dry, wet or plastic, and slurry. All of this is entirely visual and tactile, whether he's showing the parts of a tool, the steps of a process, or the variation in the material. Jason closes the Demonstration–Lecture with a reminder that he wants students to try things out:

> So it's just going to be experimental. So don't worry too much about it, OK? You want to experiment. You can make a pattern. You might smear this on to the tile [*holding a piece of slurry*]. And find a tool to make a texture in it [*pushing it with his fingernail*]. Or you can then maybe put bone-dry pieces in [*sprinkling some chips of hard clay on the slab*].

Jason demonstrates a lot in a single class, sometimes for over an hour. His demonstrations give students many options and choices about what they might pursue in their own work. Still, considering the scope of the projects and his 3-hour class sessions, Jason's Demonstration–Lectures are comparatively brief, and everything demonstrated is of immediate value in the assigned projects. Finally, everything Jason shows refers back to skills and concepts he has already introduced and developed; in this case, texturing sculptural surfaces refers back to the surfaces of thrown pots from the first semester. What he demonstrates also foreshadows upcoming concepts and skill—in this case, a tile project that uses molds.

While the five elements of Demonstration–Lecture are clearly evident in Jason's classes, his use of the structure is specific to his goals, to the context of his course and school, and to the needs of the students he is teaching, just as was Beth's very different approach to this structure.

MODELING PROCESSES, APPROACHES, AND ATTITUDES: LIGHT AND BOXES PROJECT   (EXAMPLE 3.3)

About 2 months into his drawing class at Walnut Hill, Jim Woodside introduces an assignment that focuses on light. His Demonstration–Lecture offers students information that will be immediately useful to them and is very short—under 10 minutes for this 3-hour class. Both the brevity and immediacy are prototypical qualities of this structure. Jim's use of Demonstration–Lecture is also prototypical in its use of visual images, emphasis on visual modeling of processes, and in the ways he connects previous work to the new assignment and the new assignment to the future.

Jim uses just a few words to convey the purpose of the assignment to his students ("Light light light light. That's what we're going to work on today."), but he also shows them how it connects to previous work. Students have been drawing all term from observation, and they will do so again today. "All right, what do you notice looking at the still-life today?" he asks. This is the same still-life that students observed recently when learning perspective drawing—a collection of variously sized and positioned wooden boxes (see also Example 9.2). This week, to emphasize value drawing, the still-life is dramatically lit to reveal strong shadows and highlights.

Jim reminds students of previous drawings they have done, suggesting that they use viewfinders as a compositional tool.

I want you to use the viewfinders like we have in the last couple of weeks—very, very important and helpful in a drawing like this . . . and using an eraser as a tool is not a new idea. Remember how I had said in the past to you: Using an eraser is not about correcting mistakes, that's what you do with an eraser when you take a math test [*holding up an eraser*]. Using an eraser is just another drawing tool.

In addition, he helps students imagine what finished works might look like by showing drawings that students in other classes have done already for this assignment.

Jim moves quickly through the purpose of the assignment—naming it explicitly, but not dwelling on it at this early stage in the class because he knows it will make more sense later as students experience challenges and results for themselves; he is careful to model quite deliberately and in some detail how students should approach their own work. He suggests that the project will be easier if they sit on the floor to work, "because a lot of what goes on with drawing this way is going to have to do with gravity." He shows them how to rub charcoal on their paper surfaces to prepare them and how to use a sheet beneath their drawing sheet to catch the extra charcoal that can then be returned to the jar "so we're not wasting it." He also models actually drawing while suggesting ways to begin.

So if I see a white box up there or a strong white tone on the side of one of those shapes [*pointing to the still-life*], that's where I'll start. I suggest you start with the lightest forms first, OK [*starting to draw a shape with the eraser; then switching erasers*]? You can get a little bit crisper of an edge with this eraser sometimes. All right?

The materials for the project (i.e., powdered charcoal, kneaded and gum erasers, newsprint) are common and inexpensive. Jim shows students particular characteristics of each material and tool they'll be using.

Each of you is going to have a kneaded eraser [*holding up eraser*]—do all of you know how to work a kneaded eraser? . . . it's self-cleaning, so as it gets black like that—which it will right away—as you use it on this [*pulling at eraser*]—you just sort of pull it and then fold it in on itself, and it'll keep working for a while.

He also wants students to be aware that the charcoal is messy and unhealthy to breathe, so he shows them exactly how to avoid making charcoal dust storms. This is important information for using charcoal and also a way of modeling that artists should be concerned with health and safety issues in the studio.

We want to try to keep this stuff to a minimum in the air, all right? So I don't want to see you like doing this and then blowing it [*pretending to blow on sheet*]—I don't want to have like clouds of this stuff in the air. I mean, it's not going to kill you—it's not—but it's, you know, we just want to try to keep it down so you don't start coughing all day.

In addition, Jim is aware that the technical drawing process of "pulling light out of the piece of paper" may be frustrating for his students. "Obviously this is going to be messy. You're not going to get this sort of nice, pristine perfect drawing, but you're going to learn to see this thing [*pointing to still-life*] in terms of shape and light only." He alerts them to common mistakes, such as drawing lines and filling in the shapes, rather than "going right directly to the shape." The drawing tools (erasers) are cruder and more blunt than the tools with which they're most familiar (charcoal, markers, pencils, Craypas, tempera paint), so he also uses the Demonstration–Lecture to make suggestions for how they might work. He suggests they squint as a way to see the essence of the shapes.

It gets blurry, and it gets simpler, OK? It's reduced down into real simple forms of light and dark—and that's gonna help you. . . . So here's how we're going to start this. Each of you—to begin with we're going to do an exercise, a small drawing this size on newsprint.

In addition to offering visual information about processes and possibilities, Jim uses the Demonstration–Lecture to set a relaxed, experimental atmosphere about the assignment:

Maybe we will expand to larger drawings today and maybe we'll stick to this size, but let's just start out doing this. . . . We're going to proceed with it and see how it goes. But let's not worry about that just now.

Once again, this structure accommodates the teacher's intentions and purposes for particular students in a particular context.

STUDENTS-AT-WORK

I just call it teaching.

—Kathleen Marsh

The structure we refer to as *Students-at-Work* forms the heart of an art class. Here students work independently on a project, typically one introduced to them in a Demonstration–Lecture. As the students work, the teacher circles the room, offering timely interventions on an informal basis. In a Students-at-Work session, students' primary means for learning about art is through doing. The teacher provides the resources, the challenge, and the individual guidance.

Here are the major characteristics of the Students-at-Work structure:

- *Focus on Making.* Learning occurs mainly through working with materials.
- *Independent Work.* Students work on their own, but in a shared studio space under the guidance of their teacher.
- *Ongoing Assessment.* Teachers observe and assist students while they are working.
- *Individualized Interventions.* Teachers consult with students individually and tailor the assignment and their comments to each student's needs and goals.

Though students usually work individually during these sessions, they do so under the careful guidance of their teacher and in the community of the studio classroom where their classmates are also working. The Students-at-Work structure allows for both independent work and for a collaborative and informal sharing of information, thinking processes, and understanding.

Personalized Teaching

Students-at-Work sessions offer time for teachers to shift from standing at the center of students' attention to observing students as they work. During these sessions, teachers generally work with individual students, personalizing their comments and suggestions. Teachers watch students' work in progress carefully and consult with students one-on-one. These consults may be quick or extended interactions. Consults promote thoughtful decisions. They might include encouraging remarks, brief demonstrations with the materials, questions that help students reflect on their work in progress, or extended conversations about a student's intentions for a piece or about how a particular piece relates to broader goals in the course and to the student's potential for developing as an artist.

The Role of Students-at-Work

Students-at-Work is the cornerstone of the studio classroom. In the 38 class sessions we observed, the largest percentage of time (typically 60–75%) was spent with students working independently on projects while the teacher observed and consulted with students individually about their work.

In the Students-at-Work sessions during class, students are deeply involved with the materials of the assigned project—drawing, painting, sketching, centering pots, or forming objects out of clay; thinking seriously; and making artistic decisions as they work. Students carefully observe their works, plan the next steps of their projects by envisioning changes, and explore new techniques, materials, and ideas. Students learn to reflect continually on the processes of using and making decisions about materials.

The teacher plays a key diagnostic role, observing the students working and consulting one-on-one to guide them in their work. The Students-at-Work structure has three broad roles in the studio classroom.

- Putting *making* at the center of learning (with perception and reflection growing out of making)
- Assessing work *processes* (not just resulting products)
- *Individualizing* the curriculum

Putting Making at the Center of Learning. Teachers' decisions to devote most of their classroom time to having students make art is what makes an art class a studio class. Students-at-Work sessions give students the time, space, materials, and support they need to create artworks and put into action the ideas that are introduced and discussed during Demonstration–Lectures and Critiques.

Assessing Work Processes. In Students-at-Work sessions, teachers continually assess students in all phases of their working *process*, rather than just evaluating their final *products*. They see students' plans for a piece develop, watch how students start, make decisions, and change directions, and see immediately how students respond to instruction. This observation of students as they work is the fundamental way teachers assess how students' minds are developing as they work and learn. Such immediate observation and response also allows teachers to help students in the moment, often the most effective way to instruct. Students told us that they learned more from their teacher's comments on works in process than comments on their completed works.

Individualizing the Curriculum. In a sense, teachers have two sets of curricula in a studio classroom: one for the whole class, and one for each individual student. This personalized curriculum is developed in response to the specific abilities, needs, and interests of each student. While individualizing is in no way unique to studio art teaching (excellent teachers of all subjects know how to individualize to great advantage), the studio classroom has long used individualization and can provide a model of individualized teaching for the rest of the academic curriculum. As Jim explains, "I do have goals for individual kids . . . each kid is very different. . . . [My studio class] is absolutely equally a class activity and an individual activity." By allowing teachers to gather information about how individual students work and learn, the Students-at-Work sessions enable teachers to define and carry through individualized responses to help particular students along their personal paths of development. Thus, the Students-at-Work structure supports teachers working effectively with heterogeneous skill levels in one classroom.

THE CRITIQUE

That's why we have these critiques. . . . I try to get them to realize that they need to start looking at their results very carefully. . . . I want them to start looking and getting information and applying that back to what they're going to do next.

—Jason Green

Critiques are central to a studio class—a chance for students and teachers to reflect as a group on their work and working process. In Critiques, art-making is paused, so that students and teacher can reflect on the work and the process of creation. Here are four ingredients of Critiques:

- *Focus on Artworks.* The students as a group focus their attention on their own and other students' work.
- *Reflective.* Students think about the meanings and expressions conveyed by works of art and think about what is successful, what is not, and why.
- *Verbal.* Students must put their reflections into words as they are asked to describe their working process and products and to explain and evaluate their artworks.
- *Forward-looking.* The discussion aims to guide individual students' future work and help them to envision new possibilities.

Features of Critiques

Critiques do not have a rigid format or single purpose. They are structured in a wide variety of ways, occur at many different points in the working process, and are used to further different ends. However, Critiques have two distinguishing features that earn them a place of honor in the studio classroom. First, they focus attention on students' work and working processes. And second, Critiques are explicitly social. Students share their work with the teacher and other students and get responses from them. Taken together, these two features make Critiques an important forum for helping students develop an understanding of their work and development as artists.

The Work Does the Teaching. By focusing on student work, critiques become a powerful teaching tool. Just looking collectively at a piece of art is useful for both students and teachers. When students see the range of ways their classmates have approached an assignment, they begin to envision possibilities outside their usual habits. A concept that eludes a student may suddenly "click" once seen and discussed in a classmate's work. Critiques are where students learn most genuinely from one another.

Teachers, too, find it informative to see all the work during a Critique. Doing so gives teachers a quick and powerful way to gauge where students are as a group, to see how individuals vary in relation to the group and to expert norms, and how best to help individuals and the group address their current needs in the next project.

A Community of Arts Learners. Students learn in conversation with others. While students often talk about their own work during Critiques, and teachers also generally comment on individual students' work, Critiques involve an explicit shift from individual to group work as the class comes together as a community to discuss one another's works. Critiques involve sharing work and responses with others. Students gain insight about their own art-making by verbalizing thoughts about their own work and by hearing how others talk about their work. They also learn by looking at others' works and hearing how these works are discussed. A 9th-grade student in Guy Michel Telemaque's design class at the Boston Arts Academy talked about the value of learning from others during critiques:

> After we did art pieces, we'd sit down together and talk about it. And that helps a lot because you get . . . certain opinions or advice from not just the teacher but the students around you better observing your work. And you could take that advice and use it on the next piece.

The Role of Critiques

In Critiques, students and teachers look back on art that is being or has recently been made by the students. The purpose is to understand and evaluate students' work and working process and to look forward as individual students begin to envision possibilities for how to proceed. Critiques can take many forms, and teachers structure them to suit particular students' needs and to address goals for the class as a whole. In the 38 classes we observed, there were 25 Critiques, ranging from a 2.5-minute session to a 2.5-hour-long session with seniors who had been working independently for the previous month. Critiques offer a forum for balancing the learning opportunities of an assignment with the particular needs and insights of individual students in a dynamic interplay.

Each of the teachers we observed structured Critiques differently. But for all teachers, Critiques played the following key roles in fostering learning in the arts:

Helping Students Connect Their Working Process to the Final Product. In the Critiques we observed, students' artworks are not viewed as static objects to be evaluated, but rather as a record of the students' thinking and making process. A key aim of the Critique is to make explicit and analyze the decisions that went into making a piece.

Critiques often employ a reverse engineering technique in which students and teachers try to understand how something was made; identify the effects of different decisions, marks, and techniques; and imagine how the work could have been made differently. For instance, as Jason's students pick up and examine ceramic pieces, he asks them to notice evidence of the artists' hands on the pieces and think about how the pieces appear to have been made, why they were made that way, and what they would look like had the artist made them differently.

The product is not the only thing that matters in assessment—students are praised for stretching beyond their usual style or habits of working, even if the resulting artwork is not particularly successful. Conversely, a successful piece may be criticized if the student did not venture outside his or her "comfort zone" to make it. Works are often praised in terms of the thought process behind them: "a smart solution," "a really powerful decision."

Helping Students Learn to Observe, Interpret, Explain, and Evaluate Works. Artworks can seem impenetrable to students. While students can often tell whether or not they like a piece, they have to learn to understand and notice how different aspects of a work contribute to its general effect. Through Critiques, teachers instruct students in how to notice details and patterns in artworks, how to understand what the works communicate and why, how to verbalize what they see, and how to evaluate the effectiveness of works. A key aim of Critiques is to help students explain what they see, think, and feel about work and working.

Teachers push students to notice more dimensions of the work by asking them to focus on particular aspects rather than just the whole. For instance, Kathleen Marsh asks her students to talk about the composition for each self-portrait, and Guy Michel Telemaque asks students to think about how light acts as a subject in each of their photographs. This narrower focus helps students organize their thinking about artworks and pushes them to think beyond the novice response of "I like it."

Teachers model how they want students to look at and think about artworks. They often talk aloud through their thought process as they view a work. They point out details and features that they notice, they describe what the work reminds them of or the feelings it evokes, and they articulate visions of how the piece would look if a part were changed. The aim is not to communicate an authoritative interpretation of a work, but rather to model a process of thinking about it.

Teachers may give general strategies for thinking about and evaluating work. For instance, Jim tells his senior Critique group to ask themselves the question, "What part of a work seems most extraneous? What could be taken away, and the central thrust of the work would remain the same?" He tells them this strategy can be a useful way to push work forward when there's nothing obviously wrong with it—a way to improve a piece that is already successful.

Highlighting Key Concepts in the Assignment or Course. While the assignments in the classes we observed were open-ended and not prescriptive, they often served as a targeted exploration of an artistic concept or concepts such as value, expression, line, sculptural unit, or abstraction. At the Boston Arts Academy, these key concepts were often formalized in an assignment rubric. At Walnut Hill, they tended to be more informally presented in the teacher's instructions, description, or demonstration of the assignment. Teachers often used Critiques to highlight these concepts in students' work.

In addition, each teacher had a number of key ideas that he or she touched upon over and over throughout the year. For instance, Jim repeatedly stressed the idea that technique should serve expressive purposes and that expressive, emotional aspects of works arise from the ordinary. On the very first day of class, he helped students see the expressive potential of a still-life of a collection of objects painted white, and, in Critiques throughout the year, he repeatedly revisited the relationship between technique and expression. Teachers have a variety of key ideas, such as examining the relationships between form and function, between observation and abstraction, or between the students' artwork and their lives. During Critiques, teachers point to ways in which students' work illustrates aspects of these central ideas and suggest ways students could incorporate or develop them in their work.

Guiding Students' Future Work. Critiques look back at what has been done to help shape students' work on the current piece-in-progress and on the pieces they will make in the future. Sometimes this guidance is explicit: Students receive specific suggestions, whether for the piece being critiqued or for the next assignment. The guidance may also be implicit: Teachers instill the idea that each project should be reflected on and should inform future work, as Jason said in the lead quotation for this section. Critiques encourage students to push beyond just looking at the work "as is" and help them develop the habit of envisioning new possibilities for what it could become.

Critiques extend beyond reflections on the work itself, because fundamentally they are reflections by students about themselves as developing artists. Teachers help students see elements that are characteristic of their work and help them identify strengths on which to build. Teachers learn about their students' approaches to work not only by observing the works but also by listening to what their students *say*. For instance, after a Critique, Jim noted about one student: "I think that she's really finding a way to draw here. Now I know that I know this from talking to her a lot and looking at her other drawings. But she's finding a way to draw that is really smart and really her own." Through Critiques, students develop an understanding of their personal way of working and the ways that this personal style may differ from that of other students in the class.

VARIATIONS IN USE OF THE STUDIO STRUCTURES

Teachers weave the three basic Studio Structures of Demonstration–Lecture, Students-at-Work, and Critiques together in many different ways.

ABA Shape

In the simplest model, students work in long stretches of unbroken time, sandwiched between an introduction and a conclusion. We refer to this pattern as the ABA shape: whole-group/individual/whole-group.

The class begins with a whole group gathering, such as in a Demonstration–Lecture in which an assignment or working process is explained. Or, the class might begin with a brief Critique of work from a previous class that leads into work for the current class. That's the "A" section of the ABA shape. The class then shifts to an individualized Students-at-Work session for the bulk of the class period (60–75% of the class time)—the "B" of the shape. The class concludes by returning to whole-group time, with either a Critique of the work made during the class, or a Demonstration–Lecture reviewing what was learned and highlighting what will come in the next class—this is the closing "A" of the ABA shape.

Although we saw many close variations, we saw no "pure" ABA-structured classes. Sometimes teachers would spread this ABA shape over two classes. For instance, at the Boston Arts Academy, Guy Michel, who had shorter class sessions than some of the other teachers (1.5 hours twice a week compared with 3 hours once a week), sometimes spent one class introducing and getting students started on a project (Demonstration–Lecture followed by Students-at-Work), and then used the next session as an entirely unbroken work session followed only by clean-up (Students-at-Work followed by Studio Transition). This allowed students to enter into their work deeply and lessened the amount of time spent setting up and cleaning up.

Punctuated Shape

The most common approach we observed to shaping class time employs shorter structures layered more frequently and at shorter intervals within a single class. We call this type of sequence a punctuated shape (see Figure 3.1). Here we see structures arranged in the following order: Studio Transition; Demonstration–Lecture; Students-at-Work; brief Demonstration–Lecture; brief Students-at-Work; brief Demonstration–Lecture; Studio Transition (break); long Critique; brief Demonstration–Lecture.

Such interspersion gives teachers more opportunities to refocus students on the habits that teachers intend them to learn, to help the group build thinking together about their work, and to introduce new ideas incrementally, rather than with heavy doses of Demonstration–Lecture as class begins, which requires students to sustain focus independently.

We cannot claim to know which variations are best, nor can we recommend how much of each type is sufficient, nor suggest best practices for selecting how to mix ABA and punctuated classes to result in maximal learning. At this stage of the research, we can only identify and describe the structures, habits, and shapes we observed. We suspect that there is no "most effective" way, but, rather, many ways that serve different goals and contexts. As teachers work with the structures over time, preferences and best practices will certainly emerge; future research can then compare various approaches for efficacy in promoting learning.

Figure 3.1. Time Bar Showing the Punctuated Class Shape

From Jim Woodside's class, session 1, working on the Contour Drawing Project

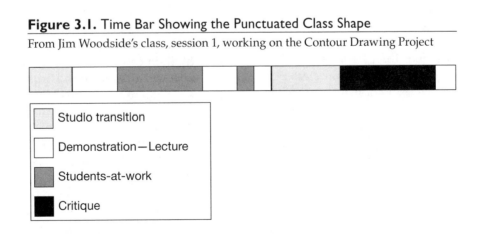

FOUR

A Fourth Overarching Studio Structure

EXHIBITION

Exhibition, in all its forms, whether it's in visual arts or science or humanities, is incredibly important to the cycle of the learning process. It's one thing to be working in your sketchbook, another to do research from a prompt that your teacher gives you, another to struggle in the studio, and yet another to go through a critique. But the exhibition is really the final, and an extremely critical, bookend piece that students have to experience—where your work becomes public. It would almost be like rehearsing and never performing. To go through the process is really valuable and to be specific and transparent about what those skills are that go into creating an exhibition really matters.

—Kathleen Marsh

Art is a public discourse.

—Steve Locke, Associate Professor,
Massachusetts College of Art and Design

In Chapter 3 we described three basic Studio Structures for learning that operate within class periods. Here we describe Exhibition, an overarching structure that typically includes the other structures and that often extends beyond class space and time, including into virtual spaces. Other overarching structures that we do not address in this book, such as long-term projects, contests, residencies, portfolios, and performances, can also be linked to an exhibition.

Creating exhibitions is an authentic practice in which artists regularly engage, and thus it is a key part of a studio education. Students need to think about their artworks as part of an ongoing, public conversation, and exhibitions help them to think in this way. In Exhibition, students engage in Critique as they select which works to show and where to place them. Teacher or student curators or guest experts may give Demonstration–Lectures on topics such as hanging techniques, website design, lighting, or curatorial principles. From planning to clean up, Exhibition involves Students-at-Work.

In addition to the benefits to student learning, Exhibition contributes to program development because it encourages high standards, and to program assessment because it makes artistic efforts visible. Exhibition can also be a potent form of advocacy, promoting programs to stakeholders. Dave Ardito, Director of Art in the Arlington Public Schools in Massachusetts, describes this process in his school system. Teachers regularly hold exhibition receptions where they converse about their programs with parents. They show student work in the school committee room, and the school board receives printed statements about the exhibitions at each of their meetings that are read aloud and televised. In this way, the board, parents, and the broader public are all informed about art program goals, materials, and exemplars.

Exhibition can take many forms: physical or virtual, installed or performed, ephemeral or permanent, a sanctioned or guerrilla installation, informal or formal, or in a curated gallery style such as is described in the classic work on the topic, *Inside the White Cube* (O'Doherty, 2000, originally published in Artforum, 1976). But regardless of the form, Exhibition is the structure that comes into play when artists "let work go"—moving it from the private process of creation by its makers to the ongoing, public process of recreation by its viewers. High-quality exhibitions are possible anywhere, and attention to the phases of exhibition can help teachers aim for the highest quality possible for their immediate purposes within their particular contexts.

Whether in a classroom corner display, a hallway, a public outside space, a blog, website, or a dedicated gallery space, an exhibition can reveal the strength of particular works, the process of making work, or—at the lowest level—may merely get something on the walls so they aren't bare. Similarly, students can be indifferent to what teachers have tacked up and not even see it, or they can be responsible for creating exhibits themselves; perhaps as small groups showing their own work, as curators of peers' work, or by maintaining rotating, ongoing displays of single pieces of their own work, updated weekly. Whatever the form, Exhibition can be a structure that promotes student learning if teachers are alert to that potential and motivated to use exhibitions in this way.

Using Exhibition well means providing guidance in how to select, organize, and display images so that they are compelling, and it means helping students think through how works might communicate to audiences. Helping students to understand the exhibition process writ large is particularly important, since it is no longer only a hierarchical, mediated practice in visual arts. Rather, children, youth, and adults now engage in public display as a regular part of their lives. Sharing art and other visual representations with wide audiences has become a quotidian experience through digital outlets (Ito et al., 2010; Jenkins et al., 2007; Lenhart & Madden, 2005; Peppler, 2010). Sheridan & Gardner (2012) claim that our models of what constitutes artistic development for all children shift as the artistic practices change—the new collaborative and public forms of youth art highlight different capacities of artistic practice and change how we conceptualize children's and youth's artistic development. When youth can and do share their artworks in digital public spheres, for example, art teachers can help them think more deeply about the meaning and implications of what they display and how.

Schools have serious constraints on space, time, and materials, and many are not provisioned for fully developed exhibitions. The traditional school practice of display bears little resemblance to artists' practices of exhibition, such as are described here. In schools, student artwork is often displayed on walls, doors, or bulletin boards in classrooms and hallways. Conventions of display include posting every student's response to a given assignment, mounting works on construction paper, and hanging works densely in grids or quilt-like patterns with little empty space. Often, scant attention is given to the aesthetics and goals of the display or to honoring the individual works.

In some schools, however, we have seen exhibitions that resemble artists' practices, and in this chapter we describe elements of those exhibitions. We hope that by examining artistic exhibition practices, regular displays of student work in all subjects can be made more aesthetic and more effective in supporting learning. A teacher or class might never stage an exhibition of such formality or magnitude as those illustrated here, but by describing in full each phase, we mean to offer a vivid image of exhibition practice to reveal how any kind of exhibition undertaken by artist-educators and teachers of other subjects can be designed and carried out to catalyze learning.

Regardless of the size and complexity of an exhibition, four phases are present to one degree or another: Planning, Installation, Exhibition, and Aftermath, as described in Figure 4.1. Depending on the context, all of these tasks might be carried out by one or more students (particularly in the case of short, informal exhibitions), or tasks might be distributed across a number of specialized roles, including curators, managers, and support staff. Here we draw on two contrasting but fully realized gallery-style exhibitions as examples: (1) exhibition of student works in a pre-practicum class taught by student-teachers at the Massachusetts College of Art and Design (MassArt), and (2) a senior class taught by Kathleen Marsh at the Boston Arts Academy (BAA).

Figure 4.1. Phases of a Gallery-Style Exhibition

I. **Planning Phase**

   Setting a Theme or Focus
   Determining Schedule, Timeline, and Roles
   Designing Publicity and Invitations
   Securing and Designing Space
   Selecting and Preparing Works

II. **Installation Phase**

   Preparing Space
   Creating Signage and Labels
   Setting Up the Display
   Setting Up the Lighting

III. **Public Phase**

   Transitioning to an Exhibition
   Ensuring Exhibition Is Open as Advertised
   Maintaining the Exhibition
   Holding Public Exhibition Events

IV. **Aftermath Phase**

   De-Installing the Exhibition
   Repairing and Storing Materials and Tools

EXAMPLES FROM TWO SITES

Saturday Studios Exhibition at MassArt

At MassArt, students who are preparing to be art teachers learn how to develop exhibitions while they teach Saturday classes at the college to elementary, middle, and high school students. The student-teachers are taking a pre-practicum course as a prerequisite to their required internships in schools, museums, or community arts organizations, either during their senior years or as students in the Masters of Teaching program. The course is designed to support them in planning and delivering lessons, and their classes are supervised by MassArt faculty. Classes are taught on eight Saturday mornings by student-teachers singly or in pairs, are 2.5 hours long, and involve up to 20 students. Each term culminates in a group exhibition. The student-teachers learn how to set up an exhibition so that they can involve their future students in some or all of the exhibition tasks that they learn to carry out at this point. The BAA faculty, including Kathleen Marsh, Guy Michel Telemaque, Barrington Edwards, Móni-ka Aldarondo, and Robert Leyen, all took Saturday Studios at MassArt, and Kathleen once taught in the program, so BAA's exhibition program grows out of that context and exemplifies its impact.

Exhibition at BAA

At the Boston Arts Academy, students' education is focused on their development as artists, and the seniors have been learning exhibition skills throughout their four years of high school. In Kathleen's words, "Every fine artist is going to have to go through this process. It's pretty rare that you go to art school and suddenly other people are hanging your work." She goes on to say, "We do build it in gradually, and then, hopefully by their senior year they've had enough group experiences that they're able to pull it together and make the show happen."

Students at BAA take four courses in exhibition, one each year. The "Zero" course, taken freshman year, introduces the foundations of the concept and practice of exhibition. The sophomore year course emphasizes communication (visual and written), audience response, and collaboration, all from the perspective of learning to be an exhibiting artist who displays her or his own work in physical and/or virtual exhibitions. The junior year course builds on those basic goals, refining and expanding on them. Its goals are to differentiate artists' from curators'

perspectives, develop ways to curate around a theme, design space, and place works to enhance meaning, quality, and viewing. Students distribute tasks in a collaborative exhibition and learn ways to provoke dialogue about their work, expand audience through various kinds of publicity and signage, present and defend their work publicly, and document and reflect on the exhibition process and its relative success.

Exhibition is included as part of the spring-term senior Studio Art 4 course, and here the seniors, not the teacher, do most of the work. The seniors' experience at BAA of creating an exhibition almost autonomously stands in contrast to the experiences of students in the MassArt Saturday courses. At MassArt, the student-teachers do most of the work for the exhibition, not the students attending the Saturday classes, because time is more constrained by the short span of the 8-week Saturday morning course.

We illustrate below the four phases of formal, gallery-style Exhibition with examples taken from BAA and MassArt.

PHASES OF EXHIBITION

I. Planning Phase

The Planning Phase ensures clarity of purpose and timely attention to necessary prerequisites for exhibition, including purpose, schedule, publicity, space design, and procuring and selecting work to display.

Setting a Theme or Focus. An exhibition is more than a random collection of work hung together. Curators or artists may select a theme or focus for a show and make selections of work to support the theme. They may also start by choosing work that seems related and refine the exhibition focus or theme as they add or delete work from consideration.

Some exhibitions begin with a theme. For example, in Professor Steve Locke's Exhibitions course at MassArt in Spring 2012, students selected the theme "M(other)." The theme drove the selection of works that were varied, but all were related to the idea that people tend to seek "other mothers" and substitutions for mothering when they are deprived of this essential nurturing relationship, whatever the reason.

At BAA, exhibition themes are variously chosen by teachers or students, or collectively. A sample of recent themes includes Neighborhood (i.e., here's what you don't know about my neighborhood); Honoring Victims of Cancer (student selected theme); Honoring Someone Who Helped Your Artistic Life; "Mistakes" (i.e., the artistic opportunities in errors); Line (i.e., the expressive variations in mark-making); Personal Biome (i.e., like a personal identity box); Muses (i.e., the students' artistic muses); Strengths/Weaknesses; Our Shared School Values; Color Use; Favorite Cartoons; Audience Participation (a theme from one of the 11th-grade exhibitions that happens in the school cafeteria); and Good Dreams/Bad Dreams.

The Saturday Studios exhibition, on the other hand, has no content theme; the exhibition simply displays works by children and youth in Saturday Studios courses (class displays within the exhibition represent their course theme). When an exhibition has no clear content theme, the challenges of making a coherent display increase and need to be addressed somehow during planning and installation.

Determining Schedule, Timeline, and Roles. Scheduling involves more that setting a sequence of dates of the exhibition—it is also important to define a division of labor. Someone needs to identify tasks, create roles that name people or teams who will undertake each task, and plan when tasks must be initiated and completed along the way. If there will be a reception or public event associated with the show, that, too, needs to be scheduled.

In Saturday Studios at MassArt, the first job for the student-teachers is to become familiar with the idea of a schedule that works backwards from the date of the exhibition, the roles and responsibilities that must be completed along the way, and the dates by which each job must be carried out.

Kathleen Marsh found scheduling to be the key to her support in what was otherwise an almost entirely independent process for the seniors.

I structured the timeline, and I structured the jobs, so everybody was really clear about what their role was, and they structured the expectations. They structured the rubric, so that they already knew what they expected of themselves and of each other in terms of how the show was going to go together. That, I think, really kind of clinched the deal, because they had it in their heads how they expected themselves to do.

Kathleen joked that her role in the Senior Exhibition at BAA "is really to drink coffee and open doors that need unlocking," so she sets the students up to work as a team to pull the show off. A good mat cutter is going to have to cut a lot of mats—more than just his or her own. The postcard designers have to do lots of work early on, since it's always a tight turn-around. One role that Kathleen always makes sure the students create is that of "boss"—someone who ensures that every job gets done and everyone is supported in doing their part. The students name this position anew each year—recently "El Jefe" (the Chief) has been popular.

Designing Publicity and Invitations. Initial planning includes thinking about publicity materials and allowing time for their design and distribution. Publicity must take into account the schedules and deadlines for all forums in which the show is to be advertised, and checks must be built in to ensure that materials satisfy the group's quality expectations in their design and fit the style guide (logos, fonts, color palettes) for the sponsoring institutions (e.g., the school or gallery).

At MassArt, student-teachers begin designing the invitation for the final exhibition near the beginning of the course, right after teaching their first class. One or two student-teachers volunteer to create designs in Photoshop and present these to the other student-teachers. Over the span of several weeks, the class considers and critiques design mock-ups during their pre-practicum classes (held during the week, between teaching Saturdays), and the teacher-designers respond by developing variations until the whole group agrees on a single design. For the informational side of the invitation (dates, times, locations), the design and font need to conform to the marketing style of the school and these are reviewed by the publications office to ensure compliance. The design is then sent to the printer so that the invitations will be ready a week before the event to give to family, friends, and teachers.

Student-teachers also need to distribute invitations to their Saturday students to take home, post the schedule of the exhibition on the school calendar, stuff invitations in faculty and administrative mailboxes, and post them publicly on kiosks and bulletin boards around the College.

Similarly, at BAA, a few students work with an outside designer to create the invitation for their show, going through a similar process of critique and revision.

Forums for publicity are constantly changing. Facebook, twitter, and palm-sized cards are currently more popular than postcard-sized invitations. Invitations can be sent via email, posted on websites, or included in newsletters, with new venues emerging all the time. The point is to consider the audience meant to attend the exhibition and then aim to communicate with this audience in the most appropriate manner.

Securing and Designing Space. It is important to consider the quantity and kinds of work to be displayed (i.e., two- or three-dimensional, time-based works, scale of the works, sound works) and any preferences of the artists (e.g., hanging on walls, in corners, or from the ceiling, placed on pedestals or shelving). Physical space must be arranged to accommodate viewing of the work and the flow of visitors. Movable walls and positions of other architectural features are decided at this point, although those decisions are all contingent and usually refined during the next phase, Installation.

The design of the exhibition space was accomplished in similar ways by the college-aged student-teachers at MassArt and the high school seniors at BAA. In consultation with their teachers and supervisors, one or two students used a gallery floorplan to plan for the placement of moveable walls, pedestals, shelves, cabinets, and other large furniture to create a flow of space from work to work and section to section within the exhibition. Sometimes this planning is done on paper "blueprints," sometimes on software such as SketchUp. The space designers determine which areas are highest visibility and select work for those locations that is most riveting from a distance. They assign a space to each class (at MassArt) or student (at BAA), considering balance across the whole exhibition and the relationship of works that are to be near to one another.

Selecting and Preparing Works. Selections of work to be displayed are made as early as possible, although these decisions are often still tentative, as they are adjusted during the installation phase.

At MassArt, student-teachers work during the penultimate class with their students to select 1–3 works each for potential display in the exhibition. Students prioritize their works, considering both how much they want a work to be shown and how much time is still needed to complete the work. Students are highly motivated in this final class before the exhibition is mounted, and an enormous amount of work is produced because of the looming deadline of the exhibition. The student-teachers curate their own class displays, working to honor the students' requests. Sometimes a student's desire to show a particular work may override a student-teacher's judgment of which is the student's best work because of a student's strong personal need to show a weaker work. Teachers make sure that students understand that selections are negotiations, first between the student-teacher and student, and

then between the student-teacher and the Saturday Studios supervisors, who are the final curators of the exhibition. Because of this negotiation, it is rare that students are disappointed when they see the choices their teachers have made for the exhibition. But of course sometimes students are disappointed, as are the student-teachers when students really need to show a lesser work. Selection is a delicate dance that must be done sensitively to accommodate sometimes contradictory values.

At BAA, students used to select work in consultation with their teacher before matting it. Kathleen Marsh told us about a student who wanted to put in her self-portrait

> because it was personal . . . but her photographs are far better. She doesn't feel connected to her photographs because she feels like a lot of them are accidental, but she has an amazing gift with light and composition in terms of photography. So we had a long talk, and I left it to her, and she hung it the way I suggested.

Because of instances like this, the school now vets work with the faculty for the Senior Show before it is hung.

The vast majority of professional and student exhibitions show final works, but exhibitions of the history of works through drafts or versions en route to the final work are very valuable in educational settings, because they show student learning. An exhibition can, therefore, display process as well as product. Displaying preliminary sketches alongside a final piece makes visible a student's decisions and the evolution of a piece. Showing photographs and internet research or other collected source materials gives insight into a student's inspiration. Explanatory text describing process, whether written by the artist or someone else, is another way to focus attention explicitly on the process of making rather than solely on the final product. It is important to consider the aesthetics of displays of learning carefully to avoid the common failing of being too text-heavy.

The student-teachers at MassArt exhibit a video that shows students in their classrooms in the process of making their works. This video is displayed as a silent, looped slide show just outside the exhibition hall. Student-teachers at MassArt also have come up with some clever solutions to the dilemma of producing a gallery-quality show while at the same time revealing student learning. For example, one student-teacher attached tabs to the bottom of finished comic panels mounted with draft works behind them. A small "lift me" icon directed viewers to find the drafts. Other student-teachers ask their students to describe their own learning in written artist statements that they post near the works. Some classes have made books of drafts and reflections presented on pedestals in front of the display. Still others show process videos on a monitor within the display of the finished works. These are promising approaches in what is an evolving set of solutions to this conundrum of revealing learning while still honoring exhibition of high-quality finished works.

II. Installation Phase

The second phase of exhibition relates to placing work in the exhibition.

Preparing Space. Preparing the exhibition space means that walls and pedestals are set in place and painted, and tools and supplies are checked (Are the hand-drills charged? Are there enough hanging pins and hammers?) and made available in the display space. There should also be an agreed-upon hanging plan. (Will work be hung around a center line or in some other arrangement? Hung floor to ceiling, salon style, in groupings, or . . . ?)

At MassArt, a committee of student-teachers arrives a few days before the installation to make sure that the gallery is ready. The gallery is supposed to be prepared by the preceding group, but it often needs work: Holes need to be patched; paint needs to be touched up. Then the space needs to be set up according to the space design, with designations for each class and a line strung or chalked at 55 inches around the entire gallery to use as a hanging guide.

At BAA, the student curators proceed similarly before work is hung. They paint and position movable walls and designate spaces for particular students.

Creating Signage and Labels. Introductory text and wall labels are written and prepared prior to hanging. Decisions that need to be made include content, choice of wording, font, and font size. Label content usually includes some of the following: name of artist, title of work, year made, materials, dimensions, but content can vary considerably.

A committee of MassArt student-teachers designs all of the signage. For the exhibition title, they select a sans serif font for ease of reading that matches the font on the invitation; determine the wording to specify the show's theme, artists, and dates; and

order the lettering from a company that sends vinyl letters with adhesive backing to be pasted on the wall. Each student-teacher also makes and hangs a sign for his or her course, based on a template designed by the signage and labels committee. The template includes the class title, a brief description of the course, its intended learning goals, a photo from the class, and students' and teachers' names. These signs provide information to viewers and help to unify the diverse classes being exhibited. Labels use the same font and are printed from a computerized label template on a laser printer, three per student, with only first and last name, which offers the most flexibility for hanging. Labels are distributed to the installers.

Setting Up the Display. Placing the works involves aesthetic decisions about individual pieces (How will works be attached to walls or pedestals to honor their uniqueness, protect their physical integrity, and allow viewing without distraction?) and general design (Where is each work placed in relation to other works and open spaces? Where should labels and artist statements be applied relative to works for consistency throughout the exhibit?). Some decisions also include functionality and safety (How is electricity conveyed to monitors or speakers and how are cords taped so they are not a distraction or a hazard?).

At MassArt, the pattern has been to hang single works bisecting the 55" baseline; two works are balanced equidistant above and below the line, and three-work stacks build from a bisected center work. This kind of hanging is very different from the traditional crowded hallway bulletin board, but also from Salon Style, another common approach in galleries that clusters works more freely. Gallery exhibition styles are constantly changing, but whatever style is selected for the exhibition needs to be implemented consistently across the display.

Works are not put on construction paper backing, but are rather placed directly on the wall using sticky putty on the four corners to position, and small-headed pins or nails for solid attaching. The goal is to make the manner in which the works are installed invisible. Once hung, labels are affixed with precision to ensure that they are correctly positioned, level, and without smudges.

Some displays include brief artist statements, either typed or handwritten. These have been displayed along with the work or in a book on a pedestal in front of the exhibition. Sometimes the student-teachers have put quotations from the students onto cards held together by rings and hung on the wall.

Setting Up the Lighting. Focusing lights is a finishing touch meant to enhance the decisions of display and to direct the viewer's attention to the works.

In the Arnheim Gallery at MassArt, the lighting is about 15 feet up on the ceiling. Because it is important to get the lighting exactly right with no glare, a gallery assistant usually sets up the lights after the hanging is complete. At BAA, the gallery has track lighting. But in other spaces, exhibitions use clamp lights when that is safe. Sometimes the constraints of lighting mean that the shows have to be short in duration.

III. Public Phase

The third set of tasks for an exhibition involves presenting the work publicly.

Transitioning to an Exhibition. Prior to opening of the exhibit to public access, all extraneous tools and materials are removed, the gallery is swept, and works are checked for details such as leveling, attachment to walls and pedestals, and positioning of labels.

At MassArt, with over 20 installer-curators displaying work, the gallery ends up full of ladders, carts, loose hardware, drills, and general mess from the hanging process. Before the show opens and after all the student-teachers have finished their installations, a group of students comes in to return tools and extraneous materials to storage and to sweep and check the exhibition for missing labels, damaged walls or works, and any other picayune details that distract from the focus on the artworks.

At BAA, ensuring the transition falls to the "El Jefe" role, and Kathleen tells us it always gets done.

Ensuring Exhibition Is Open as Advertised. The exhibition is made ready for public viewing by its opening date and opens at the advertised times. It seems like something one could expect; but in our experience, it is important to make that explicit to the installers and to insert checkpoints so that everything is ready to go.

Maintaining the Exhibition. The exhibition needs to be checked throughout the time that it is open to the public. Some maintenance is routine (e.g., video monitors need to be turned on and off at opening and closing each day). Some maintenance is needed to fix problems (e.g., work sometimes needs adjustment or even re-hanging if it falls, and may need repair or replacement if it is damaged).

On every day of the exhibition, student-teachers at MassArt are scheduled to come in and open and close the show. Anything that has fallen is rehung and/or the teachers responsible for that work are contacted to take care of it; any missing elements are identified and teachers reminded to fix them; lights and videos are turned on in the morning and off at closing time.

At BAA, the "boss" again insures that the group completes these tasks.

Holding Public Exhibition Events. Exhibitions often have an opening or closing reception for visitors at which light refreshments are served. At this time and/or at other scheduled events, artists and curators talk about the exhibition and engage visitors in conversation about the work.

The exhibition at MassArt opens to the public on a Monday and can be visited from 10–6 every day through Friday. The following Saturday features a public event when family members, friends, students, and all other invitees arrive. This reception lasts for half an hour—kept short to preserve class time—while artists and teachers remain near their work to discuss it with viewers as they come by. At the end of the half-hour, students take their pieces down and take them home. What took a full day to mount is disassembled in 10 minutes.

At BAA, the public events vary widely, depending on the course, exhibition, and location. Seniors have a formal opening in the gallery, attended by friends, family, and BAA alums. The cafeteria exhibitions exist for just 45 minutes during one lunch period. Other external exhibitions may or may not have a reception at all. And sometimes an exhibition has a more "guerilla-like" feel: Works just appear, without ceremony or fanfare.

IV. Aftermath Phase

The final phase of an exhibition returns everything to normal.

De-Installing the Exhibition. Following the close of the exhibition, work is removed and returned to the artists, and the gallery space is returned to a neutral condition (removing shelves and walls, spackling holes, repainting surfaces on walls, shelves, and pedestals). The room is swept, and tools and materials are stored to make the space ready for the next exhibitors.

Repairing and Storing Materials and Tools. During the fray of installation, organization of tools and materials devolves into chaotic disarray. Because it is important to leave the space better than when installation began, it is best to build that expectation explicitly into the timeline. At MassArt, the Aftermath Phase is an excuse to dig vigilantly through those mixed bowls of screws, pushpins, T-pins, kneaded erasers, nails, L-nails, and so forth, sorting them into organized bins; taking materials and tools off shelves and out of drawers to dust, reorganize, and relabel as needed; sweep the cobwebs out of the closets, and restock or inform someone if consumables (pins, paint, putty) need to be replaced. All of this is simply common courtesy, but it is an important consideration that is easily neglected. We make it an explicit expectation, because it is an easy one to forget once the show is over and everyone has gone home.

Similarly, teachers have to decide how to deal with the potential stacks of abandoned artworks that accumulate unless closely monitored. At MassArt, work is sent home before the exhibition (if not displayed) or from the exhibition (if displayed), and a 1-week-after deadline is set for forgotten artwork to be picked-up; faculty grimace but throw out works that are unclaimed. At BAA, students have to check-out with the department chair before they are allowed to leave on the last day of the year. They must clean out and remove every scrap of their personal effects—work, materials, clothing, everything in their portfolios, cubby, and drawer. Otherwise, they don't graduate. Kathleen says, "I know you don't know what to do with that door that you so lovingly painted. But it has to go with you."

WHAT CAN BE LEARNED FROM EXHIBITIONS

When they become artists . . . you have to put on your own shows, and you have to learn that it's a whole separate set of skills, and you need a vision . . . and you need to be able to match paint, and know how far a gallon bucket of paint will go, and they also need to know if that's something that they'd want to do.

—Kathleen Marsh

An exhibition is an opportunity for learning how to engage in art as public discourse. As true as it is that art is an expression of the artist, it is never made in isolation, but rather in relationship to all the work made by others in other places at other times. In schools, it is all too easy for students to see their work as a private expression, coming uniquely from themselves and speaking only to themselves, which convinces them that presentation is unimportant. Similarly, when posting on public networking sites online, students are likely to neglect presentation skills, lacking the inclination and alertness to understand their value in these contexts, too. Whether teachers set up the exhibition themselves, involve students in it, or students post work themselves online, it is important to think of ways to help students develop understanding of what it means to have their artist voice heard in the public discourse about art.

For Kathleen Marsh it is important to have students involved in all aspects of an exhibition:

I've been in other schools where I am the teacher who does all the matting and the hanging, but this is an art school. We're training some of these kids to be artists. We're definitely training all of them to understand the end of the cycle—the putting your own work out there, knowing how to curate and hang and measure and paint walls, putting your work out to the world, and saying, tell me what you think, give me your feedback. The big one is connecting to your audience and owning the entire process.

Kathleen believes the exhibition works against the "tendency to be lazy, the tendency to be sloppy, the tendency to settle for second best, the tendency to over-edit yourself, the tendency to say none of this is good, so I'm not putting anything in." When she asked her students what was needed to make an exhibition good, they listed "communication, productivity and rigor, time management, and accountability. . . . A distinguished rigorous and productive person takes on tasks that are beyond their own and helps without asking and does jobs in their own time."

Studio Structures Operate Within Exhibitions

In addition to being classroom formats, the three basic learning structures also operate within the larger exhibition structure, as can be seen from the examples below.

In the Demonstration–Lecture, teachers or other students or visitors might explain how to set up each component of the exhibition, or demonstrate a hanging technique, or show students how to dig out and then spackle over a screw hole to leave a flat wall, rather than repainting a wall of spackled bumps.

During Students-at-Work, teachers might help students edit their work, removing pieces of low-quality that distract viewers and leaving only those that best represent the artist's voice; reteach a skill such as leveling a work or hammering short pins into hard plaster walls; or reorganize works to balance the display or better convey some thematic meaning.

And Critiques, too, can be held profitably in the exhibition space, with students prompted to think about how the works are displayed, how their works appear different in an exhibition compared to a classroom context, where works are viewed in temporary displays. In an exhibition, students may be able to focus more on the quality of the craft, the success of the expression, and how well their intentions are conveyed to a particular audience—and if not well, why not, and what, if anything, to do about that.

At MassArt, a student-teacher who taught high school photography gathered her students in front of their exhibition for most of the last class. Students observed and responded in individual booklets, writing to each of their peers, describing what they saw in the series of three photos displayed for each student. Afterwards, students left with a rich commentary about their work by peers whose opinions they valued. Such critiques could certainly be held in a classroom, but the sustained engagement of the students in the task for nearly 2 hours suggests that something about the exhibition context itself lent a seriousness of purpose to the task.

Peer critiques can also be held along the way. Kathleen described a situation in which students told a peer—who thought his work was ready—"This looks like crap, take it back and re-do it." The student just turned around and began to work on his piece, with no resentment. Sometimes it's easier to hear critique from peers.

With the advent of the internet and social media, forms of exhibition and public discourse have changed radically. For example, the Saatchi online gallery in London (http://www.saatchionline.com/) describes its mission as providing "artists a platform to show their work to a global audience outside of the traditional gallery structure in order to connect them directly to collectors, first time buyers, and everyone in between." Photographs are exhibited on Flickr, videos on YouTube and Vimeo, and a full range of works (skin art, wallpaper art, poetry, and so forth) are exhibited and discussed on sites such as deviantART, which may be linked back and shared through the artists' social media venues (e.g., Facebook, Twitter). Artists routinely build websites to present their work. In fact, the works of some artists (e.g., as displayed on Net Art, in interactive documentary, and in virtual worlds) are created solely for the internet. Fundraising for proposed art events and projects may begin through a funding platform like Kickstarter.

In these virtual forums, a Demonstration–Lecture is likely to be an online tutorial, and Critique would probably be comments by viewers unseen by the artist. However, whether the exhibition space is virtual or physical, there are decisions to be made about the work and exhibition environment. Invitations generate an audience whether delivered by traditional means, social media, or email. Signage and labels convey information, whether creating context for what is seen or as part of the presented work, and maintenance and de-installation are still necessary presentation elements. An exhibition may also be a hybrid of traditional and emerging forms (e.g., documentation of street or performance art exhibited in a traditional gallery exhibition or online), and it may lack any gatekeeper other than the exhibiting artist, a situation that places even more responsibility on the artist to reflect on when work is ready to be shared with the public and to envision who that public may be over time.

As you are reading this, likely new virtual venues for exhibition have emerged (and ones we have identified may have declined). While learning to navigate and create within these new forums is now a necessary part of the education of aspiring professional artists, these forums also provide spheres where anyone with an idea can engage in public contemporary art practice. Any shared work may have a life beyond its initial virtual location and form, as others may post it elsewhere and alter it. Any creative product shared may stick with an artist's or art student's name long after its initial posting (even if she would prefer to delete her name or take down the work entirely).

Given that virtual forums are central to contemporary art practice, and youth (even those who do not aspire to a career in the arts) can and do participate in these new digital exhibition venues, the Exhibition studio structure can no longer be thought of as occurring only within school walls or as special occasions with the local community. Regardless of whether an art educator hosts formal exhibitions, a contemporary art education needs to help students to develop the skills, alertness, and inclination to engage thoughtfully with the vast array of ways they may share—and already are sharing—their creative works with wider audiences.

Part II

INTRODUCING THE STUDIO HABITS OF MIND: A DISPOSITIONAL VIEW OF *WHAT* THE ARTS TEACH

Watch an entire studio art class with the aim of discovering what is being taught in that class. Observers first notice students learning a multitude of techniques—throwing pots on the wheel, mixing pigments, figuring out linear perspective, and so on. Looking a little closer reveals that what is going on is a lot more complex than the teaching of technique; students are learning many other ways of thinking at the same time as they are mastering techniques.

In the classes we observed, we saw eight ways of thinking being taught, and we refer to these as Studio Habits of Mind (often shortened to SHoM). In the chapters that follow in Part II, we describe each one of these habits of mind in alphabetical order.

The SHoM are not hierarchical, as emphasized by the circular arrangement of the habits in Figure 1.2. The habits do not work and should not be taught in a set sequence that privileges any one over another. Instead, one can begin with any habit and follow its generative energy through dynamic, interacting habit clusters that animate studio experiences as they unfold.

Studio Habits as Dispositions. Each studio habit is considered as a *disposition* that includes not only *skills* but also the *inclination* to use these skills and *alertness* to opportunities to deploy particular skills (Perkins, Jay, & Tishman, 1993). A dispositional perspective is useful for teachers in identifying assignments, lessons, and projects that are truly effective. Of course, no one project has to emphasize all three dispositional elements, just as no one project needs to foster all eight studio habits. The habits and their dispositional elements are aids to support teachers' professional judgments, not substitutes or mandates to replace teacher expertise.

Skill. Each habit has its own core skills, as discussed in the chapters that follow. An assignment "works" when students at diverse skill levels can use it to develop skill in one or more habits that are just at the edge of their ability. For instance, when Beth Balliro taught color theory, she introduced the color wheel (see Examples 5.1, 7.1, and 13.1). Students copied the wheel and a few notes into their journals. Then they made paintings that required them to use color to express an environment in which an imaginary creature—a creature they had imagined that symbolized aspects of themselves—was born (using complementary colors) and died (using neutral colors). Some students in the class were skilled in the use of color and some had never thought about color theoretically before. But this assignment allowed students to enter from any level of learning and build their skills through exploration and reflection.

Alertness. "Attention, attention, attention" says the Zen master. Where, in the stream of life's experiences, can we recognize opportunities to use abilities to good advantage? Alertness is that recognition. When Beth assigned students to "spy" on their families to see how they used "vessels" at home (Example 14.2), she fostered their alertness to consider the functions of vessels. When Kathleen Marsh assigned a texture collection, to be made by rubbing patterns found outside and in students' homes, as homework (during self-portrait assignment, see Examples 5.2, 10.3), she fostered their alertness to an aesthetic element she wanted them to begin using more mindfully in their work. When Guy Michel Telemaque asked students to cut thumbnail images from popular magazines so that the images became unrecognizable and were transformed into pure design elements, he fostered alertness to the presence of design in familiar contexts. When Jason Green asked students to drink from their own fired ceramic cups, he fostered an alertness to nonfunctional elements such as sharp lips and awkward handles. All of these assignments help students develop habits of alertness to aesthetic qualities in the world around them.

An assignment succeeds in developing alertness to the extent that it helps students notice connections between their subjective experience and the world around them, guiding them to think about their experiences as visual artists do. Assignments have to be sufficiently focused to direct students' attention toward ideas valued by professionals who take visual art seriously. Assignments that address central ideas in the field of visual art provide such opportunities by offering windows into what experts consider and work with when they create and appreciate art. For example, sessions focusing on how to translate to a two-dimensional surface what is perceived in a three-dimensional world, or how to suggest the passage of time, lend themselves to this kind of learning. At the same time, assignments need to be roomy enough to leave plenty of space for the individual student's interests. Thus, a well-balanced assignment both channels and awakens perception, and in these ways, supports the development of alertness.

Inclination. Inclination refers to the motivation to put one's skills to use. Inclination can be extrinsically motivated (i.e., work completed for a grade, to please someone, to fulfill a requirement), intrinsically motivated (i.e., work completed to discover an answer or a new question, or to satisfy curiosity), or can combine external and internal motivations (Amabile, 1996). An effective assignment challenges students to put skills to use in new contexts that engage them in the process of making–perceiving–reflecting (Winner & Simmons, 1992). In great assignments, extrinsic motivation begins to take its rightful backseat to intrinsic motivation, which develops as students engage in genuine inquiry and creation.

For example, Jim asked students to use the drawing skills developed through a year of instruction (e.g., composition, value, figure drawing, quality of line) to make Cubist drawings. As he explained to his students (see Example 12.4), in Cubism, objects are depicted in all three dimensions, not by means of two- and three-point perspective, but by showing multiple and conflicting views of an object simultaneously. Jim had students make Cubist drawings by posing a student on a swivel chair that he turned every 10 minutes to face another direction. Students were to superimpose the several views of the model

in one drawing. Students struggled with this new way of drawing, while Jim showed individuals examples from Picasso, Braque, and others who had approached the challenge of depicting three-dimensional reality on a flat surface. "I want to do that," a student said, as Jim showed her a Cubist work. She did not want to do it just because it was an assignment, but because she enjoyed the challenge. For this student at least, Jim had succeeded in creating intrinsic motivation for the assignment. She was inclined to use her drawing skills in pursuit of making a Cubist drawing.

It is important to realize that alertness and inclination cannot be taught in the same manner as skills, which are usually demonstrated and then practiced—or, in a more constructivist vein, explored, named, and developed through iterative reflection and making. Alertness and inclination, however, are attitudes, and these are developed through processes more like apprenticeship—through immersion in the classroom culture developed among teachers and students. Although it is easier to test for skills than to test for alertness or inclination, full assessment of any habit of mind requires assessing all three components of the habit: skill, alertness, and inclination.

The teachers whose classes formed the basis of our original research, Beth Balliro, Kathleen Marsh, and Guy Michel Telemaque from Boston Arts Academy, and Jason Green and Jim Woodside from Walnut Hill, are seen throughout the following chapters. We also mention examples from other educators currently using our framework, but for a more detailed look at current uses, see Chapter 17.

Since publication of the first edition we have heard from many artists and classroom educators who have found that the framework also applies to other disciplines. In the habits chapters that follow, we include sections that clarify the connections practitioners have pointed out across the arts and in non-arts domains. Only further research will tell us whether these habits are the same or different when learned in a studio arts class or in academic classes, and whether these habits of learning transfer to other areas of the curriculum. Might students who develop the habit of persisting for weeks by throwing six-inch clay cylinders bring this newly developed habit into crafting and drafting essays? Might students who hone their observational skills in a studio art class apply this habit to their work with microscopes in biology class? We don't know the answers to these kinds of questions about "transfer" of learning to non-arts classrooms, but we do know that before we can talk about transfer, we first need to figure out what is learned in the primary domain of art.

FIVE

Technique = Procedures & use of tools & materials

Develop Craft

TECHNIQUE, STUDIO PRACTICE

Studio Practice = skills & attitudes for taking care of tools & materials ect.

You start and you don't know how to do anything. You make a huge mess. You're out of control. You have no technique. It's so obvious [laughing], 'cause it's so messy. And then like any craft, you have to build and build and practice and practice. And the minute you create something with control and with technique—it's just a totally beautiful moment because you know you couldn't do it before.

—Beth Balliro

They know when they need to be there. They . . . just work . . . they've just developed studio habits. . . . And they work like artists. They just come in and do their work, and they know where everything goes. . . . And that's what you want the beginning students to develop into.

—Jason Green

Perhaps the most obvious Studio Habit of Mind is Craft. When asked what they learn in art class, students are likely to respond that they learn to draw, paint, throw a pot—they equate learning art with simply learning craft. For example, they assume that learning to draw means learning to use conventions such as perspective, shading, color mixing, and "rules" of composition. They rarely think about the other habits of mind that they are using as they work—for example, looking closely, imagining three-dimensional forms on two-dimensional surfaces, conveying the expressive feeling of a form. But as Jim Woodside put it succinctly, "Art is beyond technique."

In what follows, we describe the two components of Develop Craft. Students develop the disposition to use skill attentively in various media and tools, and with conventions. We refer to this as Develop Craft: Technique. Students also develop the disposition to care for materials, tools, works, and studio spaces, and we refer to this as Develop Craft: Studio Practice. When we analyzed our videos and interviews, we labeled as Technique all instances in which students were being taught procedures and attitudes about using tools, materials, and conventions; we labeled as Studio Practice all instances in which students were being taught skills and attitudes for taking care of tools, materials, works, and studio spaces.

TECHNIQUE

Teachers demonstrate the use of tools and materials and guide students as they work. Students are meant to learn the varied properties of tools and materials and the range of ways that they can be employed in a skilled and mindful way. Students develop a sense of what they can and cannot do with different tools and materials, and they become more adept at choosing the right tools and materials for the piece they wish to make.

As students develop technique, they also learn about the elements of artworks, such as form, line, surface, value, and how to employ artistic conventions such as perspective or color mixing. While developing technique involves becoming familiar with artistic conventions, it does not require rigid adherence to them. Developing technique allows students to make informed decisions about if and when to depart from conventions or use tools and materials in new ways.

41

TEACHING THE THEORY AND PRACTICE OF COLOR: INVENTING COLORS PROJECT   (EXAMPLE 5.1)

The classroom example that follows illustrates Developing Craft: Technique. In a color-mixing class at the Boston Arts Academy, Beth Balliro teaches her students about color theory and how to use the color wheel. They put this into practice by experimenting with color mixing using acrylic paints.

Beth's Inventing Colors Project (see also Examples 7.1 and 13.1), taught near the midpoint of her second-semester course with 9th-graders, is part of her multiweek Imaginary Creatures Painting Project in which students depict themselves as mythical creatures. Two paintings are assigned in this class. In the first, as mentioned earlier, students depict where their creature was born, focusing on using a set of complementary colors. In the second, they depict where their creature died, focusing on using a set of neutral colors. The class is intended to help students gain experience with acrylic paints before they begin using them on their final paintings, where they will put into practice some of what they have learned about color theory.

Demonstration–Lecture

Beth begins her Inventing Colors session with a Demonstration–Lecture on color theory that focuses on the color wheel. Beth tells students that color theory is a topic that can be taught at many levels and requires gradual building up of knowledge.

> You're getting the basics of color theory. . . . This is a very, very first baby step. And when you're sophomores and make it back here, you'll need to know this. When you're juniors you'll further refine it. And, when you're seniors, you'll laugh because this will be so easy. OK, but right now it's the first, first step. It's the foundation. And, unless you know the foundation, you can't build upon it.

Beth directs students' attention to a color wheel she has drawn on the board. Using the wheel, she engages students in a question-and-answer session about various aspects of color theory: primary and secondary colors, complementary colors, neutral colors, and color mixing. She builds on students' knowledge, elicits and corrects misconceptions, and models how to use the wheel to envision new colors. She also explains that the color wheel is a theoretical construct that provides guidelines for color mixing, but that learning about color also involves trial-and-error mixing with the specific paint being used.

Studio Transition

While students distribute the brushes, papers, and palettes (i.e., clean, white Frisbees), Beth reminds them about how they need to care for materials (Develop Craft: Studio Practice) and shows them how to set up their palettes with only red, blue, yellow, white, and a gloss medium. She directs students' attention to writing on the board that describes the guidelines for the two assigned paintings. As students are setting up their palettes and materials, Beth checks in with individuals to make sure they understand the assignment.

Students-at-Work

As students work with the paint, Beth encourages them to experiment and mix a wide range of colors in order to build an understanding of the concepts of complementary and neutral colors.

- *Invent your own colors and use principles of color theory to move beyond basic colors.* Beth tells one student,

   > Yellow/violet. Those are opposites, so have it be mostly yellow and then mostly violet. So yellow doesn't mean only this [*holding up a yellow paint tube*]. You can mix it with a little red to have an orangish yellow, or a little white to have a whitish yellow.

   Stopping to talk with another student, she reminds him to use the painting to develop facility with color mixing and not to spend too much time locked into detail. Moving to two other students, Beth advises one to explore "endless kinds of yellow." With the second, she clarifies, "You don't want it to be just red or green, you want it to be in the family of red or green."

- *Use principles of color theory to guide your color mixing.* To a student who asks how to achieve skin tone by mixing colors, Beth demonstrates as she tells him how to make use of the principles of color theory along with trial and error to create a desired color: "Whenever you go for skin, that's a neutral color no matter whose skin you're talking about. And that's made by mixing the color and its opposite." She also points out that she's using lots of water because she wants the colors to blend. Finally she shows how to add white for a highlight, but cautions:

> If you want to get darker, you can't use black because it will make it too gray—I want you to do what a group of artists called the Impressionists did, which is to use only color for dark. So I'm going to add [*adding blue*] and this will be your dark.

- *Think of these paintings as a vehicle to develop technique in color mixing.* Beth tells one student:

> Try not to spend too much time on the drawing. Because even though we just spent lots of time talking about how drawing is the foundation of painting, today you need to learn how to mix color. That's the goal of today. It's not to create a great perspective drawing of a bridge. It's to mix color.

- *Recognize that trial and error help in learning to mix color.* Beth asks a student what he used to mix the color he wants to be a deep orange. As she demonstrates how to mix the color, Beth explains, "So if I said that orange is a little too green, add red, the opposite of green. It's a back and forth. There is no recipe because each kind of paint acts differently."

- *Try other ways to mix color once you have grasped basic techniques.* Beth confirms a student's use of red plus yellow to make orange, with the addition of gel medium to make a translucent orange. Then she challenges him:

> And now think about if you can pull in other colors to get it to be even more of a range of color. In other words, now that I've seen a lot of paintings I think, "Oh he made that with red and yellow." You want me to look at it and not even care about how you made it. You want me to think, "Ah, look at that red. How did he do that? It's a mystery red."

Beth Reflects

Beth explained to us in a post-class interview that she lectures on the color wheel and its history rather than just letting students learn through trial and error so that students will see that painting is scientific. Regardless of whether or not students become painters, "they understand that painting is not exclusively an intuitive, free, emotional process, but there is a real science supporting it, and a long history of color theory."

But theory is not enough. To explain why students also need to experiment with paint, Beth gave the following example of what colors do in practice to model differences from what the color wheel predicts:

> If you mix Yellow Ochre with Mars Black you get a green. So without any kind of blue, you can achieve a green. And that's very different from what the color wheel tells you. And it's because how they make Mars Black is with probably some dark, dark blue pigment. It's a composite color so it's not a pure thing.

In her Demonstration–Lecture, she alerts students to this gap between theory and practice. This class illustrates Beth's belief that playful assignments that prompt students to Stretch and Explore help students develop technique. She explained that when students play around, they end up having to confront technical issues. And when students are just playing around, Beth finds she can help them with technical issues in a low-stakes way without threatening their self-confidence.

With more advanced students, Beth uses a more complex and inventive approach to technique instead of explicitly focusing on the development of technical skills, as she does with beginners. "I believe in the standard 'you have to know the rules to break them,' and this connects to building technique first and then pushing beyond it and its foundation," she explains. For beginners, Beth said she might ask them to use five complementary colors, while with advanced painters she might talk about achieving space through the sharpness of edges, or by *inventing* some kind of technique. Beth also added another example: "With 9th-graders I might talk about . . . how you glaze. This is how you create a dry brush effect. With an upper-grade student, I might say 'what technique have you made up here?'"

A Dispositional View of Technique

It is easy to equate technique with skill, but skill is not sufficient. Technique must be tied to its purpose, which is making an idea visible. Our current national arts standards reveal a considerable effort to clarify the technical skills involved in working with different media, but as a field we have made less progress in clarifying the attitudes artists bring to their work. Alertness to opportunities to use techniques, and the inclination to pursue techniques both lead to the expression of meaning.

Teaching artistic conventions in isolation from what these skills are *for* fragments art education into mere training.

Skill. The skill of Technique includes the ability to use tools, materials, and the conventions of design. While learning technique involves becoming familiar with artistic conventions, it does not require rigid adherence to them. Students need to learn what they can and cannot do with different tools and materials, and learn to select the right tools and materials for what they want to achieve.

Alertness. When artists notice weaknesses in craft, they show an alertness to Technique. Without alertness, all the skill in the world is insufficient: Artists need to recognize when and where to deploy their skills, and they need to be resourceful—recognizing the potentials of available materials. Alertness to the technical potential of materials lays the groundwork for making informed decisions and leaps of insight, such as when Picasso recognized a bicycle seat could be used to represent the head of a bull. Students learning to use a new material need to be alert to its range of possibilities: the textural qualities paint can make, the range of effects afforded by a filter in a graphics program, the different methods by which pieces can be attached in an assemblage. Developing technique allows students to make informed decisions about if and when to depart from conventions or use tools and materials in new ways.

Inclination. Even when students are alert to what needs to be worked on, they must have the inclination actually to do so. Thus when a teacher observes a weak element of technique in a student's work and the student responds simply, "But I like it like that," that student may be showing a lack of inclination to appreciate the importance of technique. Students can have the ability that is needed (skill) and be aware of what needs to be done (alertness), but still not be motivated to *use* their skills to address an issue (inclination).

STUDIO PRACTICE

Studio art involves making things, and students need facility with the tools and materials with which these things are made. But some instruction must invariably involve teaching students conventions for caring for these materials and tools. We call this kind of instruction *Develop Craft: Studio Practice.*

Studio Practice refers to ways for finding, caring for, and storing materials (e.g., clay, paper, paint) and tools (e.g., brushes, wire cutters, erasers). Studio Practice also involves learning how to store one's works—labeling and dating them, spraying them, putting them in portfolios so they do not get ripped, and so forth. This is distinguished from learning how to present one's work with matting and framing, which we classified as Understand Art Worlds: Domain, because it involves learning to present oneself as an artist. Studio Practice also involves learning ways to make best use of the physical space of the classroom (e.g., giving yourself ample room for materials, placing materials such that they are easy to use where and when you need them), as well as learning about procedures that are specific to work in an art studio (e.g., wearing smocks, wearing safety glasses when using power tools).

The two classroom examples that follow illustrate Developing Craft: Studio Practice.

TEACHING THE PRACTICE OF MAINTAINING THE STUDIO: SELF-PORTRAITS IN COLORED PENCIL PROJECT   (EXAMPLE 5.2)

At the Boston Arts Academy in Kathleen Marsh's class, Self-Portraits in Colored Pencil, taught near the beginning of her fall course with 9th-graders (see also Example 10.3), students engage in a clean-up session that shows many of the features of what we came to call Studio Practice. From the first days of school, Kathleen assigns specific clean-up tasks to students in her 9th-grade class as a way of encouraging them to be responsible for maintaining their work environment. Kathleen considers it foundational that students learn the studio practices of setting up, cleaning up, coming in and out of the studio space, and finding specific tools and materials. She notes, "It's going to be a huge change from what they've been doing." Workspaces inevitably get messy, and students must learn that cleaning up is just as important as setting up their work environment.

In interviews with us, Kathleen stressed the importance of students learning to maintain their work environment, which is especially important in a shared space. If students have their own studios, the level of mess is a personal choice. But in a communal space, courtesy and efficiency dictate cleaning up. "There are so many people that use that room. That room is in use all day long. And it's got to be ready and presentable for the next class." She used the example of Alexander Calder to acknowledge how working solo differs. "I don't think the man ever cleaned up. And it didn't affect his work any. Some people have to have a clean environment to work. But I don't think everybody does." In a shared space, Kathleen added, "It's about citizenship."

Kathleen teaches clean-up as part of a work cycle. "They have to understand that their work period has a beginning and an end, and at the end, you know, the work has to go in a place where you're going to be able to find it. And the tables have to be orderly. And the floor has to be swept. That's just basic." To structure the clean-up, Kathleen assigns specific tasks so students know exactly for which part they are responsible. Assignments provide training and solve the practical problem of making sure all work gets done. Kathleen also told us that at the Boston Arts Academy there is a school-wide clean-up philosophy. "This is their workspace, so they need to work on maintaining it."

TEACHING THE STUDIO PRACTICE OF KEEPING A PORTFOLIO: LIGHT AND BOXES PROJECT   (EXAMPLE 5.3)

Midway through the first term, students in Jim Woodside's class are working on a Light and Boxes Project (see also Examples 3.3 and 9.2). They are making reverse charcoal drawings of a still-life of boxes by using an eraser to pull light forms out of paper coated with graphite. Today students are also going to learn how to care for their work by constructing a portfolio, spraying their drawings so that they don't get smudged, and organizing and storing their artworks in the portfolio. During class, Jim takes students one at a time over to the side of the room, where he helps them make a portfolio from cardboard and duct tape.

Before students start to draw, Jim explains what they will be doing and why. "I think the easiest way, the most useful way to maximize our time is for me to ask you to come over one-by-one. And then the rest of you can keep drawing." He also reminds students to spray their drawings outside where there's fresh air, to preserve them. Jim makes clear to students that portfolios help them take care of their work. Additionally, he tells them that having work organized in portfolios helps him when he grades their work.

Jim Reflects

In an interview, Jim talked about the importance of students keeping portfolios of their work. Maintaining a portfolio helps instill a sense of professionalism in students about their artwork, an important sense that takes time for students to learn. Portfolios also allow students to see changes from their early to later drafts. Seeing this history of one's working process is part of seeing oneself as an artist, and this is the reason Jim encourages students not to throw away any of their work.

> It's really important, because it has to do with how they see themselves as artists. They see the work they've produced. They see the process they've been in. And they see the history of the process. This is why I don't want them to throw things away as well. You know, sometimes I say, "If you do something that you think is a mistake and you throw it away, it doesn't mean you never made the mistake, you know. So why throw it away?"

When Jim sits down to write comments and give grades, he looks through a portfolio to view a student's work from the beginning to the end of the semester. Students looking at their portfolios have the same window onto their work and working process. They see the peaks and valleys and how hard they've worked, and this allows them to reflect on their process and progress. Additionally, Jim told us that he worked one-on-one because students in this class were young, and he wanted to sit with each of them personally as they organized their work. Here is why he had students cut the portfolios out of cardboard:

> I think it's good wherever I can to teach kids to take shortcuts about art supplies, because so many art supplies are so expensive. And the kids need to learn to be resourceful and make things—even the kids that do have money. I just think basic to being an artist is a kind of resourcefulness.

A Dispositional View of Studio Practice

Skill is rarely a challenge for students' understanding of Studio Practice—pick up the scraps, return tools to their designated places, wash the paint (carefully!) out of the brushes. More challenging is the need to develop proactive attitudes toward those skills so that the studio environment continuously supports one's learning. Artists arrange studio spaces to nurture the production of their work, and studio classrooms need to be maintained for the same reason. When teachers introduce clean-up as something artists do to help them in their work, rather than as something rigid and done because teachers say so, students develop alertness to *when* to do maintenance and the inclination to *actually do* it. What is usually seen as drudgery management becomes part of the learning agenda. It may still be unpleasant, but it is recognized as necessary and purposeful.

Skill. Gaining the skills of Studio Practice is not difficult. Skill requires learning how to keep one's materials and tools clean and how to store one's work and materials so that they are both safe and accessible—labeling and dating them, spraying drawings, putting flat works in portfolios so they do not get ripped, storing clay in plastic bags to keep it malleable, and so forth. This skill involves learning how to organize one's space so that one can work optimally (e.g., giving oneself ample room for materials, placing materials so that they are easy to use where and when you need them), as well as learning about procedures that are specific to work in an art studio (e.g., soaking clay tools in buckets to avoid clogging sinks, working with masks and in well-ventilated spaces with materials that emit toxic fumes).

Alertness. Alertness to Studio Practice requires that students identify instances when cleaning or re-organizing materials, tools, and studio space will support them in making artwork. Disarray is useful for some and impedes others, but noticing the environment's effects on the artist's process is what provokes decisions to take the time away from creating and make physical adjustments to the studio. Recognizing when to change the music, repaint the walls, or overhaul the orientation of a working set-up to natural or artificial light sources are all instances of the alertness to Studio Practice.

Inclination. Studio Practices are routines artists develop to support their working process. When teachers straighten up the classroom, they model taking responsibility in the studio. When they define and assign specific roles and tasks for cleanup, they use external motivation to build the habitual expectation that maintenance is part of an artist's daily practice. A studio routine may also aid an artist's working process (e.g., cleaning or organizing the studio as a way to pause and think about a piece from a new perspective). Any task that motivates actually making changes to the physical environment's organization and maintenance of spaces, tools, or materials develops the inclination to develop Studio Practice.

STRUCTURING A CLASS TO FOCUS ON BOTH TECHNIQUE AND STUDIO PRACTICE

TEACHING CARE OF THE WHEEL AND THROWING TECHNIQUE: INTRODUCING CENTERING ON THE WHEEL   (EXAMPLE 5.4)

At Walnut Hill, Jason Green develops students' understanding of Studio Practice and Technique in his Centering Project, introduced in the first class of the fall semester (see also Example 14.1). Here students begin to learn how to use the pottery wheel to center balls of clay. To do this, they must gain familiarity with both rules of the studio and techniques for using the pottery wheel (see Figure 5.1).

Demonstration–Lecture

At the beginning of this first class, Jason shows students where the tools and materials they will need are kept. In this 15-minute Demonstration–Lecture, he walks them through setting up materials and tools so they can begin to work. As he talks, he demonstrates each tool, shows how it works, and then gives step-by-step instructions as he models how to work the wheel, showing both correct and incorrect ways.

The following examples illustrate how Jason introduces getting set up to use the pottery wheel:

- *Jason tells students all about the tools they will need* (Develop Craft: Studio Practice). Jason informs students that they will each need a bucket for water. He shows them where the buckets are kept and fills one with water to show exactly where and how to fill them, as well as how much water to put in. He also shows students ceramics tools that they will need. He takes one of each and displays the collection on a nearby table as an example that they can refer to as they set up their own throwing materials—wooden ribs, wire tools, needle tools, and sponges—and other tools that they won't need today but will use later, like wooden knives.

- *Jason tells students how to get their clay ready for the wheel* (Develop Craft: Technique). Students will first need to get water in a bucket and set up a bat, the round flat surface on which their clay will sit as they turn the wheel and work the clay. Jason shows students how to cut clay and how to compress it. As he demonstrates, Jason

Figure 5.1. Develop Craft—Jason Green's Students Learn to Throw Clay Forms on a Pottery Wheel

A. Jason Green introduces tools to students in their first ceramics class

B. He labels drawers of ceramics tools to make them accessible

C. Jason demonstrates setting up to center clay on a pottery wheel

D. While students work, Jason advises them individually on centering

describes what he's doing. "When I'm doing this, I'm trying not to fold the clay, like these folds, really trying to keep those compressed."

- *Jason gives a detailed description of the wheels* (Develop Craft: Studio Practice). Jason holds up a splash pan, shows how this large bowl fits onto the wheels, and notes that some of the wheels are a little bit different; these practical details are critical to the students' success with the tools. He next shows how each wheel has a pedal and where the buttons are that turn the wheels on. Students will also need a bat. Jason tells students where to get their bats and how to care for them.

> Sometimes the bats aren't cleaned. You want to make sure everything's clean. So if you have clay here [*pointing to the bat*], or clay around these [*pointing to the wheel surface where there are pins that fit the holes in the bat*], you might need to take your needle tool and clean it a little bit [*holds up the needle tool*].

> Once a bat is clean, it can be placed on bat pins, and students are told to be sure that the bat doesn't rock on its pins.

> Next, Jason shows students how to form balls of clay. He makes eight balls to give students a chance to really see his ball-making technique as they work along. After they have made several balls themselves, Jason demonstrates how to center a ball of clay on the wheel. As he demonstrates, Jason carefully describes all the actions involved in each step of the process. He draws their attention to how his body is positioned, where his support is, and what he does with his hands. As he demonstrates the correct procedures, he also describes typical problems students may have and how to avoid them.

[handwritten margin note: As he models through talks through process]

Students-at-Work

Following Jason's introduction, students choose a wheel and set up their own areas for work. Jason talks with students as they work, offering comments rich in information about the studio practice of getting set up. Sometimes Jason's comments remind students of what they saw in the earlier Demonstration–Lecture, as when he had to remind students where to get their clay. Other comments offer new information, as when he told students which kind of bat to use.

When students begin to work on the wheel, Jason circles the room, closely observing students before giving advice on their technique. When he talks with students, he notes points of success and corrects errors, frequently demonstrating again as he talks. The repetition is necessary to support understanding, as each student sees new aspects of the process, depending on their constantly changing levels of understanding.

- *Jason reminds students of the assignment and gives advice as he watches them* (Develop Craft: Technique). When students first start working, Jason often reminds them of the assignment and what he has shown them in the Demonstration–Lecture. For example, stopping to look at the balls of clay one student has made, he reminds her,

> Make these really, really round. Make eight and remember you'll need a bat, which is up front, to put them on. Try to make them the same size if you can. That's good, that's good. Try not to make them too big; you'll have to use lots of muscle.

- *Jason gives step-by-step instructions to help students attend to aspects of process as they work* (Develop Craft: Technique). To a student trying the complex process of starting the wheel and centering a clay ball, Jason first advises, "Now, the first thing, you're going to put some water on it and press down on it." He then corrects how fast she is spinning the wheel. After the student has correctly adjusted the speed, Jason demonstrates and describes how to hold her hands and press the clay. Before moving to the next student Jason prompts, "Add a little bit more water now," and demonstrates again how the student should hold her hands.

- *Jason shows how the whole body contributes to centering* (Develop Craft: Technique). As Jason advises students, he moves students' hands, elbows, or feet to correct their position or demonstrates proper form himself. Jason tells one student, "Remember, your left elbow has to be braced, so you want to brace it against your hip. And then you want to put your right hand, lock it onto your left hand." As he speaks, he shows her this technique and how the clay is starting to get centered as he starts to apply pressure. After watching the student, he reminds her, "Keep that elbow down on your leg. Put pressure on the top and side at the same time, and add water very frequently."

Jason Reflects

In an interview after the class, Jason told us that he focuses on the technique of centering because that skill is a prerequisite to making any kind of pottery. He added that in the demonstration he shows how to center rather than how to make a pot because "students know they're going to be making pottery, and they know pottery is hollow. But if they don't have that basic skill of centering, then it's very, very difficult to make a pot."

Jason explained that centering is a complex and difficult skill that involves a variety of types of understanding—conceptual and physical—and that his goal in the first several weeks is for students to learn to center.

Most of them have never touched clay before. And even if you know a little bit about throwing pottery, you know what centering is, but if it's brand new, you might not even know what that term means. In some ways there are mechanical and sensory aspects and the understanding that goes along with it—understanding the language of the medium.

Jason's focus on centering is one way he works to change students' general attitudes toward materials. Jason gave us the following reason for his emphasis on the properties of clay:

Sometimes students will try to use clay to make something, and they're just making their idea and not *thinking* about the material. And they may fail, because they're not using the entire process. They're just using the clay as a construction material.

Without becoming responsive to properties of the material, entering into an ongoing dialogue with it, students are just implementing fixed ideas and might as well be using any material. He wants them to avoid naively underestimating the material's importance, which is typical of a beginning student. "They just happened to be in ceramics, so they're making this thing out of clay. But there's no reason for it to be made out of clay." This is the kind of thinking he wants students to avoid and to begin to understand how the clay is a partner in their creations.

More advanced students also have the same difficulty working with the properties of the clay. After

Jason described one student's growing frustration and difficulties, he added,

Sometimes you just can't do certain things because the materials you have won't work the way you want them to. One point I was trying to make to her is that she might not have to actually follow her design exactly, and she might have to allow the process to be more fluid.

Students vary in the ease with which they develop techniques such as centering. As Jason noted, "It takes some students weeks and weeks and weeks until they can do that." He added that sometimes he spends class time mainly going around the room individually helping those students, demonstrating to them, and correcting their technique individually.

Generative Connections with Develop Craft

In the third of his six Norton lectures at Harvard University, South African artist William Kentridge illustrates how artists combine Craft with other habits. As he walked back and forth between his drawing and the camera used to shoot his animation, *Mine*, Kentridge pondered how to transition between two scenes (see http://mahindrahumanities.fas.harvard.edu/content/william-kentridge-drawing-lesson-three-vertical-thinking-johannesburg-biography). This slow process required the maker (Develop Craft), the viewer (Observe), and the walker (Reflect) to converse with one another. It was during his walks back and forth between the camera and the drawing that Kentridge figured out how to get the film's character, a mine-owner, efficiently from his bed to the mine, a problem the artist had been pondering for days.

Kentridge's description of how he works mirrors the process described by Arts PROPEL, a collaboration among Project Zero, Educational Testing Service, and the Pittsburgh Public Schools (funded by the Rockefeller Foundation from 1986 to 1991). Arts PROPEL developed long-term projects (called "Domain Projects") involving three components: production, perception, and reflection. Production, or making, was always primary and central. Perception always grew from making: Students were encouraged to look closely at their works (and works of others) as they created. And all along students were encouraged to reflect about their process and to continually evaluate their work. Hence, reflection also grew out of making. This structure in which production, perception, and reflection interact was important to the development of our studio thinking framework. PDFs of the Arts PROPEL handbooks are available on the Project Zero website (http://www.projectzero.gse.harvard.edu/library.php).

The teaching of craft is often—though not always—central to visual arts classes. Acquiring technique gives students control over their works. And as students acquire technique, they begin to "think" with it, and that means making connections to other habits. But although Develop Craft was emphasized as an intended learning goal for every class we observed, we never saw it being taught alone. Instead, teachers cluster technique with one or more of the other habits, introducing ways to use skills with tools, materials, and conventions in the context of larger projects that require students to "think with" these skills, and not simply as tricks to be mastered for their own sake. Similarly, teachers model practices that maintain the studio as a way to support the art-making process, not as tasks to be carried out because someone said to. Teaching Develop Craft within the context of a project sets students up to learn alertness (recognizing when a new or better skill would improve the work they are engaged in making) and inclination (they are more likely to actually use skills to improve work they care about).

Using habits together develops all of the habits involved: Each one stimulates the others since they are interdependent. In the example below, a senior from the Boston Arts Academy talks about capturing light and creating variations of value in his drawing. His comments show us how Develop Craft clusters with Engage and Persist and Observe.

> It's about capturing light on something. . . .
> Once more it's about value. Because that's
> something I've been working on the past four
> years. . . . I push myself to see more variations
> and to get more detailed and to compare the
> grays. Like when I was doing my self-portrait,
> comparing the grays between one area of my
> face and the other to try to show the difference
> [see Figure 5.2].

Develop Craft pairs with Express whenever teachers assign authentic and engaging projects so that technique must be used to convey meaning. Develop Craft also clusters with Stretch and Explore and Engage and Persist (teachers might tell students to play around and keep trying); and also with Observe

and Understand Art Worlds (a teacher can encourage a student to look closely at how other artists use or approach materials and tools).

In the following example, Develop Craft clusters with Express and Reflect. As a student searches for a palette to convey a feeling of sadness (Develop Craft and Express), she might try mixing dark tones by adding black (Develop Craft). But doing so flattens the hues and can make the painting feel muddy. The student might think, "that's not sad, it's confused" (Reflect and Express). So a teacher might suggest remixing the colors using complements to create clearer, neutral tones (Develop Craft). The teacher might also wonder aloud whether confusion is part of what the student is trying to convey (Express); what if she created an undifferentiated surface texture with the paint, or perhaps blurred the edges of objects (Develop Craft and Express)? By pursuing techniques to express an intention, the student ends up reframing ideas iteratively and developing different aspects of craft to express those ideas. This example shows how teachers can help students expand the intention of their work and refine their craft to convey what they are trying to express.

Figure 5.2. Self-Portrait from a Senior at the Boston Arts Academy

Here is an example of a complex cluster involving Develop Craft, Stretch and Explore, Express, and Reflect. Kitty Condon, a teacher in the Chicago Public Schools, watched one of her 6th-graders drawing and saw the opportunity to have this student learn more about pencils in order to express meaning (Develop Craft and Express). Kitty brought over six pencils and quickly demonstrated how different kinds could be used to convey a different feeling (soft vs. strong lines, blurred vs. hard edges) (Develop Craft). As Kitty left, she reminded the student where she could get different pencils [Studio Practice] and told the student to see what she could do with the pencils, thereby encouraging her to Stretch and Explore in the service of Developing Craft and Expression. This encounter also called for Reflect: Evaluate, since the student needed eventually (but not while playing!) to judge the relative success and failure of her explorations.

What Teachers Can Do

Don't Teach Develop Craft Alone! The single most important understanding students can develop about Craft is that it is *for artmaking* and must be taught so that students experience that connection. When Craft is taught alone, it's like Delilah cutting Samson's hair—Craft's power to catalyze insight and creativity disappear. Craft is the way artists convey meaning. Contemporary artists often violate our expectations about craft and create surprise, either by using techniques in unusual ways or by using approaches that contradict expected fundamentals.

Use One-on-One Conversations During Students-at-Work sessions as opportunities to introduce mini-lessons on skill. "Here's a tool that might help you," or "Let me show you something about mixing browns," or "Have you thought about how things are attached? Let's look at what you've done and what that tells a viewer." Teachers can also build Studio Practice into these conversations. These "just-in-time" teaching moments help students develop the alertness for which of their skills to use when. "If you put your water bucket on the other side, you won't have to reach across your work and risk dripping on it," or "Your workspace is awfully cluttered. Take a few minutes to get it organized—you'll be able to find what you need more quickly."

Focus on the Quality of Craft in Relation to What the Work Conveys. "Let's look at the edges of your shapes. See how this is a hard edge and this one bleeds into the next? This one has a gap, and this one is soft and transparent. What are you saying with all those different edges? If you mean them all to be bold, you'll need to keep working to make them all consistent. But if you want a sense of disarray, think about making them more different, and where each difference should be."

Develop Craft in Other Disciplines

Every discipline involves craft, and just like the visual artist, practitioners of other disciplines need alertness and inclination in addition to skill to practice their craft well. Both surgeons and sailors learn techniques for tying knots, alertness to which knot is needed in a particular situation that comes up, and the motivation to tie it so it holds (inclination). An historian learns to find and handle primary source documents without damaging them, alert to the need to preserve the fragile and irreplaceable objects for the future and inclined to do so even when it is inconvenient. A writer learns grammar and syntax to communicate clearly, is alert to errors and to the needs of different audiences, and makes the effort to speak and write grammatically, driven by the need for listeners and readers to understand. Astronomers learn to use telescopes and to care for them, chemists to accurately weigh and measure substances because minute differences can change reactions. A singer learns the skills needed to support her breath from the diaphragm, but must also learn to recognize when to adjust her breathing technique (alertness, for example, to the shifts needed when singing long melodic vs. punctuated phrases), and be driven consistently to employ different skills as different needs arise (inclination). And every kind of work has Studio Practices. In all disciplines, professionals need to maintain their working spaces, tools, materials, and storage of products that are in process and completed: Sailors develop the motivation to care for ropes and singers to foster the health of the voice, and both develop alertness to when that is required (older ropes beginning to fray; how to sing when a cold is coming on). In each of these examples, Craft is used for disciplinary purposes.

In the next chapter we look at how classes are set up to teach students to work through frustration, to not give up, to persist and remain engaged.

SIX

Engage and Persist

COMMITTING AND FOLLOWING THROUGH

I think they learned how to work through frustration.

—Kathleen Marsh

Teachers in rigorous visual arts classes present their students with engaging projects, and they teach their students to connect to the assignment personally, to persist in their work, and to stick to a task for a sustained period of time.

In both schools we observed, this culminated in high school seniors being able to pursue a self-directed line of inquiry for a full semester. Students are taught to identify their own passions and interests and connect these to art projects, whether assigned or developed autonomously. They are also taught to focus, to develop mental states conducive to working, and to develop self-regulation (Baumeister & Vohs, 2007). They are taught to break out of ruts and blocks, and to feel encouraged about their learning and motivated to go on. For instance, a senior at Walnut Hill pursued a semester project that resulted in several dozen expressive and painterly oil portraits and other studies. He told us that his teachers gave him some feedback as he pursued his independent study but that they mostly had a "hands-off approach," allowing him to focus on what he termed his "personal learning." In his words: "I think that's where I am currently as a result of doing a lot of work and just learning from what I was doing. . . . And a lot of it, I've found, is my personal learning. I mean, the biggest element is, I think, I care about it. It's like I really want to advance where I'm going."

Teachers in rigorous visual arts classes also push their students to stick to projects and not to give up.

One 9th-grader at the Boston Arts Academy told us why he practices his drawing every day outside of class. "You can't expect to be great at it without practicing." In the words of artist Sister Corita Kent (Kent & Steward, 2008, p. 176), Rule 7 in art is "The only rule is work. If you work it will lead to something. It's the people who do all of the work all the time who eventually catch on to things." And Rule 5 complements that approach: "Be self-disciplined. This means finding someone wise or smart and choosing to follow them. To be disciplined is to follow in a good way. To be self-disciplined is to follow in a better way."

When one is engaged, one is intrinsically motivated to persist. Persisting for intrinsic reasons is what matters, not simply following directives to persist or persisting out of fear or a desire for approval. It is this habit that becomes the "still small voice" that drives intrinsic motivation, turning students from "school-success" orientation to working to pursue a full and passionate life.

Engagement is what makes someone *want* to persist. Personal engagement means that one gets pleasure out of the work itself, rather than simply working at something for some future goal. Mihaly Csikszentmihalyi (1990) calls this "autotelic" experience—experience that is self-rewarding and leads to states of flow—when one is truly engaged, lost in concentration, unaware of time, and fully focused on the moment.

In what follows, we present two classroom examples in which we see students working on projects that require sustained attention and motivation. In both classes, students wrestle with frustration and must work hard over time to meet a deadline.

DESIGNING IN CLAY:
COMPLETING THE TILE PROJECT   (EXAMPLE 6.1)

Toward the end of the school year at Walnut Hill, students are hard at work on a tile project in Jason Green's ceramic sculpture course. This project requires considerable technical skill and the willingness to stick to a task for several weeks without being able to see the end product. In an earlier class (see Example 7.2), students have designed a grid composed of nine tiles, and today their task is to finish their tiles. Students are asked to think about the shape, color, and texture of their tiles and to use the grid as a sketchbook in which they experiment with design options. As students come into class, they know what they are working on and go right to work. Jason calls this a "working class" (see Figure 6.1).

Students-at-Work

Today students must keep working hard if they are to finish the assignment by the deadline. "We will actually try to finish these tiles today, and that's a lot of work for some of you," Jason says, acknowledging that the students have a difficult task ahead of them.

Jason consults with students as they work, helping them focus on their work and stick to the task:

- *Stick to what you've begun.* Jason opposes a student's plan to start over, urging her to stick to the work she has begun. He also reminds her there is a deadline: "It won't be done by the show. That's all I can say if you want to start a new one. I would finish this."
- *Slowing down is sometimes a form of persisting.* To another student, Jason says, "So you just need to relax and take your time and build it."
- *Even if you're not happy with your work right now, it's important to keep going.* When a student says she feels her work looks "stupid," Jason gives her courage to keep on going. "You shouldn't be critical at this point, because it's so early in the process."
- *Learn to manage time as you work.* Jason suggests to a student that she find time to come to the studio outside of class so she can finish. He reminds her that she should glaze soon. "It's going to take you a while to glaze those pieces, I think. So you want to make some time in your schedule. This weekend. Friday."

- *Keep going even when you may not feel like it.* Jason tells a student to keep on going, even if she is not in the mood. "You should try to finish this today even if you don't feel like doing it. It's your last chance to get it done."

Jason Reflects

In our initial interview with Jason, he talked about how the medium of ceramics requires self-discipline because the material is continually changing and always drying out.

> I think it helps students develop habits—speedier habits that hopefully will allow or force them to think about things—and think about their artwork a little bit when they're outside of the classroom, so they don't just leave and forget about it. They have to remind themselves—you know, think about it sometimes. . . .

In our interview following this class, Jason talked about how students learn by following through, even if they don't like what they have made. By going through the process and coming up with something, students realize that not everything works.

Sometimes a class is just about working until the job is done. Jason characterized this class as a "working class" and the last "wet day," so students needed to get right to work.

> Just get work done so that we can finish things up. The goal was to . . . really get people to make decisions about things and do it . . . and that's . . . how art works when you have a deadline. And you know sometimes that's a good thing because you know your process is accelerated a little bit and you know you might have to make a quick decision or it changes the pace a little bit. So . . . that's sort of the overall goal [of this class] . . . do the work that needs to be done.

Jason also noted that students come to understand that art projects require work over extended periods of time. At the same time, there needs to be an emphasis on the way the program is set up.

> That's why we have 3-hour classes and . . . open studios on the weekends. . . . Here kids can just come in and work. . . . Time is such an important factor in doing what we do [and giving] the

Figure 6.1. Engage and Persist—Jason Green Helps Students Work on a Project That Lasts Several Weeks

A. Jason Green urges a student to continue the work she has begun

B. His students go right to work as they enter class

C. He advises a student not to judge her work so early in the process of making ceramic art

D. Jason urges another student to try to finish by the end of class as he consults about her design decisions

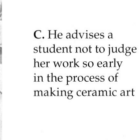

students enough time to make these things that we ask them to make.

Jason acknowledged that this was a frustrating project, and students would never have completed it if they had not been pushed to persist. He added:

> The students didn't like the project very much, but they liked the results a lot. Almost across the board I think they were really frustrated with the whole thing, because they had to use so many tools and measure things, and I think they just really had to struggle a little bit, and, also, we had a short time line.

FINISHING THE PROCESS: MAKING PUPPETS PROJECT   (EXAMPLE 6.2)

As the final project in Kathleen Marsh's fall term, 9th-grade foundations class at the Boston Arts Academy, students are working on 3-D projects. They have learned to encase an egg in a package strong enough to keep it from breaking when dropped 100 feet (see Example 12.6). This was followed by a joinery workshop with Barrington Edwards, a colleague in the visual art department at the Boston Arts Academy. In the class featured here, students are in the midst of work on a culminating project designed jointly by Kathleen and Barrington: making a 3-D puppet with two kinds of joints and five moveable parts. Kathleen and Barrington have stressed the importance of linking craft and design in building the puppets, a technically demanding project.

Just as Jason recognized the difficulty of the multistep Tile Project, Kathleen is well aware of how challenging this project is. Students have told her that they are frustrated because their puppets look unfinished. They have not yet gotten them to the envisioned endpoint. Like Jason, she feels the need to encourage the students so that they will stay engaged. For example, at one point she asks, "How many of you feel frustrated with your pieces right now?" Many students raise hands. Her next comments offer encouragement:

> I want to say for all of you that you've done an amazing job. . . . To take something [paper] that's inherently two-dimensional and make it three-dimensional is really difficult. This is a really hard thing we're asking you to do. And you're doing a really good job. So, don't lose heart, OK?

As in Jason's class, students are working against a deadline, and they know that they are expected to persist in this project in out-of-class time. Kathleen reminds students of the deadline and suggests one way they might meet it:

> You . . . only have today to work on these. . . . You may stay after school. . . . I've been sad to see that only a few people have stayed after. These three girls have stayed after yesterday, but I haven't seen many people stay after school since we began talking about this deadline, which was quite a while ago.

Students are given clear information about just what they need to do to finish this project, to help them stick to the task by making it clear what the task demands. "I hear a lot of extra conversation. I know you guys are really ready to begin, OK? And I know you are really antsy, but I want to make sure that everybody is clear about what's required."

Kathleen also reminds students of expectations, "Part of the culture of this school, and not just this department, is that there is an expectation that you are going to spend time outside of class on your work." At the same time, she tells students why there is this expectation:

> Our expectation is that you spend a little time outside of school working on things, because we do want you to challenge yourself. We do want you to go above and beyond the very basics of what we ask, and sometimes that requires more time. OK? So, sometimes you need to get into the habit and culture of staying after school.

She reminds them that all of the visual arts teachers are available in the classrooms Monday through Thursday after school.

Students-at-Work

As students work, Kathleen offers encouragement to both individuals and to the whole class.

- *Don't give up. You've done a good job.* As she helps students, Kathleen pushes and encourages at the same time. She looks at one student's sketch and prods the student to continue. "Where are your moveable parts?" "You have a lot of work to do, but you have a good start. You've got to really focus." At the same time, she offers praise for what the student has done so far.

- *Remember the task at hand.* As Kathleen walks to help a student, she express her concern for the way the whole class is starting to lose focus, "I'm very worried by you. You're all over the place, and you're not focused."
- *Re-engage with a "good-enough" vision and a feasible plan of action you can carry through.* As Kathleen pauses to help a student joining paper strips, she offers advice:

> Don't fall in the trap of having a vision that's so far away that you can't satisfy the basics of the assignment, and don't get so caught up in disappointment that it's not matching your original vision. You and many others like you fall into that trap, and one of the things an artist needs to learn is that sometimes you just have to meet deadlines and meet the criteria being asked for rather than being too perfectionist.

Kathleen and Students Reflect

In an interview after the class, Kathleen reflected on the project and on helping students to Engage and Persist. Some students need to be monitored so that they stay on track. Others Engage and Persist on their own, yet even these independent students need to be checked in a large class so they don't get lost. "You have to keep checking everybody. Making sure they're still all going in the right direction. Making sure they're not losing focus, and it's hard 'cause that class is really big."

Kathleen finds that students at the Boston Arts Academy need support to stay focused, because

> A lot of kids who come to this school do not have the kind of external support that kids who are middle-class or upper-class have. Whether it's two parents. Whether it's money, whether it's experiences, they just don't have those opportunities, so we have to . . . create structure and support.

She finds that students learn to stay on task for increasingly longer periods of time. "I noticed that their attention span is lengthening. They're learning to work in longer studio sessions. They aren't asking me for breaks anymore."

One senior said learning to persist in work was the most important thing she learned in her 4 years at the Boston Arts Academy.

> Here they force you to stick with a piece. . . . I remember in middle school you just started drawing something, you just leave it on the table and walk away. You don't have to finish it like that. And I had a real difficult problem with sticking to my work because . . . I'd have an idea and I'd be all happy about it and I'd start it. And then by midway, I'd have another idea. And I'd get the idea from the piece that I started and so I'd just digress again and start over. And they had no problem with that in middle school. It's only like keeping you busy. It doesn't matter what you're doing. Then I got here. It was only Boston Arts Academy when I really started finishing pieces and that was a big thing for me because it's like wow, I actually completed something! And I like it! [*laughing*] So it was huge, it was like a big deal for me just to finish the work [see Figure 6.2].

Figure 6.2. Charcoal Self-Portrait by a Senior at the Boston Arts Academy

A senior at Walnut Hill talks about her persistence and shows us how sticking to a project also involves

the habit of *Envision*. The end product that she holds in her mind motivates her to keep working:

"I think I've learned how to work really hard" is the first response of the Walnut Hill senior who created the sculpture shown in Figure 6.3 when we asked her what she saw as her important learning over 4 years of art classes. The sculpture is inspired by her idea of creating a 3-D mosaic with wood blocks and is a good example of her work ethic. Working from a pixelated 2-D image of gears, she describes her initial process: "I put [the pixelated image] in a gray scale so that for each different scale I made a block a different length—the lightest blocks were the longest ones and the darkest blocks were the shortest ones. So I had to plan everything out before I actually started to do it." However, after cutting all the blocks to scale, planning their assembly, and constructing it nearly to the top, she realized that the sides of the circle were not going to connect properly and the structure was not stable. She had to disassemble the parts of the circle, figure out how to make it work to her envisioned goal, figure out the dimensions that would make it both connect and not lean, and then recut the wooden pieces. Her engagement in creating this piece, envisioning how it would look when done, and her commitment to good craft combined together to help her to persist: "I'll get halfway finished and I'll just be like, 'ugh, I don't want to do that anymore'. . . . But when I get to that point I'll just look at what I've done . . . that's what gets me through it, just thinking about what the end product is gonna look like." She told us that as a senior she explicitly set challenges to make herself work hard: "I pick ways of building things that are very tedious, very meticulous work. . . . I make it really difficult for myself to get done. I make it difficult because I pick such tedious things, and I like it when I get stuck because I have to work so much harder. I don't know, I just like to work."

Figure 6.3. Wood Sculpture by a Senior at Walnut Hill

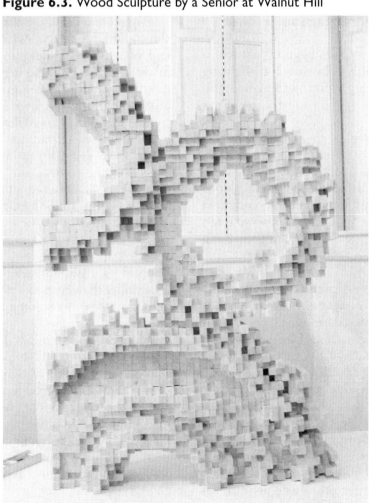

In our final interview with Kathleen, she talks about the importance of passion, which we see as the high end of engaging and persisting:

> The thing that we talk a lot about as a school is that other thing that you look for, which is the unmeasurable thing, which we call "it," or "the twinkle in the eye," "the hunger," "the desire," and we don't measure it. We certainly talk about it, we certainly note it, we do write about it, but we don't measure it. There is no way to measure it.

Both Jason's Tile Project and Kathleen's Puppet-Making Project challenged students and grabbed their interest. The projects were within the students' abilities yet were novel and exciting. The projects also gave plenty of space for students to take a personal approach to the task. Teachers often played the role of gently keeping students on task and making sure they persisted in their engagement.

A Dispositional View of Engage and Persist

Engage and Persist extends beyond just working hard. Developing this habit involves figuring out how to start and keep working in meaningful ways.

Skill. The skill that makes engagement possible is self-awareness. Students need to be able to identify their interests. Skills of persistence include strategies to work through obstacles to continuing, such as taking a break, asking for someone to comment on one's work, standing back and looking at one's work from a new angle, or working on something else for awhile.

Alertness. Alertness to engagement requires that students recognize what engages them and notice when they feel engaged. Alertness to persistence means recognizing the obstacles to persistence, such as feeling stuck, overwhelmed, sleepy, distracted, or frustrated, and knowing that this is the time to pull out all stops and use the skills of persistence.

Inclination. The inclination to engagement means seeking out opportunities that are engaging and finding what is engaging in work that is assigned. The inclination to persist arises when one is engaged—if you genuinely care about what

you're doing, you push through obstacles until you are satisfied. The inclination to persist also depends upon self-efficacy—the belief that you can get better. As Carol Dweck (2000) has shown, when students believe that intelligence is something that can be improved through effort, they work harder. When they believe that intelligence is fixed and "you have it or you don't" (an entity theory of intelligence), students are less likely to challenge themselves and more likely to give up.

Generative Connections with Engage and Persist

In Jason's Tile Project and Kathleen's Puppet-Making Project, Engage and Persist was not taught in isolation. Engage and Persist often pairs with Reflect when students become aware of obstacles that need to be worked through. Engage and Persist pairs with Express because working on a project to convey personal meaning is engaging; in addition, the most engaging projects are usually ones that allow expression of personal meaning.

Engage and Persist also frequently pairs with Observe and Understand Art Worlds—when students look at artists' work and practices and use these as inspiration. For example, a 9th-grader at Boston Arts Academy identified as a graffiti artist and resisted broadening his skills. By his senior year he had become interested in his African heritage and chose to look closely at African masks. This study resulted in a painted self-portrait in the style of an African mask (see the color insert, "Sam's Transformation Over 4 Years"). Observing the art of another culture broadened him, and he found that graffiti was only one of the ways of working that engaged him.

The example below shows a cluster of Engage and Persist, Envision, and Stretch and Explore, as Jason helps a student sustain an experimental attitude rather than rush to a premature solution in the initial stages of envisioning her "unit sculpture."

Jason: Before you start that, I want you to think about the little coil. Think about that and think about other forms or shapes of clay that you might use rather than just that little coil—maybe three or four different pieces of clay that you could repeat to build. . . . (Envision)
Student: So you don't want me to do the pine cones?
Jason: I didn't say that.
Student: You want me to experiment first. (Stretch and Explore)

Jason: First, yes, rather than just starting, I want you to experiment with some different types of units. Some might be very geometric, some you might just grab and shape in your hand quickly. (Stretch and Explore in the service of Engage and Persist).

What Teachers Can Do

Teachers can help students engage by setting up projects that include choice, a practice often under-emphasized (Douglas & Jaquith, 2009; Jaquith & Hathaway, 2012). They can ask students to think about the activities they choose to engage in during their free time—such activities are likely to be what they care about. They can also ask students to keep personal sketchbooks to gather ideas and images that intrigue them and that can be used later. This helps not only to get students to work in the moment, but also to develop their disposition to engage continuously in their work.

Sometimes teachers need only to encourage and praise efforts at persistence (e.g., "you're doing a great job here"). At other times, developing this habit takes the form of either creating tension by urging students to keep going (e.g., playing energetic music; saying "don't stop now, keep at it"; or "you have only a half hour left to work"), or reducing tension, by, for example, playing relaxing music to help students focus.

Perhaps most importantly, teachers can help students Engage and Persist by nurturing their self-efficacy—reminding them to be alert to excessive self-criticism and encouraging them not to give in to negative self-talk. Teachers can also help students develop self-efficacy by showing students what they can accomplish if they Engage and Persist.

Engage and Persist in Other Disciplines

Getting good at anything requires persistence. Much has been written about the 10,000 hours required for expertise, whether the activity be gymnastics, violin playing, chess, or feats of verbal memory (Ericsson, 1996; Ericsson, Nandagopal, & Roring, 2009). Even the most gifted child prodigy needs to work hard to develop and actualize her inborn abilities. And engaging work is the key to persistence in any discipline.

SEVEN

Envision

THINKING IN IMAGES

I try to get them to think about how they would choose an object as a source, and then abstract from that object to make a sculpture.

—Jason Green

In studio classes, students learn to think in images when they are developing their works. They think in images as they come up with an idea, as they progressively re-conceptualize their work, and as they imagine the steps to get there.

Envisioning and Observing are ends of the same continuum. When observing, one looks closely at the outside world. When envisioning, one imagines and generates images of possibilities in the mind.

Consider the relationship between Observe and Envision in observational drawing. The artist observes and then uses a medium to give form to what she sees. The translation from model to representation requires envisioning. Artists aim to capture not only the surface aspects of their models, but also the underlying structure and geometry—for example, the axis of the head versus the axis of the body, the torso as a trapezoid, the triangular or overlapping relation between two figures. Artists may also emphasize aspects of a pose (e.g., location in space, tension in a part of the body) or choose a composition that suggests associations or narratives.

In work that is not done from observation, the continuum is less clear, but it also exists. Artists work from mental images that are themselves derived from having observed the world.

Here are some of the many ways students were encouraged to *Envision*

- Generate a work of art solely from their imaginations, rather than from observation.

- Imagine how their work would look if they made specific changes. Here, the skill of *Envision* is used in planning a work.
- Make a "unit," repeat it, and then combine the units into sculptural forms. This is an example of another kind of envisioning focused on "improvisational" planning.
- Imagine all of the ways they can vary a line, a shape, a color, or a composition.
- Imagine implied forms in their drawings—forms that cannot be seen in full because they are partially occluded.
- Observe the underlying geometry of a form and then envision how that geometry can be shown in their work.

Two classes are featured in this chapter, and both demonstrate two kinds of *Envisioning*—imagining and planning. Imagining is an activity that is required for planning a work, and it can be done in a host of ways.

PLACES FOR AN IMAGINARY CREATURE: INVENTING COLORS PROJECT   (EXAMPLE 7.1)

At the Boston Arts Academy near the conclusion of Beth Balliro's spring term course with 9th-graders, we see students continuing to work on the Imaginary Creatures Project. They are using acrylics to paint a mythical creature situated in the landscape in which it was born or died (see also Examples 5.1 and 13.1). The creature cannot be seen; thus it is envisioned.

Students-at-Work

As students work (see Figure 7.1), Beth repeatedly finds ways to focus students on one form of Envisioning—generating images from the imagination:

Figure 7.1. Envision—Beth Balliro and Her Students Consider Ways to Paint Environments Where Imaginary Creatures Lived

A. Beth Balliro works on color with a student

B. Beth and a student consider how a landscape expresses character

C. Beth urges a student to envision how to vary the color

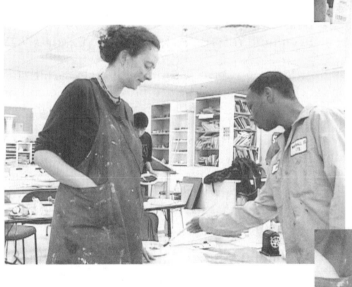

D. She wonders with another student how to expand the range of colors in a work

- *Imagine where your creature came from and create a landscape for the creature.* Beth asks a student to think explicitly of what he is trying to represent. "Wherever you think that beautiful creature can burst out of a seed. Where would it be? . . . a greenhouse, or a pot, or a windowsill, a crack in the sidewalk."

- *Create an imaginary landscape that tells a narrative.* Beth tells a student:

  > I want you to think about how you can tell a story with your landscape. I'm having you come up with where they were born, because to do that you will have to . . . have in mind a place and not use characters to show it. . . . I want you to have a landscape that has a story, and, in this case, I want you to think more deeply about your character.

- *Envision where the light is coming from in the landscape.* Beth asks a student to think about light. "Where is the light in this forest coming from . . . day or night? What time of day? What kind of light? Is it foggy? Bright and shining?" Beth also asks students to look closely at their work (Observe) as they plan, to see how it might grow (Envision).

- *Determine where on the page a new color could be used.* Beth asks a student, "Think about if there is a place where you want to include a color that's different than these."

- *Envision variations of a color.* Beth prods a student working with two colors to envision more variations of the colors. "OK, so you have red plus yellow . . . you have orange, think about how many oranges you can get."

- *Think of how to make color translucent and layered.* Beth asks students to think about how to layer colors "so you can still see the value shining through."

Beth Reflects

When asked to give this class a title, Beth called the class "Inventing Colors." As explained in Chapter 5, students were learning to envision new colors out of primaries, motivated by their struggles to envision a mythical creature that could in some way represent themselves, in landscapes of its birth and death. When asked why students should learn to invent rather than copy, Beth replied that when students just follow tradition, their work is "so much less interesting than when they invent. So, that's

why I didn't want to lead them by requiring that they look at references." Beth also thinks it's important to have students learn the relationship between drawing from imagination and drawing from observation because "fantasy drawings will be much better if you work on observation." (Figure 7.2 shows a painting resulting from this project.)

Figure 7.2. Birth Painting by a 9th-grader at the Boston Arts Academy

DESIGNING IN CLAY: BEGINNING THE TILE PROJECT   (EXAMPLE 7.2)

In Jason Green's classroom at Walnut Hill, students are beginning a tile project near the end of their second-semester course in ceramics. In this class, they are assigned to create nine tiles pressed from molds. They place objects into the molds to press out individual textured tiles. They must think of each tile in relation to the whole, as in painting, because the nine tiles, each 5-inches square, must form a piece that can be hung on the wall (see also Example 6.1).

Students-at-Work

As students work, Jason frequently asks them to envision the next steps in their work. Below are Jason's interactions with two students as he prods both to think of what they might do next with their work:

- *How might individual tiles function as a single piece?* Jason tells a student, "I want you to think of how the tiles relate. Have something that connects them together between the tiles." To another, he says, "You need to know what each

tile will look like before you start making it."
He further warns her to avoid carving all nine
pieces separately; she will need to think in terms
of a grid.

- *What would your work look like if you tried
  something else?* Jason asks the student to think
  of the basic things that make up the design. He
  then asks her, "What would happen if you did
  it on each tile, so you didn't have to carve nine
  pieces of plaster?" (This also nurtures the Studio
  Habit of Mind Stretch and Explore, because
  Jason is encouraging the student to consider
  options.)
- *What do you plan to do?* Jason asks a student what
  she plans: "You have to decide if you want the
  middle out, coming closer to you. That means
  you will have to cut these little squares."
- *What technique might you employ?* As the student
  struggles with her grid drawing, Jason suggests
  that she think of how she might execute what
  she plans: "You could cut something like this
  [he picks up a straight piece of wood] and have
  it go into the mold, and you would get a nice
  straight line."

Jason Reflects

In an interview after this class, Jason noted that
the project requires advanced planning, which we
refer to as Envisioning. "They're making all the decisions about their artwork when they're not actually working on the clay." He also stressed that in
this project, students have to "figure out" ahead of
time (Envision) the end product before beginning
to build the object. They must envision how the
forms will be reversed after clay is pressed into the
mold.

Jason said his goal was to have students envision
their own product and not follow a set of automatic
steps: "What I don't want to do is give them the recipe for making art, because there is no real recipe."
Instead, Jason's goal is to help students find their
own solutions: "I want to give them the tools so that
they can be innovators and come up with their own
problems and their own solutions and their own
questions."

One might at first think that Envisioning occurs
only when artists work from imagination. But Envisioning also occurs when working from the model
or when combining imagination and observation in
works. Every time artists plan next steps they are
Envisioning. Every time they step back and ask
themselves how the work would look if they made
some kind of alteration they are Envisioning. The
teachers asked students to plan and to imagine revisions in their works. Thus students gained considerable practice in working from mental images.
Envisioning—the ability to imagine and to generate
mental images—is a disposition important in many
domains. And visual arts classes are perhaps the
arenas in which this disposition is most consistently
fostered and demanded.

A Dispositional View of Envision

Skill. The skill that makes Envision possible relates to using mental imagery. Students need to be
able to generate and manipulate visual images in
their minds as they imagine how they want their
finished products to look.

Alertness. Alertness to envisioning requires
that students recognize when it is important to re-
imagine their work. Students creating observational work need to recognize that the translation from
model to work is not direct; it is mediated by their
imaginations. There are many ways to represent
what is seen, and it is up to them to imagine how
they want to show what they see as they translate
observation to the work of art they are creating.
Students creating work from imagination need to
recognize moments to re-imagine their product
and realize that there are many ways to proceed.

Inclination. When artists put their imaginations
to use as they are planning and/or creating works,
they show the inclination to Envision. Without support, students often skip or give short shrift to the
envisioning process and move directly into making,
without doing the mental work of exploring their
ideas. Without specific attention to Envisioning, cli-
chés come to the surface, students stay stuck in their
existing schemas, and works tend to be uninspired
and say little that is new. The envisioning process
is what sustains artistic investigation and leads to
innovation.

What Teachers Can Do

Some typical approaches to support the skill of
envisioning include regular use of sketchbooks,
making thumbnails and storyboards, and sus-
pending the commitment to final decisions by, for

example, using tracing paper to make revisions or gluing collage elements only after trying out many different compositions.

Teachers can help students envision by setting constraints such as "make ten sketches before you start the work" or not giving students glue until they've arranged a collage three different ways. Another technique is playing the "what if" game by asking students to imagine how their work would look if. . . . What if you moved this part over here? What if you darkened this corner? What if you repeated this red over here? What if you showed the figure more from the back? All of these prompts push the student to generate and manipulate a mental image, to put off the final decision, and to imagine greater possibilities in the work.

An antidote to the problem of "first idea" is shown by a practice in Olivia Gude's Spiral Curriculum (a Saturday program at the University of Chicago), where she teaches her pre-practicum art-teacher students to employ Surrealist games as envisioning tools that surface unconscious ideas, forms, and intentions useful to the creation of provocative works. By smoking paper, preparing papers with inkblots and splatters, or using random selection processes of dice, spinners, or blind choice, students' imaginations open in ways that avoid the constraints of their usual ideas.

Generative Connections with Envision

Envision—the habit of thinking in images—commonly clusters with Observe and Develop Craft. Kimbell and colleagues (2005) describe this process as "The Interaction of Mind and Hand":

> The concrete expression of ideas not only clarifies them for us, but moreover it enables us to confront the details and consequences of them. . . . Cognitive modeling by itself—manipulating ideas purely in the mind's eye—has severe limitations when it comes to complex ideas. . . . It is through externalised modeling techniques that such complex ideas can be expressed and clarified, thus supporting the next stage of cognitive modeling. It is our contention that this inter-relationship between modeling ideas in the mind, and modeling ideas in reality is the cornerstone of capability in design and technology. (p. 21)

This kind of embodied thinking—making envisioned ideas real by crafting with materials, observing what is done, and then tinkering both with the idea and the material—is central in art making.

Envision also often pairs with Reflect—the habit of metacognition. Asking students to talk about their works can help them become clearer about their goals and their judgments, prompting them to re-envision and go on to revise. Judging when a work is finished also requires that Envision interact with Reflect and Express—to recognize when one's vision has been achieved.

Envision also clusters with Stretch and Explore and Engage and Persist. When students are dissatisfied with what they have made, they have to envision something new. And this often requires being willing to stretch beyond what they know how to do well and to experiment. One must be sufficiently engaged in the project to persist in exploration.

Envision also frequently interacts with Observe and Understand Art Worlds. Students can look closely at works by other artists—in museums and galleries, in books and reproductions, and online—to help them envision what they might do in their own work. Students can also learn to envision how to work by studying artistic process—something readily available to every classroom teacher through the high quality videos of contemporary artists' practice that are now available online (e.g., Art21, Spark, TateShots).

Envisioning often surfaces in complex clusters of habits whenever artists describe their process. A freshman at Walnut Hill explained his thought process as he responded to a drawing assignment:

> Well, when I did the drawing (Develop Craft) it was supposed to be about the way the whole room looks and the way everything just comes in to the subjects (Observe). But there are a lot of . . . things around that would distract from what I was trying to draw (Reflect: Evaluate). So I did change things around a little bit. I tried to make things as much as I could point to the middle here (Express). . . . I think it's mostly the stuff that I left out that helps support the piece (Envision, Reflect: Evaluate) (See Figure 7.3).

Envision in Other Disciplines

Envisioning—the ability to imagine and to generate mental images—is a disposition important across domains. This disposition is consistently demanded and fostered in visual arts classes.

Athletes often rehearse what they are going to do using mental imagery. For example, Mary

Whipple, coxswain for the rowing team at the 2012 Olympics, explained how she visualizes what she will say in a race and how she gathers her rowers together in a quiet dark room before every competition; they all close their eyes as she talks them through the coming race (http://www.nytimes.com/2012/08/02/sports/olympics/voice-of-authority-directs-us-womens-rowing-team.html?src=me&ref=general).

A scientist envisions patterns to form conclusions; an historian avoids the problem of presentism by envisioning the mindset of a different era. Choreographers envision dances; composers and conductors envision the sounds and silences of music; and playwrights and directors envision dramatic stories.

Writers imagine and re-imagine plot structure for writing scenes. Filmmakers imagine a narrative in time and motion while creating storyboards for a film. Architects use sketches and Computer Assisted Design to imagine a building that is translated into a three-dimensional model and drawn in blueprints to convey their vision to others for execution. Engineers envision how parts of machines can work together efficiently—in their minds, in sketches and physical models, and using 3D modeling on computers. All of these responses employ envisioning and moving back and forth between envisioning and observing.

In the next chapter we consider how students learn to go beyond technique to express a personal vision in their work.

Figure 7.3. Charcoal Drawing of a Studio Class by a Freshman at Walnut Hill

EIGHT

Express

FINDING MEANING

The strength of the drawing is going to depend very much on the evocative nature of the space.

—Jim Woodside

Express is commonly associated with arts classes. Often people equate expression with free and undisciplined venting of emotion. But expression is really about meaning of all sorts—feelings, concepts, and ideas.

Works of art convey meaning through the symbol system of the art form. In his book *Languages of Art* (1968), philosopher Nelson Goodman distinguishes two ways of symbolizing: "representation" and "metaphorical exemplification." A painting of a crying child is a representation of sadness. It is literally a picture of a sad person. When works of art symbolize through metaphorical exemplification, they convey qualities that the works do not literally possess: A painting can be metaphorically sad, loud, or agitated just through the way it uses line, color, composition, and allusion. A piece of music can express brightness or ease through its timbre, tempo, and consonance. Dance uses such elements as gesture, force, level, and speed to convey meaning.

When we look at a work of visual art, we do not see only what is represented (a landscape, a portrait); we also grasp its non-visual, metaphorical properties. When a violinist plays with great skill but no feeling, the audience is left cold, and the critics take their revenge. When listening to Beethoven's third symphony, the Eroica, the audience is meant to feel a host of emotions, from triumph and nobility to mourning and solace. Works of art cannot be reduced to verbal messages to convey their meaning, and great works of art are always more than great craft.

A senior at Walnut Hill told us how she learned about the centrality of expression:

I came . . . to this school and I basically just was thinking about skill and showing skill and, you know, trying to create depths and dimension and just show what's real and show that I can present it in a real way. And that's the perfect example [referring to her realistic apple drawing]. . . . But with my self-portrait, it clearly shows how I'm more . . . working with myself and . . . who I am. . . . It's very personal, it's more deep, and it's not about presenting something in a realistic way. . . .
It still has a lot of skill in it. . . . But the whole general idea of what I'm trying to present has changed. And I grew a lot through that because basically when I came here I started to have a lot of skill but I didn't really know what to do with it or how to connect it with my thinking. (See Figure 8.1)

While representation as a form of symbolization is not limited to the arts, metaphorical exemplification is specific to the arts. We named this habit Express to refer to the making of meaning in both ways.

In the following two classes, we see students learning aspects of expression. In both, we see examples of class structures and interactions with various students that encourage them to go beyond technique to create something with evocative meaning.

Figure 8.1. Self-Portrait by a Senior at Walnut Hill

DRAWING FOR FEELING: FIGURES IN EVOCATIVE SPACE PROJECT (EXAMPLE 8.1)

At Walnut Hill in Jim Woodside's Figures in Evocative Space Project (see also Examples 12.1 and 15.2), students learn to convey a mood or atmosphere in their drawing that evokes something about the psychology of the figures in the drawing. Jim moves students away from thinking about representing a single figure, as they had in previous classes, toward thinking about figures in relationship, telling a story in an evocative space (see Figure 8.2 on page 68).

Demonstration–Lecture

Five months into his drawing class, Jim introduces his students to the concept of drama and narrative. He poses a male and female student together at opposite sides of a space. He asks the rest of the students to think of the models as kids just hanging out. He contrasts this kind of drawing with more standard fare in which he had asked students to draw an isolated figure he set up for them. He makes comments, encouraging them to be expressive in their drawings.

- *Jim asks students to use drawing to express a dramatic relationship.*

    I'm trying to set up a kind of dramatic lighting . . . a lighting that seems almost mysterious or evocative. . . . I want this to be set up like a kind of stage. . . . You know, when you think of actors on a stage, you don't just think of the personalities, but you think of the whole story being told. You think of the lighting. You think of the kind of environment being implied, right?

- *Jim asks students to think about what is implied, suggesting that they think as if they were movie directors and show their decisions in their drawings:*

    These two people are elements in a drama. . . . What I'm asking you to do is move beyond the idea of just drawing a figure in an art class, which is what we've done for the last couple of weeks. Now I'm asking you to think more about the emotional content, the relationship between the two, the drama, the mystery.

- *Jim asks students to Express the relationship between the two figures in the empty space between them:*

    You're going to have to include all this space, this empty space. Now that's going to be a big challenge in your drawing, because something is going to be in that space, you know? There's gonna' be the wall, the blackness of the window, but more importantly, what's the sort of emotional content and character, and what do you get out of that drawing? Let me re-phrase that—the strength of the drawing is going to depend very much on the evocative nature of this space.

Jim also introduces paintings by Edward Hopper and Richard Deibenkorn and leads a discussion about these paintings' evocative, emotional content (see Example 12.1). In addition to his focus on Express, he fosters Understand Art Worlds as the students learn how their work relates to that of professional artists. He helps them Observe, as students learn to see light and value by looking closely at works of art, and he asks them to Reflect: Question and Explain, as they are asked to describe qualities in the work.

Students-at-Work

Jim consults with students as they work on a series of quick, compositional sketches (3–5 minutes each), and then on a longer drawing on better paper:

Figure 8.2. Express—Jim Woodside's Students Learn to Express Emotional Content in Their Figure Drawings

A. Jim Woodside focuses students' attention on light as a source of drama in drawings

B. His students begin drawing figures in dramatic lighting

C. As students work, Jim talks to individuals about their work

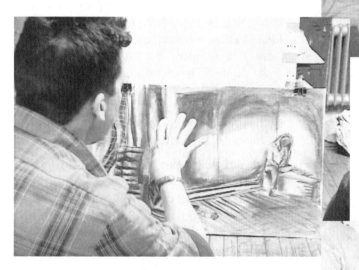

D. Jim encourages an uncertain student to heighten contrast in his drawing to show the dramatic relationship between the figures

- *Notice the expressive light on the face of the female model.* Jim directs a student's attention to the strong, very clear light on one side of the model's face and the dark values on the other, and says, "That can be all the information you need. A sort of very mysterious, wonderful light across one side of her body." This consult also fosters learning to Observe as the student is shown how to look closely at the model.

- *Create a dramatic sense of receding space by exaggerating perspective.* Jim puts tracing paper on the drawing to demonstrate as he suggests to a student that he include in his drawing pictures on the wall "because if you put them on in perspective, it's the perfect way of telling the viewer that the space is going back. But you can make that even more dramatic if you like, exaggerating the diminishing side of the picture." This consult also fosters the learning of Develop Craft: Technique, as the student is encouraged to use the rules of perspective mastered earlier in the semester, and the learning of Observe, as the student is encouraged to notice space around the models and use it to express an intended effect.

- *Use the technique of erasing to convey a dramatic feeling of light.* Jim suggests that a student use the technique of erasing. "This drawing is the type of drawing that sort of works from darkness backward instead of putting darkness on." He also asks the student to recall a project from several months ago, when he covered the paper in charcoal and erased into it (see Examples 3.3, 5.3, and 9.2). "In a way, there's a similar thing going on here, where bits of light are worked out of darkness." Jim asks for permission to erase the student's drawing a bit and describes what he's doing. "In certain areas where it's important to show the weight of the figure, go back in with your eraser. You know, heighten that contrast in certain areas." This consult also fosters the learning of Develop Craft: Technique, and is a good example of how students are taught to be alert to craft (and develop technical skill) in the service of expression.

Critique

During the class, Jim uses several short Critique sessions to point out how specific compositional decisions determine the kind of relationship conveyed between the two figures. Students' works, taped onto drawing boards, are leaned informally against the wall for all to sit before and contemplate. Jim praises students' success at making decisions in their sketches about what they want to express. In discussing the drawings, he directs students' attention to expression as "powerful decisions starting to be made, starting to emerge out of your sketches."

During the Critique, Jim notes how one student has created a strong statement of isolation by the choices made. He points to small, discrete figures and suggests the power of really exaggerating the distance between them. "Maybe it's a statement about the lack of communication between the two figures."

Jim further compares the expression of the deep space in the drawing to another student's drawing that is flatter. He points out how the dramatic angle gives the picture a less stable effect and how the student's choice to include architectural elements (wall and floor) is really the substance of the drawing. "It's not a portraiture, it's just arrangement of shapes."

Jim also shows the class a finished drawing of the same kind of scene by a student in another class to explain what he means by telling a story. He points out the power of the open space and the way the drawing is done with just a hint of light around the otherwise anonymous figure. Finally, he comes back to the idea of a stage set. "When I talk about telling a story, I'm not saying that you're illustrating an event, a story, but I'm saying that you're implying a drama, a sort of living drama between figures."

Jim Reflects

In our interviews with Jim, he talked about how he strives to teach students to find personal relationships in their art and how he never teaches technique alone. "It is about connecting the art to your life and to the world and your place in the world." Jim talked about why he never wants to teach just skills and then go on to content and expression. "It is not [only] the skill of drawing that they are learning. It is very much the making of a mark in the world as expression; and, to me, that might be something that is more interesting and more exciting for them."

For Jim, the teaching of technique is only part of the picture. "I have had kids in drawing that could draw better than I could, but they really couldn't push it to another level. There is just not depth in their work." He tries to help students see how an idea, like drawing the figure, connects to a world that they relate to and understand. "Whether it's them with their parents in the kitchen or whether it's kids hanging out in Harvard Square, there's a kind of drama to everyday life." And what hits you first when you look at a work of art is not its technique but its evocative properties.

In our final interview with Jim as he reflected on the year, he said that the assignments do get more interpretative as he moves through the year. They are more evocative in terms of expression, but he stressed that expression cannot be conceived of in isolation from other aspects of drawing.

DRAWING FOR MEANING: IMAGINARY CREATURES PROJECT   (EXAMPLE 8.2)

At the Boston Arts Academy, in Beth Balliro's Imaginary Creatures Project in the middle of her second-semester course with 9th-graders, she stressed that students should express personal meaning in their work. The students are each making a mythical creature that expresses something about their own personality. They are going beyond representation to create something with connotative, evocative meaning. In an earlier class, students wrote about what inspires them ("What is your muse?"); (see Example 10.1). Now with this inspiration in mind, Beth helps them to do a pencil sketch in which they think of themselves as a mythical creature—part human, part animal. As students worked, Beth encouraged them to identify properties through which to convey personal meaning in two ways:

- *Decide which aspects of character to express in the mythical figure.* Beth asks a student several questions to get him to think about which aspects of his character he wants to express in his mythical figure. "If you could be any character, would this be the one? A warrior? What about you is the most dominant part of you?" Beth also reassures the student that he is already steps ahead in the challenge of making a drawing that synthesizes man and beast. Now he has to make sure he is ready to commit to this drawing as the basis for a big painting later.
- *Decide how your drawing will express that character.* Beth urges a student to put her figure of a mermaid into action so that it expresses more power, and so that the mermaid expresses something about the student's self. She

encourages the student to make "not just any old mermaid but your own mermaid. . . . Instead of having a portrait of a mermaid, see if you can put it in action." When the student responds that mermaids have power over the waves, Beth replies, "Yes, so that tells part of her power."

Beth and a Student Reflect

In an interview, Beth talked about how she was indirectly trying to influence the student who chose to make a mermaid—trying to get her to think about the viewer and make a creature that conveys something to that viewer. Although she really didn't want the student to do a mermaid, she didn't want to tell her not to do a mermaid because the student was invested in a lot of draft drawings of mermaids, and "she was pretty psyched up about the mermaid thing. But in my mind I'm thinking, uhh, a mermaid!" Beth wanted the student to avoid being "clichéd":

> Art that is clichéd doesn't engage the viewer, and art that presents something intriguing does engage the viewer. So, I don't know that she's ever thought about the viewer before. I'm trying to get her to see the work outside of herself as something that conveys something to a viewer.

In our initial interview, Beth told us why learning to be expressive is so important for her students. "They have equally not really found their voice, in a way that it can be heard. I think being an artist is figuring out how to get yourself heard." In a later interview, Beth talked about how it is that students can discover their voice in an art class but still struggle in an academic class. Here she has brought up the vexing issue of transfer. Whether students can discover their voice (and thus something about their identity) in an arts class and have this discovery generalize outside of art class is a question ripe for investigation.

A Dispositional View of Express

People often think of expression in art as the unruly expression of feelings. As we define it in the Studio Habits, however, Express requires a great deal of skill to work its magic.

Skill. Gaining the skill of Express means learning how to create a work that goes beyond craft to convey meaning and feeling. And this can be achieved both through literal representation (e.g., expressing agitation by depicting an agitated crowd) as well as through metaphorical means (e.g., expressing agitation by using vibrating colors).

Alertness. Alertness to Express requires that students become familiar with and exploit the expressive potentials of the media in which they work. For example, when working with the concept of memory in collage, a student might use familiarity with translucence, transparency, and opacity to create layers suggesting the history of an event dimmed by time. Or when working in clay, familiarity with a wide range of surface treatments might allow the creation of objects like those by artist Marilyn Levine in which clay takes on the look and feel of leather jackets, purses, or shoes (http://www.marilynlevine.com/artworkframeset.html). Artists are alert throughout the making process to the potential implications and interpretations of the aesthetic choices they make with craft.

Inclination. The inclination to Express means actively pursuing meaning when making and viewing artworks. We do not mean by this, however, that works are coded representations of ideas. And making expressive work is not a linear process, since meaning often evolves along with the piece, and sometimes artists do not consciously or explicitly understand where a work is taking them. But the inclination to Express means following the work as it evolves into its final form, remaining aware of its meaning and feeling.

Generative Connections with Express

Express often pairs with Develop Craft, since artists manipulate materials into forms that convey meaning. By using Develop Craft in the service of Expression, students learn to use techniques for what they are intended—conveying visual meaning. But any number of habits might surface in a cluster with Express and Develop Craft, including Stretch and Explore (playing around with ways to use materials that might suggest various meanings); Engage and Persist (pursuing expression of some particular meaning over a sustained period of time by systematically investigating qualities or approaches to materials and techniques); Observe (noticing particular qualities of materials that evoke some idea or feeling); and Reflect (when students

talk about and judge their own success in conveying meaning with different materials).

A complex cluster that combines a number of habits is well-illustrated in an example from a 12-year-old in MassArt's Saturday program. A middle school student was exploring found-object sculpture. As he looked around the array of materials available in the room (Observe; Develop Craft), he noticed the tab on a cardboard box. "That tab looks like the symbol for pi!" he exclaimed (Express; Reflect: Question and Explain). He noticed that this tab was part of many boxes in the room (Observe), and he set about claiming them all by cutting them off carefully with a matte knife (Engage and Persist; Develop Craft). Then he played with the pile of pi-tabs, exploring ways to arrange and attach them as he built up a column of contrasting negative space and positive shapes (Develop Craft, Stretch and Explore). "Look! It's the Leaning Tower of Pi-sa!" (Understand Art Worlds; Express; Reflect). His historical/mathematical pun revealed found-object sculpture as having the potential for parody and humor, and he continued his explorations in this way for several more classes, creating a series of works that referenced word-play and humor about historical places, events, and people.

Express also pairs naturally with Understand Art Worlds. An artist who paints the figure in 2012, for example, paints in the context of painting's history. Female nudes were the object of the male gaze for centuries, which has implications for figural subject matter now—who is looking or meant to look, and what is meant to be seen and thought by seeing the work (e.g., issues of power and powerlessness). Some artists decide how to think about audience in relation to the expressive intention of their works, as when designers negotiate with their clients or artists address particular audiences explicitly. Others claim fealty not to the audience at all, but only to an idea—that is, to how the artist perceives an idea's representation.

Teachers can help students learn to express by viewing and discussing examples of artists' work and videos—such as those from Art21, the PBS series on contemporary art, artists, and themes—in which artists think aloud about their works and working processes. How do the artists think about meaning in their works? How do they wrestle with connecting Develop Craft and the subtlety of ideas when they are working? What evidence suggests that meaning evolves or is pre-determined? By asking students to observe and discuss examples of authentic practice, teachers can help students to focus on the challenges of creating meaning in artworks.

What Teachers Can Do

The most central support teachers can offer around the habit of Express is to keep meaning at the center of the art-making process, immersing students in ongoing discourse about meaning. The desire to use one's art-making to evoke thinking and feeling drives forward the effort to express, even when that is a long and tedious process. Assignments need to address meaning, either by specifying a theme or helping students to find their own from their explorations, brainstorming, and reflections. Works need to grow from inspiration and concept wherever they surface throughout the process of making. Instead of creating assignments by media (e.g., our "clay" unit or our "watercolor" unit), teachers can help students identify what they want to express and then show them how to use materials, tools, and the elements and principles of the visual arts to explore that meaning. Even a beautifully crafted work of art can be empty and without interest, just as an ugly one can be evocative and moving. This realization can motivate young artists to strive for more than just high-quality craft. Critiques, too, need to focus as much on meaning as on craft, identifying possible relationships between them. It makes no sense to perfect the craft first and then think about what to convey.

Express in Other Disciplines

All of the arts involve expression. Poetry uses words and punctuation for rhythm, sound, and connotation as much as denotation. Interior designers arrange furniture and use light, color, and texture to create environments that evoke particular feelings or functions. In theater or dance, the performance conveys meaning and feeling through the nonverbal symbol system of the domain—the style of the set, costumes, and props; the manner of speaking or body language in dialogues or duets; and the movement and energy of a character's entrance or exit. And music, too, expresses meaning, whether nonliteral or narrative—for example, through dynamics, rhythms, and harmonies.

Expression in the form of metaphorical exemplification is seen outside of the arts as well, in any kind of good writing, regardless of the discipline. Writers strive to write with a personal voice that evokes atmosphere and feeling and that strengthens the meaning they want to convey. This is true not only for poets and novelists but also for non-fiction writers such as historians, science writers, or political columnists.

NINE

Observe

REALLY SEEING, NOT JUST LOOKING

Keep investigating things around you. . . .
Looking is the real stuff about drawing.
—Guy Michel Telemaque

Artists use the habit of Observe everywhere. They observe the world around them, the works of other artists, and their own works as they develop them. Students in the art studio are taught to look more closely than people ordinarily do and "learn to see with new eyes." When teachers tell their students to look, as Guy Michel Telemaque does in the introductory quotation above, the students may think they really see already. But observing goes beyond looking and means moving beyond habitual ways of seeing. Students need to learn to notice things that might otherwise be invisible and therefore unavailable as content for thinking. Really seeing is the Studio Habit of careful, mindful Observation.

Students are taught to look closely at the following:

- The model or source from which they are working
- Their own artworks as they evolve
- Art processes modeled and artworks created by the teacher in demonstrations
- Artworks created by other students
- Artworks by artists past and contemporary

Teachers help students notice more by pointing out nuances of color, line, texture, and form. They point out the underlying geometry of a form and describe the expressive properties of a work, including its stylistic and compositional elements.

In the two classes that follow, we show how students are taught to observe. Both teachers have their students use a viewfinder (a small piece of cardboard with a rectangle cut out of its center), a tool artists have traditionally used to aid observation.

SEEING WITH NEW EYES: USING THE VIEWFINDER (EXAMPLE 9.1)

In Guy Michel's first design class of the term at the Boston Arts Academy, students learn to look through a viewfinder with one eye, so that they can learn a new way of seeing—seeing the world as elements in a composition. He tells them, "Instead of painting what we see, we're going to see what you would paint." This is meant to help them select what they want to put on a page.

Demonstration–Lecture

Looking through the viewfinder helps students learn to see objects as only lines, shapes, and colors in a frame. Guy Michel tells students:

Forget that you are looking at a bucket or a person's hair, or a table and a chair, and all these things. Forget that these are objects that have any real definition. I want you to simply concentrate on the lines that are created . . . in what you see.

Guy Michel talks about what he sees when looking through the viewfinder. He turns and holds the viewfinder up to a desk.

Right here I am paying attention particularly to the way this line goes diagonally across this frame, and then there is another little line underneath it that I can see has a little bit of a distance. It's a different color, different texture, and the line is thicker because from my perspective this line is a little thinner than this line down here.

Guy Michel explains how, when you look through a viewfinder with one eye, you lose depth perception and start to see the world as if it were a two-dimensional picture. Instead of seeing one thing in front of another "all you're seeing is [that] one thing stops where another thing starts. And that is all design, because one color in a shape stops and the other starts."

Students-at-Work

Guy Michel hands out viewfinders, and students practice seeing the world as design (see Figure 9.1). As they look around the classroom and hallway, Guy Michel keeps students focused on this new way of seeing by engaging in observations with them. Guy Michel asks individual students, groups of students, and sometimes the whole class to do the following:

- *Vary how the tool is used.* Guy Michel explains what to notice when looking through the viewfinder with one eye. "Think about how things look different when you hold it close to your eye or closer to the object."
- *Focus on design elements.* Guy Michel asks students to forget what they are looking at and just think about the surfaces.

  Is anybody having trouble forgetting that they're looking at something that they already know? . . . Forget that you're looking at somebody's arm or a table. Just think about the shapes, the colors, the lines, and the textures and the value of things as they change as you move the viewfinder around.

- *Notice, think, and respond.* Guy Michel asks students to talk about what they see differently by using the viewfinder: "Do you notice something that you're not used to paying attention to?"

Demonstration–Lecture

After students have investigated the classroom and hallway, Guy Michel gathers them in the classroom and uses a magazine cover with an image of a building and a poster on the wall to help synthesize what they've learned—paintings don't have to be seen as what they represent; rather, they can be seen as simply a surface of colors, shapes, patterns, textures, and forms. "That little change in thinking is what I want you to concentrate on." He concluded by introducing a homework assignment that connected the "new way of looking" to the course focus on design: Students created sheets of numerous thumbnail sketches that each combined one circle, triangle, and square, in an effort to find those designs that best conveyed the idea of motion.

Guy Michel Reflects

When we asked Guy Michel to give this class a title, he called it "A New Way of Seeing," or "Seeing the New." He explained that his goal is to "change how they look." "We're seeing what we are going to paint," he says as an explanation for using the viewfinders.

The goal of looking more closely, he explained to us, is to demystify the act of drawing and realize that the challenge of drawing a complex object is no different from the challenge of drawing a simple one.

What happens is they think, "I can't draw a person." But if you say draw this pencil they probably won't say that. But really . . . the lines are just different. So make the line that corresponds to what you see. Turn it here. Shadow it here. It's stripping away what it is and just painting the lines.

Guy Michel is, in short, teaching students to look closely so that they can begin to draw what they never thought they could draw. The first step, he tells them, is to learn to see.

SEEING THE WORLD AND PUTTING IT ON PAPER: LIGHT AND BOXES PROJECT   (EXAMPLE 9.2)

For Jim Woodside's Light and Boxes Project at Walnut Hill, students learn to think about the relationship between the world and their drawing. Students use the viewfinder to see the world anew and then go one step further and think about how they can put what they see onto paper.

Early in the fall semester, students file into Jim's classroom to find a pile of wooden and cardboard boxes in neutral tones stacked at a variety of angles in the center of the floor (see also Examples 3.3 and

Figure 9.1. Observe—Guy Michel Telemaque's Students Learn to See with "New Eyes"

A. Guy Michel Telemaque asks students to use a viewfinder to "see what you would paint"

B. He guides students to see design in the environment outside the windows

C. He tells students to forget that they're seeing objects and focus on just lines

D. Guy Michel explains that viewfinders help people see objects as just lines, shapes, and colors in a frame

5.3). The students gather around this unusual "still-life," and Jim gives them each a viewfinder. As did Guy Michel, Jim teaches his students how the viewfinder helps them see, and as a result, helps them draw more accurately.

Demonstration–Lecture

Jim shows the students how to look through the viewfinder at the still-life from many angles, and he explains how the viewfinder can help them decide about the composition of their drawings:

> This is a really great way to isolate what you want to work on to get a sort of preview of it, to figure out, most importantly, how it relates to all four sides of the paper. If you look through that you'll start to get a sense of, "Is there enough in that composition to occupy my drawing? Is there too much? Do I need to move in closer? Do I need to step back?"

Jim explains that students are also going to be working on perspective:

> We're still talking about line, but the main emphasis of what we're going to work on today is going to be perspective, geometry, one- and two-point perspective, how to arrange these shapes in a logical way, in a way that makes sense, in a way that is representative of the space that exists here in real life, on your two-dimensional surface.

Before students start drawing, Jim holds up the viewfinder and explains to the class how to use it to plan a composition:

> As you look through the viewfinder, look at all four sides. Don't just think of the top and then the bottom, you know, like we tend to look at the earth and think of the sky and the ground. Look at all four sides of the hole in the cardboard, because that's how you're going to start to think about all four sides of your piece of paper, in terms of the composition. Think about how the lines work, intersect, interact, with all four sides.

Students are given newsprint, tempera paint, and brushes as their drawing tools and materials. They are told to draw the outlines of the boxes only, and to concentrate on how one form relates to another in space. "Learn to see shapes," Jim tells them.

Students-at-Work

Jim circulates, watches, asks questions, and encourages students to use the viewfinder. Occasionally he speaks to the whole group, but usually he talks to one student at a time. For example, Jim helps one student see the major vertical organizing lines that structure the still-life. "Most of the things in the still-life are set straight up and down, OK?" He also suggests what the student might do next:

> So if I were you, I would stop on this part right now and get some of these straight verticals in, like maybe that big pedestal there, or maybe that box down there if that's in your view . . . so you can work these big diagonals against that.

Critique

After students have made a preliminary drawing, Jim puts all the drawings up on the wall and holds the first Critique of the 3-hour class. He begins the Critique by asking students to look at their own drawing and think about what's *wrong* with it. The Critique moves fluidly into a Demonstration–Lecture.

Demonstration–Lecture

Using student drawings as a reference, Jim puts up a blank sheet of paper on which he draws boxes as he talks about principles of perspective drawing. He introduces some terms, writing them and illustrating them simply—horizon line (eye level), one-point perspective, vanishing point—and draws boxes in various positions above and below the horizon line. Jim shows students an old movie projector case and demonstrates how perspective helps to understand the simple overall shape of the case and to look beyond the minor details—handle, latch, etc. He explains why they should first draw the general shape of the rectangular projector case, and as he lifts the cover to reveal the projector itself, only later to alter that same shape when depicting the specific details of the projector:

> Whether you're drawing a person or the most complicated thing in the world, you want to see it in simple terms first. It really helps to understand things in simple geometric terms first.

Jim makes a connection to the way he asks students to think of the figure:

> This is the same thing as when you draw a person. I'll tell you as we draw the figure to learn to break it up into geometry. If you just think of like the chest and muscles and arms and everybody's different shape, it can be overwhelming. But if you think of someone as just a cube and another cube attached, it can really help to simplify it.

Much of what we hear in this Demonstration–Lecture is similar to how Jim talked to individual students in teacher–student consults during the Students-at-Work session. But here, he talks to the entire group, making reference to individual students' works, thereby moving seamlessly back into Critique.

Critique

Before beginning another round of Students-at-Work, Jim helps students talk about what they see in their own and others' works that they think is more or less successful. Students discuss point of view in different drawings and the importance of intentionally choosing the point of view in a drawing. Jim concludes by telling students, "So these are the kind of thought processes and choices you should make with every single drawing."

Students-at-Work

Following the Critique, students return to working on the still-life, this time drawing it armed with the rules of perspective. With one student, Jim demonstrates perspective drawing by placing a piece of tracing paper over the student's drawing and then drawing from the student's viewpoint. As he draws, Jim explains and points out to the student aspects of the display and how he is capturing these in the drawing. "Where is your horizon line?" he asks the student. To the student's reply he answers, "Right, so that means this is significantly below your horizon line, right? OK, so let's just say that the vanishing points are off here, they're somewhere but it's imaginary, off your piece of paper." Jim continues to draw and direct the student's attention to the drawing.

Jim also focuses the group's observation on other students' work. He holds up a drawing and directs

students to observe the expressive quality of charcoal in this work.

> She's got this beautiful, very hard angular drawing of the objects, OK? But for the interior it looks like she's just sort of pretty much rubbing her fingers in toward the inner shape, taking that charcoal and pushing it in. Pretty simple solution, but I think it comes up with a really powerful expressive result, don't you?

For a student who is really struggling, Jim demonstrates how to get the horizon line right by working directly on the student's drawing. While marking on students' work is controversial among art educators, Jim and his students share an understanding that this classwork is an exercise, not a work of art, and therefore, his marks do not violate the integrity of the students' expression. Nevertheless, Jim respectfully asks the students' permission before adding his own lines to the paper. Then, as he draws, he explains his marks:

> OK, where is your horizon line? Do you know? It's about right there, right? So why do you have these going up? I'm going to do it right over, OK? [*Drawing on student's drawing.*] Your horizon line is right there, OK? You'd see a little bit of the bottom, don't you? So if I'm looking at it, it's going be like this.

Jim and Students Reflect

In an interview, Jim spoke about some of the reasons he taught this class as he did. He explained that if you look through a viewfinder at the still-life, "you're basically looking at an abstract piece of art" by becoming aware of all four sides of the piece of paper. "If you look through the viewfinder at a still-life, which is just boxes and shapes, you become immediately aware of lines intersecting on all four sides." This is a complex way of looking at a work, and most students don't think that way "but the viewfinder helps them to and it's a great thing. It just gets the visual clutter out of their assignment."

The value of critiquing your own work is to help students learn to see and "to be able to look at your own work after you've done it and do more than just be pleased with yourself." In looking at the work of others, you learn. And posing a question for the group means each student had to think, "OK, I might get called on to say what is wrong with my picture. I better look at it and pay attention." In reflecting with us after class about the Critique, Jim explained, "I wanted them to look at their own drawings and analyze them in a right–wrong/yes–no fashion." This was not intended to be a deeper critique of their thinking and expression in their work. Students were simply to find a box that just didn't look right. The form that the Critique takes follows its purpose.

Jim explains how the goal of teaching perspective is to get students to see the simple geometry underlying the forms: "It's hard for kids to see things simple. I think that simplification is a goal in art." He explains,

> Brancusi, the sculptor, had this great quote that I might even have said to the kids, "Simplicity is complexity solved." It comes up in big sophisticated ideas in art and also in things like this. So when you draw the human figure I try to get them to see the form. It's the forest through the trees sometimes—you see the big picture.

When asked to give this class a title, Jim called it "Living Use of Perspective and Composition." He means to show students how the skill of perspective drawing can be used in all drawing—it is a way of grasping the architecture underlying form. In his post-class interview, Jim explained why he does not teach perspective just by having students draw a box in isolation, but rather asks them to Observe the principles of perspective in what they see. "By having them draw a whole still-life, they're

making a work of art. They're not just drawing a box and learning how to do it." By embedding the skill to be learned in the context of artistic challenges, students don't merely learn the skill itself, they learn to use the skills for their own purposes.

As students learn to see, their observational drawing skill improves. One 9th-grader at Walnut Hill realized how far he had come in his ability to Observe when he talked about his first still-life. He told us why he thought the drawing was not accurately drawn: "I didn't really *look* at it. I just saw what I thought I saw and just drew. And I didn't really like break it down" (see Figures 9.2 and 9.3)

Students carry the habit of Observation outside of the classroom. A Boston Arts Academy senior told us how she began to notice perspective in the environment after learning about it in an observational drawing class:

> I remember walking down Lansdowne Street. I looked at the way that the street goes in, and it's exactly what he was talking about how things fade into . . . space and it's a vanishing point at the end. . . . And I was like "OK, and so this art stuff does make sense." [I noticed it before] but I didn't understand why I saw it like that.

Figure 9.3. Late in the 9th Grade, a Student Explains That He Looks More Carefully Now by "Breaking It Down"

Figure 9.2. A 9th-Grader at Walnut Hill Explains That in His First Drawings He Drew "What I Thought I Saw"

Even a beginning student noticed how he was starting to look at things differently. A 9th-grader at Walnut Hill commented on this: "When you're painting . . . it's an extremely different way of looking at things than when you're not. Because you see things, or at least I see things, in huge blocks of light and color. . . . You look at things differently."

A Dispositional View of Observe

David Perkins (1994) refers to the habit of observation as having an "intelligent eye." Students who spend time in classrooms such as Guy Michel's and Jim's are getting continuous eye training. There is looking, and then there is seeing. Students learn that looking is not always seeing. Their eyes are now opened.

Skill. The skill that makes Observe possible is really looking. When artists look carefully they can override the schemas that lead people to draw hands too small, eyes too high, far away objects too large. The art historian E. H. Gombrich (2000) refers to the process of making, which always involves schemas, and matching, when schemas are complexified by observation.

Alertness. Alertness to when to employ observational skills requires that students recognize the need for careful observation during the artistic process. Such opportunities arise regularly. They arise when noticing something unusual and before committing to a composition (an interesting face on a bus, an oddly shaped object on the sidewalk, the way the shadow of an easel interacts with a pattern on the studio floor). They arise from the realization that something is "bugging you" (Jim Woodside's words), or not working, or that a work seems stuck. Even when a work seems finished, artists alert to the possibility that there may be more work to be done will stand back and look more deeply or invite others to look at the work with them. These kinds of alertness prompt artists to consider what they are seeing, how they are looking, and what might extend their looking and renew the process of taking in information.

Inclination. Artists spend significantly more time looking at a model from which they are drawing than do novices, who look primarily at their drawings (Solso, 2001). When artists notice something that would benefit from further observation,

the challenge becomes actually putting to work their looking skills. By making the effort to look longer or more broadly, they demonstrate the drive or *inclination* to Observe. An artist might remind himself to stand up and look at his work from various angles, levels, and distances. Or she might pause her making to look at other artists' works on the web, in the library, on videos, or in galleries and museums. She might take out her sketchbook and browse through it or make new sketches. Or she might leaf through her portfolio. While responsive actions may vary widely, the point is that the artist does something to see more and better, and that informs the process of making.

Generative Connections to Observe

Teachers prompt students to Observe in relationship to using other habits. Observe pairs naturally with Envision—it is sometimes difficult to see where one of these habits ends and the other begins. When teachers guide students to imagine ways to change their work, they are prompting students to observe, then reflect and envision. Observe looks out to the world; Envision looks back into the mind. They are interdependent habits, often with a nearly instantaneous connection from the observed to the envisioned, and back again from an envisioned image to further outward observation.

Teachers can ask students to observe the works of other artists and to think about how to use what they see in their own work (Observe, Understand Art Worlds, Reflect). Observe clusters often with Understand Art Worlds and Reflect since the works made by others define the aesthetic context in which every artist's work is seen and judged.

Teachers can help students learn to observe how and how well their choices of materials and tools affect the meanings expressed in their work (Observe, Develop Craft, Express, Reflect). Reflect comes into this process when students use information from observation to consider how well they are conveying their intended meanings. They must think about what they are trying to express, look closely at their work, and decide what to change and how to make alterations.

What Teachers Can Do

Teachers can help students develop the skill of Observe by encouraging them to remember to look and to slow the looking process down. They can point out interesting observations they make in the normal flow of the day—nuances of color or light, line or texture, interesting shadows, unusual illusions or effects, or the underlying geometry of a form (Perkins, 1994). They can describe the expressive properties of a work, as well as its stylistic and compositional elements. They can also suggest common strategies used by artists to help themselves see more: using viewfinders to see possible relationships and compositions from a variety of angles, looking from different distances and levels, using lenses to magnify objects, squinting so that images blur, focusing on negative space, and closing one eye to flatten shapes. Teachers can help students develop the inclination to observe by having them keep sketchbooks to capture impressions and gather information as it comes to their attention, archiving a resource of images to be used at will.

Observe in Other Disciplines

The centrality of Observe in the visual arts is easily apparent, but this habit is important in all art forms, even though sometimes it takes a non-visual form. To develop their craft, dancers watch themselves work in front of mirrors, and choreographers pay close attention to the movements of people, animals, and objects to get ideas. Actors observe people, settings, and situations to develop an interpretation of a character, and they review rehearsals and performances of others and of themselves (attending to their own behaviors on stage and in mirrors, photographs, and videos) to assess effect and quality. Musicians observe, too, with eyes, ears, and bodies—their postures, embouchures, and fingerings; the conductor's facial expressions, gestures, and body language; musical scores; and, most obviously, the sounds and silences of the music itself.

Observe is also central to all of the sciences. The photographer Eadweard Muybridge used photography to study how animals and humans move. Similarly, a biomedical engineer might use contemporary imaging technologies to study human movement while designing prosthetic devices for amputees. Chemists observe chemical reactions, physicists observe the behavior of matter, and biologists form conclusions from observations of the natural world. Historians observe photographs, films, and events as well as texts. Mathematicians observe phenomena and logical relationships in order to model them algorithmically. Linguists and language learners observe patterns of speech and behavior. Observation is so fundamental to understanding that it seems almost superfluous to name its occurrences. But recognizing the ubiquitousness of observation across domains may help identify connections among the many different ways that have been developed for investigating the world.

TEN

Reflect

QUESTION AND EXPLAIN, EVALUATE

My goal . . . is to have them . . . question the way they do things. And lose bad habits and develop new good habits.

—Beth Balliro

I'm trying to . . . give them the questions that they should be asking themselves while they're making something. Or after they've made something.

—Jason Green

When we're talking about looking at artwork, whether it's one in the museum or your own or your classmate's, it's still that slowing process; it's still that trying to separate the difference between interpretation and description.

—Kathleen Marsh

Reflecting about artistry, making judgments about art, and thinking about what constitutes beauty are processes at the heart of the field of aesthetics. The classes we observed were filled with aesthetics discourse—which we refer to as the habit of Reflect.

We make a distinction between two forms of Reflect. Artists reflect metacognitively when they explicitly consider their works or what they are trying to do, why they used a particular technique or color or composition, what meanings they are trying to convey, and so on. We refer to this type of thinking as Reflect: Question and Explain. Question and Explain is used by professional artists during critiques and reviews, in artist's talks and statements written by artists to accompany their work, in curatorial statements for an exhibition, and in art history and art criticism.

Artists evaluate when they interpret and judge the aesthetic success of their own and others' works. Evaluation involves some kind of direct or implicit comparison of a work with other works or with envisioned criteria or goals, and it always involves considering quality. We refer to this type of thinking as Reflect: Evaluate. Evaluating shows up in professional artists' working process (e.g., deciding on next steps or when a work is finished), during critiques and reviews, and centrally when viewing works by other artists and in the related fields of art history and criticism. Sometimes artists just know when something works even though they cannot say why. Because our research focused on teacher student interaction and teachers used language to help students learn to reflect, our examples emphasize verbal forms of Reflect: Evaluate.

Making evaluations of works of art is a sophisticated process. In the words of Elliot Eisner:

> Making judgments about how qualities are to be organized does not depend upon fealty to some formula; there is nothing in the artistic treatment of a composition like the making and matching activity in learning to spell or learning to use algorithms to prove basic arithmetic operations. In spelling and in arithmetic there are correct answers, answers whose correctness can be proven. In the arts judgments are made in the absence of rule. (2002b)

Both kinds of reflection involve the construction of meaning. Students think about their own artistic goals and those of others. Both also involve self-knowledge: Students learn about themselves and their reactions and judgments as they evaluate work, whether their own or that of others. And both involve consideration of quality: Describing work is prerequisite to evaluating elements of varying levels of effectiveness. Evaluation involves some kind of comparison of the work with other works or with the envisioned final work not yet achieved.

QUESTION AND EXPLAIN

In the first two classes that follow, we show how students are taught to Question and Explain. In both of these classes, teachers use questioning to help students focus on a particular aspect of their work and to reflect on what they are making and how they are working.

DRAWING YOURSELF AS MYTHICAL: IMAGINARY CREATURES PROJECT   (EXAMPLE 10.1)

Near the middle of the second-semester class for 9th-graders at the Boston Arts Academy, students in Beth Balliro's class have recently visited the Boston Museum of Fine Arts. Beth talks about how a museum is a house of muses—and the muses are the keepers of the arts. Today students are asked to paint their muses—themselves as mythical creatures. The creature must be semihuman and must express something about the student's self. Students look at themselves in mirrors as they imagine their muse (see also Example 8.2).

Demonstration–Lecture

Beth first asks students to write about what inspires them. On the board she writes the following three questions for students to answer:

- What/who is your "muse?"
- If you had mythical powers, what would they be?
- What would your weaknesses be?

As she gets pens and brushes out, Beth pursues these questions with individual students. Next, she hands out ink and packets with photocopies of mythical creatures from African and Native American cultures that students can use to help them envision their creatures.

Students-at-Work

While students draw their mythical creatures, Beth circles from student to student, pressing them to explain how the character they are drawing in fact reflects something about themselves (see Figure

10.1). Here are some of the questions she asks students to encourage them to develop the habit of Question and Explain:

- How would this be you?
- What part of this character would be you looking in the mirror?
- How's it going to be you?
- Tell me about it. . . . How is he part you?
- What kind of character is this? Do you really want to be this character?
- And how is this you, the glasses and the eyes?
- So this is you plus what? You said some cat and what did you say? Some type of cat. . . . So how do the eyelashes make it seem half-human, half-animal?

Beth sometimes points to specific parts of a drawing and asks students to explain what they did or are trying to do there:

- So did you just use a brush?
- How did you get this detail? It's beautiful.
- Tell me about those ears.

Beth Reflects

In an interview after class, we asked Beth to say more about her questioning techniques. She talked about two ways to help students learn to Question and Explain: Asking students to answer their own questions for the next 10 minutes, and having students keep journals in which they write about process on a daily basis. In this class, though, she has a minimal goal in mind: getting students to talk about their art-making process. That seems clearly attainable for all her students and is a first, simple, and concrete step in their development.

The habit of reflection helps students become independent workers and become "able to self-monitor so that they can eventually be autonomous," Beth explains. She believes that becoming reflective can help art students gain confidence when they are in academic classes in which they may not be strong students. "I want them to be able to articulate their process and articulate how they're different from other students." They can "figure out how to be more of a presence and how to advocate for their own growth in a way that allows people to hear them."

Learning to be reflective about one's work and to advocate gives the emerging artist power in today's art world. "Part of their responsibility, I think, as artists is figuring out how to get yourself heard."

Figure 10.1. Reflect: Question and Explain—Students in Beth Balliro's Class Represent Aspects of Their Personalities in Mythical Creatures That They Create

A. Beth Balliro prompts a student to pause and think about his work

B. She leads students in reflecting on their visit to the museum—a "house of muses"

C. Beth guides students to reflect on their personal muses

D. She urges students to consider what personal characteristics they could emphasize in their mythical creatures

BUILDING OBJECTS IN RELATION:
COIL SCULPTURE PROJECT   (EXAMPLE 10.2)

In Jason Green's Coil Sculpture Project near the start of the second term of ceramics at Walnut Hill (see also Examples 3.2 and 12.5), when the focus has shifted from wheel-throwing to sculpture, again we see students being asked to Question and Explain their work. Jason asks students to look around the room to find two objects that could serve as the referents for a hand-built ceramic sculpture created with coil technique. The assignment is challenging because students are not to make a copy of the objects, but rather to create a new object that combines parts or all of the two objects they are using as models, varying scale as their intention dictates. Additionally, the sculptures must not have a flat bottom. The students are not making pottery, which is flat on one side so that it can stack on a shelf, but sculptures, which are built to be viewed from all sides. Students also have to make two experimental tiles with textures on them. From these tiles, they will choose the patterns that they want to use as the "skins" of their sculptures.

Students-at-Work

All of the techniques students have learned thus far will be used in this project. As students begin, Jason circles the room consulting with individual students.

- *Describe your plans.* "Do you know what you're going to do?" Jason asks a student as he prompts her to explain how she plans to use a light bulb. Later he returns to the same student to ask, "What about this form? What's the whole thing going to look like?" Jason questions another student to help her think how she might build with coils. "What's your object?" "Do you want to make the whole thing?" "Which part of it?"
- *Justify your choice as an aesthetic decision.* "What do you think is interesting about this? What do you like about it?" As Jason probes further, he asks the student to look closely at her chosen object and think of how it is used. Then he asks how her sculpture might be like the toy she has chosen. To a student combining a funnel and shell, Jason asks, "What do you like about the shell?"
- *Assess as you work.* "How is that coming?" After the student nods that it's OK, Jason talks with her about what she might do next. "What are

you doing now?" The student and Jason talk about what she might do next because her sculpture is too wet to work on any more today.

Jason Reflects

In an interview after this class, Jason said he hopes the students will begin to internalize the questions he poses and get better and better at the habit of Question and Explain. He explained that posing questions helps students become aware of the choices they make as they work, a process he described as follows: "They have to identify the choices they've made during the process and experiment as well, and just be able to reflect on the process or reflect on what they've made afterward." He added that "when students say, 'Well, this is the way I like it. This is the way I want it.' I say, 'Why do you want it that way?'"

A Dispositional View of Question and Explain

People sometimes distinguish between making and thinking. This is how art classes come to be seen as "non-intellectual" or "non-academic." But art-making requires serious thinking, and Question and Explain ties directly to Common Core State Standards for English Language Arts. One form of thinking called for in art classes is metacognition about one's working processes, which we refer to as Reflect: Question and Explain.

Skill. The skill of Question and Explain requires developing the technical and expressive vocabularies needed to explicitly consider one's goals, works, and working processes. It also requires the ability to think metacognitively, conveying that thinking by speaking and writing.

Alertness. Alertness to Question and Explain comes when students realize occasions when self-questioning and explaining could be helpful to advance the process of making. In the words of Sister Corita Kent (Rule 8): "Don't try to create and analyze at the same time. They're different processes" (Kent & Steward, 2008, p. 176). Such occasions arise when artists are stuck, blocked, or confused, when a work seems to be finished, or at the beginning and end of work sessions or classes. As the quotation implies, artists also need to develop an alertness to times when self-talk or comments by others constrain the forward movement of work; at these times, they need to learn to shush their too-critical interior voices for a time or find quiet spaces away from others whose opinions are not yet welcome.

Inclination. The Inclination to Question and Explain develops when students recognize the *need* to pause in the making process and think about what they are doing and where they are going. Pausing often feels unnatural during the flow of making, but it is important to take the breaks that disrupt the flow periodically. In Jim Woodside's 3-hour afternoon classes, he insisted that students put down their materials about halfway through and take a walk outside—just to clear their heads and see anew once more. While walking over for a snack, the students talked with each other and made notes in their sketchbooks. Similarly, Jim frequently paused the action of classes for mid-process critiques in which students generated new ideas from others' responses and their own new perspectives. As students see the value of such pauses, they can internalize the inclination to pause and reflect.

EVALUATE

Near the beginning of the school year at the Boston Arts Academy, the new 9th-grade students in Kathleen Marsh's class have been working on a series of four self-portraits in colored pencil (see also Example 5.2). Kathleen begins today's class with a Critique followed by a Students-at-Work session (see Figure 10.2). We briefly describe the Critique and several Students-at-Work interactions to show examples of comments likely to help students learn to Evaluate.

DRAWING VALUES IN COLOR: SELF-PORTRAIT IN COLORED PENCIL PROJECT (EXAMPLE 10.3)

Kathleen asks students to put up their partially completed drawings for all to see. Then she asks students, one at a time, to select a peer's drawing and describe it using some of the vocabulary terms listed on the board. Students were then encouraged to Evaluate the work in process by thinking about choices they had made and Envisioning changes that they could make to their own drawings. Kathleen said that she placed the Critique at the start of class so that she could redefine the goals of the self-portrait assignment through this low-stakes evaluation. She wanted students to focus their attention on value and composition. To support this shift in focus, she highlighted student work that showed good use of value, and she asked students to think

more about background (to develop Express) and the placement of the face on the page (to Develop Craft in the techniques of composition).

Critique

Kathleen initiates the Critique with a reminder to use this chance to practice vocabulary to articulate positive evaluations of each other's draft work:

I'd like a few people to pick out the vocabulary words—and here they are listed on the board—that you see evident in your classmates' drawings. . . . You guys have really done an excellent job. And I'd like you to describe what it is that is excellent about these pictures. Pick one image and describe what you think is skilled or excellent about it, and use some of the vocabulary words in describing it.

A student begins, "OK, I like the outline there and . . ." When the student hesitates, Kathleen asks, "Can you walk up and point to it?" With this prompting the student points to a drawing and explains more: "Because it has a lot of *value*. Because on the right side it goes from dark to light and you can see different colors on the dark side. And on the light you can see just light. Like a little yellow and that's probably it."

Kathleen reinforces the student and turns to the student whose drawing is being discussed for self-evaluation. "I'd like to hear what you have to say about this. Apparently what you're doing is you're building up layers of color." The student responds. "Yeah, but I only did it on one side. I was going to get started on the second one." In what follows, Kathleen prompts the student to evaluate possible next steps in using color and value.

Kathleen: OK. So what else are you going to do today? What are your other plans for this piece?

Student: I'm going to make it look like real flesh, like flesh color.

Kathleen: OK, and . . . [*She waits for him to finish her sentence.*]

Student: And I'm going to leave it that light on one side.

Kathleen: OK, and what are some of the other colors that you're planning to use to create your skin tone?

Student: I was using like the yellow and light brown and peach and pink. I'm trying to get it to look like real flesh.

Kathleen: OK, can I make three suggestions?

Figure 10.2. Reflect: Evaluate—Kathleen Marsh's 9th-Graders Follow a Critique with a Students-at-Work Session

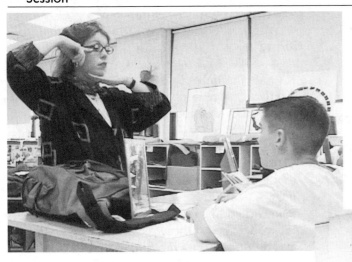

A. Kathleen Marsh shows proportions of a human face by using her own face as an example

B. She guides a student to evaluate his own work

C. She talks with a student about how his drawing can control where a viewer looks

D. Kathleen explains how she is evaluating a student's drawing

Student: Uh huh.
Kathleen: Yellow, red, and a tiny bit of blue.
Student: Blue?
Kathleen: Yeah.
Student: OK.
Kathleen: Why would I say blue?
Student: Because it's a cool color. You want to mix two warm colors and a cool color.
Kathleen: It's a cool color. Blue is the color of your veins [*pointing to the veins in her face*]. And there is some of that in the transparency of your skin. A tiny bit. And also what makes brown? And I actually said this to a bunch of you on Monday. What are the colors that make brown?
Student: Red, yellow . . .
[*Kathleen calls on another student.*]
Student: Red, yellow, and blue.
Kathleen: Red, yellow, and blue. All the primaries make brown.

Having evaluated the need for mixing primaries to achieve flesh tones, Kathleen demonstrates the need to create different colors of brown because of the variety of flesh tones. Kathleen has all the students extend an arm into the middle of the table and observe their skin.

Students then move to discussing color in another student's work. When a student points to a self-portrait that he really likes, Kathleen probes for more explanation of that judgment. "OK, what is it about this that you really like?"

Student 1: Opposite. It's like the whole different contrast of the white and the brown is just there, you know.
Student 2 [the student whose work is being discussed]: It works out smoothly.
Kathleen: OK, but are you finished? How much white do you plan on leaving in your drawing?
Student 2: Umm, not much. Only the eye and some of the light . . . are coming from the other side. Like where the white is now is where the light source is coming from, but it's not done.

Often evaluation requires metaphorical thinking, as shown by the next student to speak who says, "I don't think he finished it, but I still think it looks really cool. It's all . . . it looks like you're standing there and all of a sudden a big flash of light comes and just brightens everything." Kathleen responds that this is a good perception and another student adds, "I thought of nuclear war."

A student teacher who has been with Kathleen all term joins the discussion.

Student Teacher: How many different colors did you use on the part that you actually finished?
Student 2: About like seven or eight.
Student Teacher: What were those colors?
Student 2: Yellow, purple, blue, brown like some brown orange, and a goldish color. Orange and a pink, like a pink. Or a mustard or something.
Student Teacher: So you use a lot of colors that you don't actually end up seeing as isolated colors within his face. But they all lead up to the illusion of the three-dimensionality of his face [*pointing to the portrait*].

Kathleen offers further information to enhance students' abilities to articulate their evaluative observations about the challenges of using the color wheel:

All of you guys are taking very different approaches to the use of color. [Student 2] has decided to make his colors really intense and keep that intensity throughout his drawing. And we've discussed how that might become problematic, because you're really working with that saturated color and you're going to continue to do that. Right? So I think you're figuring stuff out about color. Right? Because normally I would say start with thin layers and build up. But he's sort of layering as he goes. And that can be dangerous because you may run into problems that you aren't able to fix later. But you're figuring it out.

Students-at-Work

After the Critique, students work on their own portraits as Kathleen consults with individuals. To foster the habit of self-evaluation, her evaluative comments mix praise with advice for how a student might proceed:

- *Look at the subtle changes in skin color.* Kathleen praises a particular part of a student's drawing and draws the student's attention to a place where he has shown the subtle change of skin color when seen through glasses. "Nice contrast in your skin between what's behind your glasses and what's on your actual skin. Remember we talked about that? How the glasses change the color of the skin behind them? You did a really nice job with that."

- *Decide if your composition is accurate.* Kathleen helps a student see that the viewer does not know where to focus because of his composition.

> This still isn't touching any side of this page. You've got a floating head there. You need to at least connect this to the bottom and somehow figure out how to connect [the] drawing to [the] sides of the page. Why would I ask you to do that? . . . It makes that a bigger scale, but why is that important in terms of composition?

Kathleen points to parts of the drawing as she continues. "I am your viewer right now, so I am looking at your drawing and you want to be able to control where I look. . . . So your glasses really help and draw me into your face. But you need to figure out ways to lead me around your page."

- *Compare your drawing with your face.* Kathleen asks a student to see how her drawing does not capture the way her face is actually built. "My sense is the light is not hitting you exactly in half like that." As she talks, Kathleen gestures to her own face to demonstrate relationships.

> Look at yourself. Generally speaking, your earlobes meet the bottom of your nose. So I think your ears need to be maybe a little bigger . . . and that will inform where the bottom of your nose is. And that will tell you where your lips will be. . . . Also look at the line of your lips. It's much curvier than what you have here, OK? Close your lips and look in the mirror.

This comment from Kathleen also prompted the student to Observe.

Kathleen Reflects

Kathleen believes that her 9th-grade students are not yet ready for a full-blown critique.

> I think it takes time to work up to that point. . . . So we're not there yet in the 9th grade. Just to get everyone [to] talk in an orderly fashion and listen to each other talk. That's where we are. We're not there yet, the full-blown critique yet.

Kathleen used to consider effort as part of the grade, but she now believes that grading for effort does not show students where they need to improve. "It's not fair to them, because it's not giving

them a really clear picture of what specifically they need to be working on." So Critique helps students learn about the qualities of work that matter. They are a kind of formative assessment.

Critiques also provide students with the vocabulary they need to talk about their work. She described many of her students as "intuitive art-makers." "They do what they feel without much vocabulary attached to it. So we give them this vocabulary that begins to really describe what they're doing." This helps students set clearer goals and also provides a basis for conversations between teacher and student.

Kathleen said that reflecting on one's portfolio and exhibiting work are two other ways students learn the habit of Evaluating. By keeping a portfolio and reflecting on it, students can see and articulate how they've grown, both of which help structure a student's thinking. She believes that exhibiting one's work is like a formal extension of an informal class critique.

> Assessment happens on many, many levels, and of course in the older grades, I really believe that exhibition is a really key assessment tool, because I think in the act of sharing a work, and showing your work, you begin to—it's like releasing your baby. Once you release it, then it really becomes a separate entity. And that's when I think we really begin to look at the work and begin to grow.

As discussed in Chapters 4 and 16, when students graduate from the Boston Arts Academy, they must exhibit their work formally and talk about their work to a panel of outside experts. They must talk about their goals, their working process, their strengths, and their weaknesses, and they must answer questions. Students reported the value of this, saying, for example, "My perspective changed after my review because I was treated not as a child artist, but more as a young adult with artistic abilities." In short, when students are asked to reflect about themselves, they see themselves being taken seriously; they see their own interpretations valued and thus they gain confidence in their abilities to think about themselves as artists.

A Dispositional View of Evaluate

Evaluation is a central reflective habit in the arts because of the omnipresence of both formal and informal critiques and because of the continual push to step back and judge whether something is or is not moving in the right direction.

Skill. Underlying the skill of Evaluate is the ability to make interpretive claims and judgments about works of art and to justify these claims using evidence. Of course, there are no absolute "right" or "wrong" judgments of the quality of works. Judgments are shaped by socio-historical context and individual taste: revolutionary works that were once reviled, such as Duchamp's "Fountain" (a urinal mounted for display in a gallery) may be revered later as an historical benchmark (i.e., as a revolutionary icon of the type of work called "ready-made").

Alertness. One of the dangers of evaluation is that students may become paralyzed by self-consciousness. Alertness about when, how, and what to evaluate calls for students not only to realize when to make judgments but also when to suspend them. Sometimes students simply need to keep working and hold off on any evaluation—silencing their internal critic so that they can work from intuition without second-guessing themselves in the process. At other times they need to pause their making for moments of "light" judgment—taking a step back from their work to think about where they are going, what is working and what is not, and why. And at still other times, they need to be able to listen to judgments of their works that others offer, even when these are critical. Deciding what to do with such judgments is yet another piece of alertness—some are good to keep and others should be let go. Discerning which is which requires alertness to the delicate balance between internal and external demands.

Inclination. The inclination to evaluate requires that students do not get stalled by taking a stance of relativity. Just because there are no right or wrong answers does not mean that every response is equally good or bad—in fact, quite the reverse. There are many rich solutions to any given challenge, but there are even more poor ones. Students need to experience for themselves the difference that tiny choices make in how a work is perceived, in their own works and in the works of others. As students get into the habit of learning from non-hurtful criticism, they come to value the potential of the evaluative process more and to recognize how it helps their artistic process move forward.

Generative Connections to Reflect

Whenever Reflect is added to the operation of a habit or cluster of habits, those habits are strengthened and deepened. Every habit can link with Reflect. Teachers can pose questions to help students talk about their techniques (Develop Craft), their levels of investment (Engage and Persist), how they are coping with a mistakes (Stretch and Explore), how thematic meanings are conveyed in works (Express), and so forth.

Question and Explain is tightly linked to Observe. When teachers circulate during Students-at-Work sessions, they ask students to describe what they are doing, explain why, and make judgments. None of this can be done without looking closely. Evaluate and Observe connect, because as people evaluate, they focus attention to specific aspects of the work, honing observational skills.

Careful observation also keeps students from making facile evaluations (e.g., "I like that work because it's graffiti and I like graffiti"). When teachers evaluate, they are typically evaluating something specific, whether the technique, the expression, or the observational skill is revealed. Thus, when a comment aims to teach the student to Evaluate, it usually is also teaching another habit as well.

What Teachers Can Do

Ultimately, teachers want students to internalize the process of question and explain and the process of evaluation, so they regularly ask students to step back and focus on some aspect of their work or working process. This kind of metacognitive talk about process occurs far more often in art classes than in traditional non-arts classrooms. Teachers can ask students to keep notes in their sketchbooks and write blogs about their changing processes to foster development of a reflective inner voice—all in the language of words in order to supplement the emphasis on visual symbols that students think with when they work with art tools and materials.

Teachers can nurture Evaluate by setting regular (even daily) reflective assignments, asking students to reflect privately in front of a video camera (sometimes called "video confessionals"), and holding frequent, mid-process critiques that allow peers and teachers to offer information in response to work-in-progress. Art teachers frequently evaluate student work informally as they move around the room while students are working, and they also evaluate more formally during some kinds of Critique sessions and in culminating reviews of students' portfolios of work. Students can learn from these consultations and critiques how to evaluate themselves and others. Thus, students in visual arts classes are learning to make aesthetic judgments and to defend them, and because they are engaged in continuous self-assessment, they have the opportunity to learn to be self-critical and to think about how they could improve. Creating such a classroom culture and immersing students in it is probably the most effective way a teacher can positively influence a student's disposition to Evaluate.

As a senior at the Boston Arts Academy told us, "When I was younger, I wanted to hear people tell me, 'Oh you're doing so good. That's so beautiful.' And now I just want to grow. So by just hearing the good things, you don't grow" (see Figure 10.3). A freshman shows us that already in his first year at Walnut Hill, he has become able to evaluate his own work critically. Looking at some work done early in the year, he tells us, "I don't think these are particularly well drawn. Because when I did it . . . I'd draw the head and finish it and then move on down the neck and into the arm. Draw everything piece by piece instead of drawing the whole figure, which is what I gradually learned to do" (see Figure 10.4, which the student felt was not drawn piecemeal).

Reflect in Other Disciplines

It is impossible to do great work in any discipline without reflection, but too often schools do not expect students to reflect. Public reflection happens more often in arts than in non-arts classes because of the ubiquity of the critique structure. But classrooms can all benefit from public reflection. For example, in Japan, which ranks high in international comparisons of mathematics education, an observer might see elementary students working in groups on a single, open-ended problem for an entire class period. The groups then present and are critiqued on how they approached the problem rather than on their final answers. By reflecting publicly, as is traditionally done in studio classes, these mathematics students internalize a focus on process that supports their success in mathematics.

As another example of public reflection in non-arts classes, Hetland asked her 7th-grade history class to present their research in process and respond to questions from their peers. As a result of challenges from their peers, the students refined their research focus and buttressed their conclusions with stronger evidence. Whenever student work in progress is made public and students engage in peer review, students have the opportunity to reflect on their processes and those of others and to evaluate products as they evolve into their final forms.

Figure 10.4. Late in the 9th Grade, a Student at Walnut Hill Reflects on How He Used to Draw Figures "Piece by Piece Instead of Drawing the Whole Figure"

Figure 10.3. A Senior at the Boston Arts Academy Describes How This Reclining Pastel Figure Shows That He Has Learned to Learn from Critique

ELEVEN

Stretch and Explore

TAKING A LEAP

I hope to teach the kids how to think differently.
—Guy Michel Telemaque

You ask kids to play, and then in one-on-one conversation you name what they've stumbled on.
—Beth Balliro

At its core, Stretch and Explore is divergent and transgressive, a central component of creativity that is modulated by convergent thinking. New ideas come from pushing at the boundaries. In the words of John Cage, "We're breaking all of the rules. Even our own rules" (Kent & Steward, 2008, p. 176). Artists always try new things and reach beyond what they have already done. They play, take risks, explore novel associations, and make mistakes, not deliberately, but routinely and inevitably. For artists, mistakes are opportunities—they lead to problem-solving as well as to something more at the core of creativity—problem-*finding* (Getzels & Csikszentmihalyi, 1976). New problems to solve are discovered through exploration. In the words of artist Sister Corita Kent (Kent & Steward, 2008, p. 176), Rule 4 in art is "Consider everything an experiment"; Rule 6 is "Nothing is a mistake. There's no win and no fail. There's only make." And Rule 9 declares the importance of the playful attitude included in the habit Stretch and Explore: "Be happy whenever you can manage it. Enjoy yourself. It's lighter than you think."

Artists Stretch and Explore by using the practice of conditional thinking: What if I try it this way, or this way, or that? They seek out the unusual, push beyond the limits of what is understood, and stride into the unknown as if they knew where they were going and what they were doing. Artist Bunny Harvey, for example, once said that she looks for odd found objects on daily walks, then plays with these forms in juxtaposition to inspire new ideas for her paintings. Artist Brice Marden painted a series of large works with a continuous line in the 1990s using flexible dowels two to three feet in length. And artist Rachel Perry Welty expands what people normally consider to be art media by making art out of the detritus of daily domestic life, such as twist ties, grocery stickers from pieces of fruit, gum wrappers, and voicemails.

In what follows, we describe two ceramic sculpture classes that show how students are taught to Stretch and Explore. Both teachers encourage students to reach beyond what they can already do and to play with alternative directions and possibilities.

INTRODUCING THE MEDIUM: SKETCHING IN CLAY (EXAMPLE 11.1)

At the Boston Arts Academy, Beth Balliro begins her ceramic sculpture unit for 9th-graders in the first class of the semester by having students "sketch in clay." Many of the students have never touched clay before. Now they must play a "game" in which they mold creatures out of clay and then destroy them. The end product is not important; only the process matters. The goal of the first part of the class is to get students used to digging their hands into clay. By working quickly and then smashing what they have made, students lose their inhibitions and learn to experiment—to sketch in clay—rather than create a perfect finished clay product. After the game, students work on a final creature that they will glaze and fire, so they experience quickly the entire process of wet clay to fired piece.

Students work in groups, sitting around small tables. A chunk of clay sits on each table, and Beth starts the game by telling one student to pick up some clay at his table and make "a creature that flies." After a minute, Beth stops him, holds up his creature, and says that he has made a creature that gives a sense of a creature that flies. Then she asks him to smash it. To the class she says, "The first thing I want you to get at is how to work quickly. The second thing, which is maybe even more fun, is destroying it."

Next, Beth asks one person at each table to pick up the clay and quickly make "a creature that slithers." After a few minutes, Beth tells each maker to smash what has been made and pass the clay to the next person, who will then make a "ferocious" creature. The process is repeated again when the next student at each table is asked to create a "gentle" creature. As they work, Beth moves from group to group, commenting on how each is doing. She tells them it is hard to just "dive in" to the clay and "smush things around." She adds, "Some of you guys might have trouble doing that. Especially some of you that like really clean lines and perhaps like to draw with pencils. Sometimes it's a really different thing to work with clay. So I want to commend you for all diving in. That's why we did that."

Students are learning to be messy and experimental—learning that this kind of mucking around is an important part of the artistic process. After the game, they each begin to work on their own imaginary creature that will be kept, fired, and glazed.

While Beth moves among students as they work, she finds ways to encourage them to keep working experimentally. "You might say, 'Here's a pencil, and I'm going to use the back of the pencil and roll it across the clay, and I'm going to experiment.'" The following are other examples of comments meant to help students learn to Stretch and Explore:

- *Don't worry about how the piece will end up.* Beth encourages a group of students to play freely without concern about how their pieces end up looking. She says that she wants them to have something in mind, "and then I want you to play and play and play."

- *Experiment with expression through texture.* Beth encourages a student to "think about what kind of texture it might be. Is it a furry part or is it sharp and shiny like a beetle?" She suggests that he can explore ways to create texture and should remember the finger marks another student used in her piece.

- *Experiment with tools.* Beth offers ideas of tools a student might use to experiment: "There's

a couple of screws and things on the window sill over there and they make really good tools, sometimes, things that aren't really tools. You might play around with that, too."

- *Discover new techniques through play.* Later, Beth will teach specific techniques, but right now she wants students to discover techniques on their own, through play. Such experiences reinforce an understanding that techniques are solutions others have come up with for problems they have encountered. Students learn that when they have a problem, they can use techniques others have created, or can invent a technique to solve it themselves. To a student struggling to stick clay together, Beth says, "There are specific ways to do it, but I want you guys to play around in this first project. Just go with that and see what happens and maybe you'll learn a new technique with doing that."

Beth Reflects

Beth talked to us about this class and about teaching students the habit of Stretch and Explore. Taking risks is an important part of growing as an artist, which Beth says she is constantly trying to reinforce in her students. Her students "need to be able to risk what they're already good at" and not be trapped by the "safety net of style." Beth also talked about her own growth as an artist and the importance of stretching beyond her comfort zone.

> When I'm really working hard and doing good work, it's not fun at all. I hate it, and that's how I grow as an artist. I struggle through it, and I feel out of my comfort zone, and I'm exhausted, my arms hurt, and that means that I'm working hard, and that I'm growing as an artist.

One of Beth's articulated goals for the Sketching in Clay class was for students to lose their inhibitions about working with the medium of clay and about being "precious" regarding their work. She wanted students to free themselves of the goal of trying to make everything perfect and smooth. She had them smash their first pieces so they learned to let go, a strategy she has also tried with painting. When asked why she did not teach students about hollowing out their forms so they were not too thick to be fired, Beth told us that this was just one more constraint she wanted them at first to be free of.

As much as she can, Beth wants students to learn from the materials rather than through explicit instructions.

> If I had more time, I would have them learn entirely from the materials. And let them learn, and then fail, and then have things, you know, break and explode and all that, and then they'd learn that way.

Capitalizing on mistakes, she says, is a major consideration in ceramics.

> It's not all about perfection and dominating a natural material, but it's letting the natural material do what it will. So if something cracks, if somebody has a piece that cracks, I don't want them to freak out and think it's broken. If you have a crack, well, let's fill it with gold. And let's make that what the piece is about.

When students are playing, Beth believes they are more able to take suggestions and criticisms than when they are working on a piece that must be finished in final form. She told the story of a student who had a "white page issue" and how "it's easier for him to address it, deal with it in kind of a low-risk painting, which was a play painting, than in a highly refined major project." She added, "I think my hope is when they play around, stuff will come to the surface and then we can address issues in a less tense way." Beth also reflected more generally on how students at the Boston Arts Academy are not allowed to learn passively: "This is not just going to school. You can't just follow these rote things that other schools may have asked you to do. You have to really step outside your comfort zone and push yourself in all kinds of areas."

BUILDING FORM:
REPEATING UNITS PROJECT   (EXAMPLE 11.2)

For Jason Green's third ceramics project in the second semester of his mixed-age (grades 9–12) introductory ceramics course at Walnut Hill, students learn to plan in a responsive or "improvisational" way, by creating a unit and then repeating that unit to build a larger form. Students are learning to adopt the attitude of "what would happen if . . . ?" They cannot know what the end product will be like from the initial unit. They discover as they go.

In their first two projects, Jason's students learned traditional methods of hand-building—coil and slab. Today they learn a method of building based on repeating units, a method that is common in nature and often used in clay, as when walls of clay bricks or roofs of clay tiles are built. They are to create a unit and then repeat that unit over and over to build a larger form. He talks to them about different kinds of units and explains how the way that the units are put together determines the form of the resulting sculpture (see Figure 11.1).

Demonstration–Lecture

Jason encourages students to begin by playing around with different kinds of units. "I want you to experiment," he says. He discusses examples of forms from nature that are built up out of repeating units—a wasp's nest, a pine cone. He shows a small wall of bricks and a sculpture comprised of stacks of the same cast bottle, layered over and over. The task for today's class is to create small experimental models trying out various units and exploring ways of joining these units into a whole.

Students are asked to decide how units will be joined. Jason tells them to consider whether they are "going to be piled or stacked or are they going to be compressed together or glued together." Students are told to play with showing how the units are stuck together to reveal rather than conceal the building process. "You want to think about showing, if you stack things together, if you stack coils together, and assemble them; when you score, leave the connection and don't smooth things over." Jason refers to this kind of experimentation as "thinking with the clay." Here are some examples of how Jason helps students learn to Stretch and Explore as they think with the clay:

- *Experiment with a range of different forms.* Jason stops to talk with a group of students. When one tells him her plan, Jason tells her, "Rather than just starting, I want you to experiment with some different types of units. Some might be very geometric, some you might just grab and shape in your hand quickly." Jason suggests to another student in the group that she go even further and build using "dramatically different units."

- *Experiment with techniques for making and joining units.* Later, Jason returns to both students to talk further about different ways they could work with building from their units. To one,

Figure 11.1. Stretch and Explore—Jason Green Asks Students to Consider "What Would Happen If . . . ?" in His Unit Sculpture Assignment

A. A student consults with Jason Green about the units she has created from which to make a sculpture

B. Jason encourages a student to play with her idea of "wings" for her unit sculpture

C. He tells a student that he wants her to experiment

D. Jason demonstrates combining natural forms such as wasp's nests and pine cones he suggests she might build something large by connecting together the pieces she has built already. Jason tells the other that he can tell her unit was made with the slab roller and suggests, "Think of touching the clay in a way you haven't touched it before. Is there a way you can make a unit just from your hand or from another tool that's not a ceramic tool?"

- *Think conditionally and experiment with what the clay can do.* Jason uses conditional "what if" language to urge a student to think of possibilities for building a unit based on a wing. He asks, "What if you just tried flattening pieces of clay and building a wing out of this?" "What happens if you start alternating and building the sculpture up this way?" He also asks a student to make clay do unusual things: "Think about Jackson Pollock, because his painting was a result of his process. He would drip the paint in a certain way. How could you drip clay?"

- *Invent some different tools.* Jason tells a student to experiment with tools, including invented tools: "I want you to also do some more experimentation before the end of the day and make some things with your hands and with other tools that aren't ceramic tools."

- *Take advantage of accidents and let things just happen.* "You are actually building a sculpture over there but didn't know it," Jason says as he points to a small pile of similar pieces of clay. He tells the student this is because they have a certain similarity and suggests maybe she try to see what she could build from them. He adds, "Those are interesting units because you weren't thinking about them too much when you made them."

- *Experiment with different versions.* Jason talks further with the student who originally based her unit on a wing and explains why he is urging her to think about several versions of the same idea.

> I want to put you through different ways to think of getting at the same idea. So if it seems like I don't like what you're doing, I like everything you do, I just want you to sometimes do different things so you can learn some more and see different ways of using the clay.

Jason explained to us that one of his goals for this class was to get students to explore ways to act on the material of clay: "I want them to research the material more than their idea of what their sculpture is going to be in the end, which is tough for them because I'm setting them down this road and they really have no idea what they're going to be making."

Jason and Students Reflect

Jason further explained why he wanted a particular student to think about the unit and not the final product: "The final product will emerge. Thinking about what the end result was going to be limits her." He added, "I'm really trying to get them to stretch and push the material and themselves, and take some risks and do some things that they might not normally do."

Jason also talked about his own habit of stretching and exploring as an artist: "That's what I do. I try to continue to ask questions, and because of that, my own processes are continually changing. I don't make the same things over and over and over again." A freshman at Walnut Hill said the same thing to us:

> If you know what you're good at and you just repeat that over and over again, you're never going to get anywhere . . . you're just stuck doing the same thing over and over again because you know you can. And that's taking the easy way out. And you're not really going to go really far with that, I don't think.

A senior at Walnut Hill identified the habit of going beyond the given assignment as central to what she learned in high school: "I think the most important thing I've learned is thinking outside the box. Coming up with interesting solutions to interesting problems." She told us about how, in response to a multimedia assignment in her junior year that asked her to make a book, she explored different ways of conceiving of books. "I didn't want to make just any old regular book, so I started thinking of different structures that kind of had pages or had covers." She ended up creating an Asian-inspired fan with the different segments representing pages of a book (see Figure 11.2).

And another senior at Walnut Hill told us what he had learned about not focusing always on creating a finished piece of work: "I think . . . you get to a point when you're doing art where you have more to learn from going and doing a new piece than refining the one you've already got . . . you can see the progression through different works."

Figure 11.2. A Junior at Walnut Hill Pushed the Form of Her "Book"

A Dispositional View of Stretch and Explore

The disposition to Stretch and Explore may be less dependent on skill and more a matter of an attitude—alertness to creative connections and the inclination to put them into action.

Skill. The skills involved in Stretch and Explore include the ability to make novel associations, to diagnose by analysis how outcomes failed, to conceive of tasks that take-off from illogical premises and follow them to their logical conclusions—even when this pushes beyond the artist's ability level and makes failure likely. Stretch and Explore is the skill of dismissing the censors, deciding to push beyond the urge to merely repeat previous successes, and keeping critical voices at bay while adopting the unconscious abilities of a child adept at play. This is what leads to problem-finding.

Alertness. Alertness to Stretch and Explore means recognizing the possibilities everywhere for trying new things, seeing where that takes you, and making novel connections. It means recognizing when benefits may come from thinking divergently and the times to infuse art-making periodically with play and randomness in order to move the process forward strategically. It means seeing the errors as creative opportunities.

Inclination. The inclination to Stretch and Explore means the willingness, even the desire or need, to innovate. It can grow from dissatisfaction, from curiosity, from confusion, from boredom—anything that motivates a reach beyond the quotidian and into the realm of novel possibilities.

Generative Connections to Stretch and Explore

Stretch and Explore often pairs with other habits that support and extend its creative core. For example, teachers pair it with Develop Craft when they ask students to experiment with new materials and techniques; students can invent new techniques with tools and materials, such as when Sara Stillman asked her kindergarten through 5th-grade students in Oakland, CA to do everything possible to alter cardboard. This pairing easily becomes a cluster when Express is added, since messing around produces unusual outcomes, which convey new meanings if they are recognized and used in art-making. Extending the cluster by adding Envision (thinking about what's to be made) and Reflect (thinking about what's been made) further extends and consolidates what is learned.

Stretch and Explore becomes more generative when combined with Envision. When teachers ask students to think about "what if," students begin to envision new possibilities and then try them out. Adding Observe into this pair results in explorations being noticed, which then can catalyze further investigation.

Stretch and Explore is also tightly linked to Engage and Persist. When students are highly engaged, they are more likely to keep on trying new things; and when students persist for long periods of time, they are more likely to find the edge of their competence and step off that edge. As discussed in Chapter 7 on Envision, another common cluster is the triad of Stretch and Explore, Engage and Persist, and Envision.

What Teachers Can Do

Teachers can help students develop the inclination to Stretch and Explore by infusing their conversations with encouragement to try new things: "See what would happen if . . ." "How else could you have done this?" "Don't worry about mistakes, just be brave . . ." They can encourage students to be willing to embrace mistakes, stumbles, and failure as steps along the way to innovation. Artist Oliver Herring's "Task" events are effective ways to introduce students to the value of play. In Task, participants each write "something someone could do" on a slip of paper and put it in a box.

Each participant then takes a slip and carries it out in some way. When they finish, they write a new task slip, put it in the box, and take another. The process unfolds with the development of more and more playful tasks, releasing a spirit of possibility that is hard to match. Similarly, MassArt professor John Crowe assigns students the task of "making fifty mistakes" and surprises them in the next class by asking them to choose one mistake to "elevate to a work of art." Students may not at first have the intrinsic motivation to generate ideas by playing without a censor for extended periods. Assignments such as Task and Fifty Mistakes provide extrinsic motivation; the goal is for this motivation to become intrinsic.

When teachers encourage students to Stretch and Explore, they strive for what David Perkins calls "optimal ambiguity"—tasks that are clear enough to communicate a direction and open enough to allow infinite solutions. Teachers who want to encourage this habit do not tell students exactly what to do. Instead, through the level of challenge in the assignments and the responses teachers make as students work on those assignments, teachers urge students to play around, to take risks, to discover what can happen, and to try out alternatives.

Teachers also allow students adequate time to stay with a line of inquiry long enough to pursue the kinds of conditional thinking involved in Stretch and Explore. At both Boston Arts Academy and Walnut Hill, we observed a process where students were gradually supported to move from responding to open-ended assignments given by the teacher to pursuing a self-directed and sustained line of inquiry that allowed them to explore the possibilities in an area of interest. As one senior working on a series of expressive oil portraits describes the process,

> We [the student and Jim] have a little bit of a back-and-forth, and then it gives me a little bit of a direction, and it gives me something to think about, and then I go out and implement that in the next, say, ten pieces I do. . . . I think they almost have a bit of a hands-off feeling or approach to it. And a lot of it, I've found, is my personal learning. I mean, the biggest element is, I think, I care about it. It's like I really want to advance where I'm going.

This sustained self-directed stretching and exploring is also an expectation of advanced art classes, such as those in the International Baccalaureate, Advanced Placement in studio art, and Teaching for Artistic Behavior (TAB) (see Jaquith & Hathaway, 2012; Douglas & Jaquith, 2009).

Stretch and Explore in Other Disciplines

Teachers of all subject areas typically hope their students will learn to think not only critically, but also creatively. Although it is in the art studio where creativity is stressed most explicitly, no creative breakthroughs are made in any discipline without a stretch, and exploration is the way thinkers stretch. Stretch and Explore is therefore the core of creativity across all disciplines. Viewing creativity as the sole purview of the arts curriculum is a common problem in schools. Students need to learn to Stretch and Explore in every school subject. For example, in the Odyssey of the Mind program, designed to foster collaborative creative problem-solving, students are given challenging problems with no predetermined solution and many "loopholes." Problems can range from a hands-on engineering challenge (building something based on limited materials) to coming up with a new interpretation for a work of literature.

In the current educational climate, mistakes in non-arts classes are often seen by students as shameful, humiliating, and to be avoided. Teachers in academic disciplines could learn from art teachers' emphasis on playful mucking around and embracing mistakes as opportunities.

TWELVE

Understand Art Worlds

DOMAIN, COMMUNITIES

Part of my role is to demystify art throughout the year.

—Jim Woodside

The most powerful experiences in art history that I have witnessed have been in my studio classes, not necessarily in my art history classes.

—Beth Balliro

There's strength in ideas . . . and working together toward a common goal.

—Kathleen Marsh

By "Understand Art Worlds," we refer to the process by which students come to understand the many art worlds in which artists (including designers and architects) engage: contemporary, modern, ancient, prehistoric, non-western, outsider, folk, popular, and so forth. Even outsider artists do not work in total isolation: artists and artworks always respond to works that have come before, consciously or not. We divide this Studio Habit of Mind into two components, *Domain* and *Communities*.

Understanding the *domain* means familiarity with the full range of art: from contemporary art practices (e.g., Damien Hirst's dead animals in formaldehyde; Félix González-Torres's candy spills; Marina Abramovic's interactive endurance performances) to the origins of human art—e.g., knowing that, as reported in *Science Magazine*, the earliest known forms of human art were actually non-representational designs rather than the famous bisons on the cave walls of Altamira and Lascaux (Pike et

al., 2012). As students gain access to fuller ranges of artistic responses throughout time and across cultures, they can develop their own voices in response to those conversations.

Understanding *communities* means learning about and participating in the discourse community of artistic practice—people who are concerned and knowledgeable about art, including artist-teachers, student-artist peers, teaching artists, local artists of all kinds, contemporary artists everywhere, and past artists. Artists are in dialogue, real and imagined, with a community that speaks the language of art around the globe and throughout time; those working now and those from the past. Understanding *communities* also means learning about what Csikszentmihalyi (1990) has called the "field" of art—the galleries and museums, and the people who guard and open their gates, including museum curators, gallery owners, and other artists. Together, these gatekeepers decide whose work will be exhibited and immortalized. While social media and other cultural forces are breaking down traditional systems of control, access, and authority, gatekeepers still exert powerful influence on what the public and various specialized audiences consider to be great or worthy. Artists need to respond to the gatekeepers in one way or another along a continuum running from acquiescence to abject transgression, and student-artists need to come to understand those interactions.

The community component of Understand Art Worlds also includes working with peers. When students collaborate on a group project, such as the creation of a library of ceramic molds (Examples 3.2, 10.2, and 12.5), or the Egg Drop Project (Example 12.6), they work in a team. When they work on individual projects, they share tools and materials, help each other by providing suggestions, and learn by looking at each other's work. In all of these ways, students come to see art-making as an activity that is carried out in the company of peers. One Walnut Hill senior told us, "I think working like this . . . made me be able to respect other people a lot more and have a better understanding of other people and who they are."

DOMAIN

Students are taught about the *domain* of art (works of art, both contemporary and historical). While art history is not usually taught in a systematic fashion in studio arts classes, teachers often ask students to look at works or reproductions of works of art that relate in some way to the project in which the students are engaged. Students are taught about their own relationship to the domain of art, considering the similarities between the problems explored in their own works and those explored by established artists.

Students often talked about how their own art-making grew from looking at how other artists had solved problems. One of Jason Green's students tried to imagine the process behind artists' work so she could connect it to her own work: "When I see the other sculptures, I imagine about them, their process—how did the artist make this? How did they work? I imagine about the process. When I think about that, I can get ideas."

We first present examples that teach about the domain of art (artworks) and help students see the relationship between their own works and those made by professional artists. In these examples, students come to see that they are working on visual problems similar to those that artists are dealing with now and/or have dealt with throughout the centuries. They also come to see how they can learn from and be inspired by these artists.

CONSIDERING REPRESENTATIONS: FIGURES IN EVOCATIVE SPACE PROJECT   (EXAMPLE 12.1)

Recall Jim Woodside's drawing project, Figures in Evocative Space, described in Examples 8.1 and 15.2, in which he sets up a "scene" with two models, far apart from each other, just "hanging out." He emphasizes that "these two people are elements in a play here, elements in a drama." He wants students to use drawing to express a dramatic relationship.

To illustrate his point, Jim provides models of artists expressing relationships evocatively in paintings by Edward Hopper and Richard Deibenkorn:

This is a very famous painting done by Edward Hopper called *Nighthawks*, done in 1942. OK, now, if you can see it, what's the sort of feeling you get from this, what's the emotional content? [Students suggest quiet, late, drowsy.] Quiet, late, drowsy, how is that implied? It's a very quiet painting, that's a really, a really perceptive remark. And I really like that you said that, 'cause what you're starting to do is describing it not just in paint terms. It's a very quiet painting, it's late at night, the figures are small in relation to the space, the way that they're relating to each other, they're all sort of, if you look closely there, I know this is just a little picture here, but if you look closely they're all sort of in their own worlds. . . . He thought very carefully about the relationship between the figures and how that was going to be implied.

This is by a painter called Richard Deibenkorn . . . and while this painting is not as emotional as the Hopper *Nighthawks* painting, it is very much about how figures relate in a larger space. You can see the artist working in his studio, and this is maybe the model. It's a very standard scene, a very ordinary scene. The figures themselves are not really individual, are they? They're just elements there, just sort of props in an overall drama.

Jim has shown the students the Hopper and Deibenkorn paintings to inform their thinking about the current drawing challenge he has posed to them. He explains, "So this is the kind of . . . thinking I think will be helpful if you need to have an image in mind as you begin something like this." During the Critique following the assignment, students discuss how they expressed emotions similar to those in the Deibenkorn and Hopper works.

Jim Reflects

After the class, Jim spoke with us about how the image helped the students appreciate the challenge of the assignment, how he hopes students will move beyond "academic" art to expressive art, and how such paintings can help students understand what he is getting at:

When they look at [the Hopper] they don't think . . . "look at the figures," they think . . . "it's a late mysterious night.". . . And there's figures in there and they don't seem to be talking to each other and they can all understand immediately, even though it's a very dated image, they can understand that idea of hanging out late at night.

DRAWING INSPIRATION FROM IMAGES: AFRICAN POTTERY PROJECT   (EXAMPLE 12.2)

Students working on Beth Balliro's African Pottery project near the beginning of their second-term 9th-grade class at the Boston Arts Academy are making a textured clay surface inspired by the patterning in African pottery (see also Example 3.1). They begin by looking at ceramics from three areas of Africa. Beth explains that this will give them some context within which to consider what they are about to start making. She focuses students' attention on packets of images she has distributed that illustrate varieties of African pottery. She asks them to notice the patterning and select three designs that they like. To get the students to think more deeply about patterns, she also asks them to make sketches of the patterns they see around their house. The goal of the project in class today is to begin to make three coil vessels, each of which has elements from the pottery of the three regions of Africa that they have studied, both here and in their humanities class. The challenge is to make the form and the pattern match.

The students also learn about John Biggers (1924–2001), an African American artist who studied the art of various African cultures. Students look at his drawings, as well as at images of pottery from Africa. Beth explains that she has chosen Biggers because he's an artist whose work was inspired by African art, as theirs will be.

Beth Reflects

After the class, Beth explained to us that she wanted her students to learn to respect another culture's art as John Biggers did. She hopes that her students will be inspired by this and will go on to research the art of another culture on their own. She also hopes to get her students to understand that art can be functional and does not just need to hang on museum walls; again, Biggers exemplifies this understanding. "I want them to think about art in everyday life and how they can actually make things to use and have them be artful and share them with people."

DESIGN INSPIRED BY OBJECTS: CERAMIC SETS PROJECT   (EXAMPLE 12.3)

The final project of the term in Jason Green's beginning ceramics course at Walnut Hill is to make a ceramic set, a group of objects that work together, and that includes one pouring vessel, such as a tea set (see also Example 13.2). Before they begin, Jason shows them a wide variety of "sets" made by ceramicists, objects that he has brought to class for the students to study and touch. He holds up specific objects and talks about how they were made. He explains how a glaze was applied. He holds up a ewer and explains what it is. He holds up some jars, pointing out how they were crafted:

Look at how these handles are made. These are pulled . . . to give this sort of elegant curve. This spout and this spout are made from slabs, flat pieces of clay, see, and they're joined right here [*pointing to the joint*]. You can look at these different types of lids and how they work. This is a special locking lid [*removing the lid from the pot and reinserting it*]. That's a nice handle [*pointing to the handle*], huh?

Jason also points out that some of the objects have designs stamped onto them. "These are put in with stamps [*motioning to impressed designs in the teapot*], so if you wanted to try stamping, we have pieces of, lots of pieces of scrap wood or pieces of plaster. You can use anything as a stamp." Jason points out how some of the pieces are made using techniques the students have already learned. "This is made using that wax resist like I showed you and just taking a very small brush and putting the glaze where I want it."

As he holds a free-form pitcher, Jason compares it with Jackson Pollock and abstract expressionism: "This is abstract expressionist, using the clay very quickly, then using lots of slips, very quickly dripping slips." Jason holds up another object, explaining that it was a sculpture made on the wheel. "Just a sculpture with this hole as the aperture where light is supposed to shine through and then hit the table." And about another object by the same artist, "The bottom is added on and this is just an oval thing, but you can see how this easily could be some sort of pot." Jason is trying to stretch his students' conceptions of the possibilities of ceramics (also nurturing the disposition to Envision).

After studying the actual objects, students are directed to look at books and postcards and images on the computer (including images of ceramics from the Sung Dynasty in China) for further ideas. "I want you to think about just the different varieties of form and different approaches to touching the clay." Like the students in Beth's African Pottery class, Jason has his students draw their inspiration here from the art of a distant culture. Such exploration extends students' imaginations through connections to the ongoing conversation conducted in the world of practicing artists.

Jason Reflects

After class, Jason spoke to us about how he believes that looking at works by ceramicists can open up students' minds to new possibilities. He wanted them to see many options. He particularly wanted them to see subtle variations in form and to relate form to function. He believes that this kind of looking will encourage students to try new ways of working with clay:

I brought in some historical stuff for them to look at . . . some of them have seen some historical ceramics. . . . It's just to show them these slight variations in forms and how they might relate to how the object is used. And just again in many ways trying to open up . . . their minds to all the different possibilities and variations that are available to them. . . . I want them to . . . be able to investigate . . . new ways of working and touching the clay. So I think it's good . . . for me to bring in examples that they can look at visually and also things that they can touch, and you know, learn as much as they can from that and observe as much as they can. . . . One thing I think I'm trying to also show them is there's such a huge variety of vocabulary available to them.

STRUCTURING A WHOLE CLASS
TO FOCUS ON DOMAIN:
CUBISM PROJECT   (EXAMPLE 12.4)

After presenting the examples above, we want to describe one class in depth to show how learning to Understand Art Worlds: Domain can become a thread through the three structures of Demonstration–Lecture, Students-at-Work, and Critique. For Jim Woodside's Cubism Project at Walnut Hill,

students examine Cubist paintings before and during their efforts to make a drawing in a Cubist style.

Demonstration–Lecture to Present the Project

Late in the spring term of his year-long drawing course, Jim introduces students to Cubism and has them make drawings based on what they have learned and seen. Jim shows a Cubist painting by Picasso and explains that this is in the style of "Analytical Cubism." "It's the first kind of Cubism," Jim says.

Literally invented by Braque and Picasso together. OK? They literally made it up around the first decade of the twentieth century—1907, 1906, around that time period. Now I'm going to give you a really quick lesson on this, and then we're going to start and you're going to do your own Cubist drawings.

Jim holds up a reproduction of a painting by Delacroix to show the contrast case—a painting that is *not* Cubist. What differentiates it from a Cubist painting, Jim explains, is that it has depth. The surface is two-dimensional, but the artist created an illusion of the third dimension. For the Cubists, the illusion of depth was "a lie" and so they rejected it. Instead, they wanted to show what was real. "What's real is this piece of paper, the flatness of it. So in a way, they were sick of lying. Now that's an exaggeration. Don't ever tell anybody that that's why Cubism started because they were sick of lying. But there's a little bit of truth to it."

Jim goes on to explain how Cubism differed from perspective drawing:

All art at that point, around say the turn of the century, the 19th to the 20th century, all art was about depth, perspective. . . . You're looking into it. You're looking into a picture. . . . Cubists come along and here they're looking at their canvas. Here's their big white canvas [*holding up large piece of paper*], and it's flat. It's flat. Two dimensions. One, two. How can we draw a picture of the world and somehow honor this flatness? Make that part of the idea? Make that part of the directness, the honesty of it. . . . They come up with this idea which ends up being called Analytical Cubism.

Jim follows this explanation with an example:

And what they thought was that if I'm going to draw [student's name] sitting there and I want to do it on a flat surface, I'm going to somehow acknowledge all sides of her. The front, the side, the back, and I'm going to put it all on the same piece of paper. So in a way, I'm taking the three-dimensional world and I'm putting it on a two-dimensional surface in a way that makes sense, that's logical and that's honest . . . it's important to understand why it ended up looking like this. It's not just a style. There was a reason behind it.

As he holds up several reproductions of Cubist paintings, Jim asks students to talk about how each one "denies depth." He points out how one of the paintings violates perspective:

You know how I taught you in two-point perspective that as things go away, they get closer together? Look at this. This artist makes them get wider right there. That's not by accident. Why is the artist doing that? To make it flat. Why would they want to make it flat? Because the paper's flat and that's more honest. That's more logical. That's more contemporary, any of those words. But that's more real. Do you understand the idea? It's pretty deep stuff. It's pretty heavy stuff.

Jim then shows students Picasso's revolutionary Cubist painting, *Les Demoiselles d'Avignon*, and offers an explanation. "Picasso is trying to imply all sides of the figure, the front and the back at the same time." He shows them a few more Cubist works:

These are what early Analytical Cubism looked like. What does the word *analytical* imply when you hear it? Analyze. It sounds pretty dry, doesn't it? It sounds pretty boring. It sounds pretty, like, analytical. And they wanted it to be that way. Think about it. Think what I'm saying. They wanted to honor the flatness of the surface. It's about analysis, like a doctor almost. It's not about wild expression. It's about how we can make it more clear, analytical, logical, honest. They didn't even want to use a lot of color here. . . . Maybe I'm making too much of the word *honest*, but it's not trying to trick anybody. It's not trying to show you a picture that doesn't exist.

Students-at-Work

Jim immediately moves students into their own drawing. "Think about trying to draw in that style today. Think about trying to draw the front and the back of somebody's head at the same time." He engineers this by placing a model in front of the class for 10 minutes, then rotating the model a quarter turn each 10 minutes that follow. Students must continue with the same drawing. As Jim explains, "You're going to be forced to draw several sides of him on the same drawing."

As students draw, Jim circles the room speaking with individuals about their work. He often reminds students about the core idea of Cubism. When he spoke with one student, he said, "What you end up with is something that generally looks pretty flat. You know, meaning that you don't really look into deep space. And you know, as I said, the paper's flat. That's what those guys liked." He tries to connect what a student is doing to Cubism: "They were inventing a new way to make art based on the materials. The flat paper. . . . So you already know how to do this. . . . It's just you're feeling, like, how can I draw like Picasso? If you need answers to this stuff, try to think about the Picassos." He is teaching his students that paintings by master artists can provide them with answers to problems that they are trying to solve in their own work (see Figure 12.1).

Demonstration–Lecture

Before the Critique session, Jim uses a short Demonstration–Lecture to reinforce the challenges and solutions of Cubism. He brings out another Cubist painting to show the similarities between this painting and the students' work. He directs students to look at the mouth. "It's a profile of a mouth, isn't it? And yet the lips are in front. So he shows you side and front in this almost ridiculous cartoon-like way. . . . That's what we're doing." He also underscores how what the students had done today is a continuation of the same things they had previously worked on in large drawings last week.

Jim stresses why Cubism is something worth understanding:

It's a really important part of the way art is taught, the art of the last 100 years. . . . Cubism is a part . . . of what you should understand about art, about Western art, 20th-century art. And it's a very big part of the way that we

Figure 12.1. Understand Art Worlds: Domain—Jim Woodside Asks Students to Draw in a Cubist Style

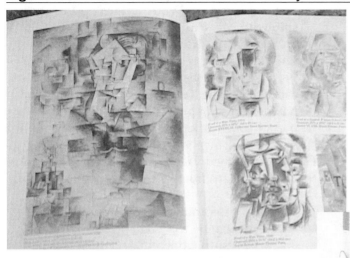

A. Jim Woodside shows students Picasso's drawings to support their learning to draw in Cubist style

B. Jim wants students to develop a "casual relationship" to art in the past

C. He explains that Cubism was motivated by wanting to depict the three-dimensional world honestly on a two-dimensional surface

D. Jim wants his students to understand that "art doesn't happen in a vacuum"

work, the way that we study. And Cubism it-self is just a style, but that idea of the flatness is what I want you to remember.

Again Jim relates Cubism to other things his students have studied:

> If you need a simple way to think of it, think of it as the opposite of perspective. . . . I showed you before, months ago, weeks ago . . . about two-point perspective [*drawing*]. And how a railroad track goes way back in space. . . . And this is your canvas [*drawing*]. And this is your railroad track going back in space. If you're doing a Cubist painting of it, there's your railroad track [*drawing*]. Right. It's flat. It's right here. Now this is really a simple illustration, but I'm only saying it to you as a way of thinking about a kind of oppositeness of perspective. And why? Because remember, the canvas is two-dimensional. . . . Cubists thought that the image itself needed to be a reflection of the two-dimensional canvas.

Jim Reflects

When we spoke to Jim after class, he offered these reasons for wanting students to understand Cubism. First, students should understand the logic behind the emergence of Cubism:

> Cubism . . . was the most important . . . new movement in painting. . . . Kids can get a handle on this. . . . I think that they can start to understand or be curious about underlying . . . concepts in other contemporary art. . . . There are fairly concrete things to grasp on to, in terms of understanding it. . . . It's important for them to understand that it's not just a new look, it's not a new style that came out, there's a reason behind it. There's logic to it that somebody was after.

He went on to explain that students should learn to use works by professional artists on a regular basis:

> Students need to develop a kind of casual relationship to art in the past. To just go look at books, just flip through them, just get the stuff in their head. . . . It doesn't have to be this almost religious event. . . . You can flip through a book,

and read a little bit here or there, browse around on the internet, and you . . . develop a relationship with it, just as you would with a person. . . . To develop a casual relationship is also to develop a living relationship. . . . The work has purpose for you beyond just historical significance. It's living, and interesting, and alive, and maybe you can imitate some of it [and make it] part of your work.

He also explained that students need to recognize that one can learn from art without copying.

> It's really important to understand the difference between the copying and learning from, and art doesn't happen in a vacuum, it's not all . . . magically generated from inspiration. [Art] happens from work, and it happens from knowledge, and it happens from seeing other works. In some cases imitating them, borrowing things . . . this is what artists of the past have done.

We asked Jim if he thought students should study art history in a separate course. He explained that he prefers his method—making connections to historical works of art when these works are relevant to what the student is working on at the time. He added, "I try to get them excited about it and draw connections. In my mind, that's more important at this age than an official art history class." Thus, the disposition to Understand Art Worlds is inextricably fused with *making*. Students, Jim believes, gain a deeper understanding of works from the past when they see a direct relationship between these works, brought right into the art studio, and their own efforts.

A Dispositional View of Understand Art Worlds: Domain

When students work in isolation from work made by others, such separation leads to solipsism, triviality, and "school art" (Efland, 1976, 1983). When students learn about the domain of art, they can use artists as models of thoughtful process and see the potentials of artworks as sources of new ideas and standards of quality.

Skill. The core skill of Understand Art Worlds: Domain is the ability to seek information and stay informed about the cultures of art and artists. The skills of Understand Art Worlds develop when students actively seek to learn from artists' works and practices in order to inform their own art-making. Both browsing and careful examination of the works and practices of other artists in relationship to their own projects are ways to build skill in this habit. Sometimes this means researching a particular question (e.g., How do artists create depth in two-dimensional works? or Which contemporary artists create impossible spaces in their paintings?). Skills include calling up the resources for specific topics by searches on the web, in libraries, and in museum archives. Once resources have been identified, artists need to know what to look at and for, and how to document and store the information acquired for later reference.

Alertness. Alertness to the domain of art is recognizing when, in the process of making, an artist needs to seek something within the works or practices of other artists. In response to a teacher's or peer's comment, a student might stop working to go look up a particular artist or artwork or a collection of works from a particular era, style, or medium. Similarly, alertness might move from looking to making: When students look at the works of others, they should be alert to what they might use in their own studio work. Alertness to the domain also occurs when looking at the work of others in Critiques: By noticing particular technical, conceptual, or aesthetic qualities in the works of others, artists can make connections to their own works and process.

Inclination. The inclination to understand the domain of art requires a willingness to pursue new ideas, techniques, materials, and formal solutions by using artworks made by others and by interacting with other artists. Some students hold the misconception that artists should not take ideas from others, and thus resist this process. It also is easy for novices to become stuck in the process of making and not develop the drive to pause long enough to inform the making process by interacting with work made by others. Artists build inclination by using that muscle. They set up regular practices to familiarize themselves with art and artists by going regularly to museums, galleries, and openings and by subscribing to museum websites; and to publicity from local museums and galleries by following blogs and online forums and by reading arts journals, magazines, and the arts sections of newspapers.

COMMUNITIES

Students are meant to learn about their own relationship to broader art communities. They practice with their peers in classes and think about how they might fit into art communities, what they might do after graduation, and what they have to do to get there. They learn how to present themselves as artists by matting and framing their work, making slides, creating a portfolio, hanging a show, and applying to art schools. All of these activities are ways in which students are learning to become professional artists. Of course, most students in art classes will not go on to become artists. But learning to understand the challenge of balancing tensions between autonomy and collaboration in creating works of art is important for both serious and casual students of art.

In this section we describe two classes in which students are learning about community as they collaborate on group projects.

CREATING A LIBRARY OF MOLDS: COIL SCULPTURE PROJECT   (EXAMPLE 12.5)

For Jason Green's Coil Sculpture Project in the middle of the second semester of his year-long introductory ceramics course at Walnut Hill for a mixed-grade group of high school students, students create a library of molds to be shared later by all the students in the class as they make "skins" for their individual ceramic sculptures, an assignment that encourages students to share while at the same time pursuing their own work (see also Examples 3.2 and 10.2). Each student is going to make three different kinds of plaster molds. One will be a large slab with a texture all over the surface (the texture mold). Jason tells the students that "this is a very fast way to get a whole bunch of texture. So we're going to start building our sculpture using all different textured slabs. And we're going to share, OK?" Students will also make a sprig mold and a stamp mold. A sprig is a small mold that yields a piece of clay that can be attached to the surface of a sculpture.

After all the students have made these molds, they will then begin to make a textured surface for their ceramic sculpture. Making this "skin" will be "a very additive process. You're going to keep adding to the surface. And it's going to be lots of different types of textures."

To make their ceramic "skin," students will be able to make use of parts of the textured slabs created by other students. "So we're all going to be making a lot of molds. And we're going to have a library of molds, so that you can have a sculpture made from all different types of textures." While students spend this class period working individually on their molds, they know that they are working to create a library of textures to be shared. As they work with the plaster molds, students also share batches of plaster.

Jason Reflects

Jason stressed the importance of collaboration when we spoke to him. He thinks it is important for students to see how others have solved a problem and for them to learn from that solution. Students can also learn by eavesdropping: When he works with students, Jason responds to the individual, but he is aware, too, that other students are listening.

FOCUSING ON STRENGTH AND FORM: THE EGG DROP PROJECT   (EXAMPLE 12.6)

It is not difficult to create collaborative projects in studio classes, and, indeed, visual artists such as muralists, filmmakers, or architects do create work collaboratively. However, such collaboration has not been the norm in the discipline of visual arts. Perhaps this explains why we rarely saw team projects and more often saw teachers set up ways for students to support each other even though they were working autonomously.

Kathleen Marsh's class described here, the introduction to the final sculpture unit in the first term of the 9th-grade class at the Boston Arts Academy, is one of the few examples we saw of a group project. She divided the class into teams and gave each the same challenge—to create a container that will keep an egg from breaking when it is dropped from a banister down several flights of stairs. Each team is given one piece of foam core, three pieces of oak tag, ten straws, and a raw egg. They have an hour and a half to come up with a solution, to "create a safe haven for your egg," as she tells them. Students know there will be a prize for the winning team (or teams), and that winning means dropping the container and not breaking the egg. Another prize will go to the team that makes the best visual design. Thus, there is one prize for strength and one for aesthetics. Students must work together to solve this problem—there are no individual contenders (see Figure 12.2).

As students work, Kathleen moves around, directing comments to the groups as well as to individuals. In the interactions that follow, we see Kathleen focusing her students' attention on working together:

- *Look at a solution devised by another group.* "And can I just show you this?" Kathleen asks as she shows one group what another group of students has done to help them think of what they might do in their own work. "If you make strips out of your oak tag and fold them like this, you can make springs."
- *Remember you are not working alone on this project.* Kathleen continually reminds students that they are working together on the project. "Maybe two of you can do that while [she] is doing this?"
- *Keep in mind that resources are shared, and don't be selfish.* One group has used several eggs, leaving none for some teams. Kathleen expresses her displeasure: "You guys really put another team in a jam, and I'm not happy about that."

Kathleen Reflects

When we interviewed Kathleen, she explained why she believes collaboration and teamwork are important:

- Each student brings a different kind of skill to the group.
- Collaboration is a way to gather ideas and is also motivating because it is fun.
- When students work in a group, they keep each other in check so that the teacher does not have to play this role.
- Working in groups toward a common goal helps students transcend barriers of class and race.
- Collaboration is a skill that artists need, and many of her students hope to go on in the arts.

Although many visual artists still work individually, collaborative teams that use "ensemble" techniques, which historically were more central to methods in the performing arts, are increasingly common in the field of contemporary visual arts. Learning to work in and with artistic communities is valuable to art students for appreciating current practice. Working in communities also offers possible connections to the performing arts and to non-arts endeavors, such as science or interdisciplinary

Figure 12.2. Understand Art Worlds: Communities—Kathleen Marsh's Students Work in Teams to Create Containers That Will Keep an Egg from Breaking When Dropped Four Stories

A. Kathleen Marsh offers suggestions to groups as she circles the room

B. Kathleen shows a group another possibility to consider in their design

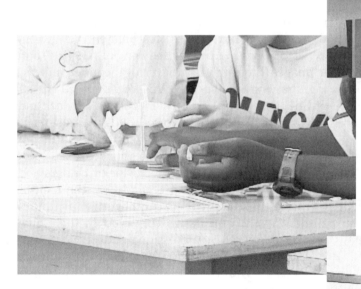

C. She tells students to "create a safe haven for your egg"

D. Kathleen reminds students to work as a group

projects in which teams of disciplinarians from a range of domains work together toward shared ends. Again, though, whether the collaborative skills and attitudes learned in visual arts classes transfer to other learning contexts is a question worthy of empirical investigation.

A Dispositional View of Understand Art Worlds: Communities

Skill. The core skill of Understand Art Worlds: Communities is the ability to work with others, not only by collaborating but also by learning how to talk to others about their work (using specific language during critiques, rather than merely saying "I like that" or "That's awful") and by learning ways to respond when work is criticized—either by considering and/or using constructive advice or by dismissing respectfully advice that is off-the-mark (e.g., "Yes, that would be interesting work; it isn't the work I'm making, however"). Other times it's creating and using libraries of resources, as when MassArt student-teacher Robert Leyen brought in five figure models in spandex from which students created a photographic archive to share for use in students' expressions of pose and gesture in developing their works about social attitudes.

Alertness. Alertness to communities is required for times when interacting with others might catalyze progress on a work in process. Or alertness might involve being attentive to opportunities to participate in a collective artistic experience or to submit work for exhibitions or prizes, resulting in field recognition.

Inclination. The inclination toward Understand Art Worlds: Communities means the willingness to work on collaborative projects, and even when working solo, to listen to and seek out the advice and reactions of others.

As students learn about artists' worlds, they connect what they do in school art classes with what practicing artists do now and did in the past. They learn about art history by consulting the works of artists to help themselves solve visual problems. When working on portraits, they compare how various artists have depicted people in the past and the ways they are doing so today; when working on light, they consider the range of ways that artists have grappled with portraying light. Understanding art history is

thus always connected to the student's own "making." Students also learn about the artistic community—the people and institutions of the art world sometimes called the field. This is part of teaching students to become professional artists, which is something many of the students we studied aspire to be. But even for students planning to study and work in other fields, learning how galleries and museums operate, learning to present their work professionally, and learning to respond to and critique the works of others are skills that help them connect their school artwork to the art world outside the school walls. And of course as students begin to work collaboratively (when art projects, for example murals or videos, call for team work), they come to see the act of making works of art as an ensemble activity.

Generative Connections to Understand Art Worlds

Understand Art Worlds never operates alone. It can be used in pairs or larger clusters involving each of the other seven habits. It often pairs with Observe, since it is by looking closely at, listening to, and reading about artworks and working processes of artists that students learn about the domain and communities of various art worlds. Teachers encourage students to ponder what they see in words (Reflect) and in images (Envision) and to convey their ideas in writing, drawing, and speech. This four-pronged cluster of Understand Art Worlds with Observe, Reflect, and Envision allows students to consolidate understanding of the connections among their work and that of others, including works by professional artists.

Similarly, when this core cluster of Understand Art Worlds, Observe, Reflect, and Envision focuses on the aesthetic approaches of other artists, it attunes students to the meanings conveyed in their own works and works by professional artists (Express).

Understand Art Worlds also links with Engage and Persist. One route to deeper engagement in a work is to search for opportunities and ideas in the work of other artists. When students are deeply engaged in an investigation of particular styles, artists, and/or works (using the core cluster described above of Understand Art Worlds, Observe, Reflect, Envision), the artists' works and practices may open students' minds to new possibilities and make them more likely to play with the ideas and techniques they notice (Stretch and Explore). That motivates them to make their own works (Develop Craft). Develop Craft, of course, is also a common pairing with Understand Art Worlds: Students can study the works of other artists to learn new techniques.

What Teachers Can Do

Students need to see how what they learn in school connects to what people do outside of school. Just as students in mathematics class need to see the relevance of mathematical modeling in daily life and to understand how mathematics is used in the real world, students in the visual arts studio need to connect what they learn in art class to what practicing artists do and to what art worlds are like, now and in the past. Without such context, students are left without a compass for reflecting on their efforts. But it is important to recognize that, while Understand Art Worlds overlaps with the discipline of art history, there are also clear differences. In art history, the goal is to teach a body of historical knowledge. When studio teachers help students to Understand Art Worlds, their goal is to help the students see connections between their own ideas and work and those of other artists, and to learn from the works of others in order to enrich their own process and works.

Understand Art Worlds: Parallels in Other Disciplines

Understand Art Worlds helps students connect their own work to that of professional artists. Students in all school disciplines benefit from making connections between what they are learning and what professionals in that discipline are doing and why. Thus, students in a history class would benefit from learning what contemporary historians are writing and thinking, the variety of methods that they use, and how publishers decide what gets into history textbooks. Students in a biology class would benefit from learning the kinds of unanswered questions being tackled and who makes decisions about which research questions are funded. Every area of study has a domain (works and knowledge created) and a community (gatekeepers and colleagues). Familiarizing students with these resources inspires and informs their efforts to develop understanding in that discipline.

We next consider how the Studio Habits of Mind are integrated with each of the four Studio Structures for learning.

Part III

INTEGRATING STUDIO STRUCTURES OF LEARNING WITH THE STUDIO HABITS OF MIND

Imagine walking into a studio classroom. Students are standing behind easels, using vine and compressed charcoal and black oil pastels on newsprint to draw a human model who sits hunched against a wall. Cool jazz plays softly, and bright lights cast shadows on and around the figure. The teacher is standing behind one student, silently observing him at work. After a while, she speaks to him briefly, points to the model, and lays a piece of tracing paper over the drawing. She quickly redraws several lines, says a few more words, and moves along to other students. She continues her rounds, stopping, looking, talking, and modeling processes and possibilities in short conversations with individuals.

A knowledgeable observer might surmise that the lesson's focus is value—students seem meant to learn to represent the variations of light and shadow on the figure. The spotlights are set up deliberately to emphasize the natural shadows that fall from the figure's contours; charcoal and oil pastels, black, without the confusion of color, are media that readily convey variations in light and shadow. But as we listen in more closely to the conversations between the teacher and her students, we only sometimes hear her emphasizing this element of developing craft. Yes, she talks to her students about value, but she frequently mentions other elements of drawing—line, edge, composition. She also talks about the "feel" or "directness" of various marks and areas of a drawing, as well as accuracy in representation. She engages in a discussion about "how to take that further," and another

discussion about the similarity of one student's approach to a particular contemporary artist, Philip Pearlstein.

She's talking about everything! In these brief personal conversations, teachers may focus on a single idea or process or Studio Habit of Mind, but, often, they address as many as five or six, or even all eight of the Studio Habits of Mind in a single, short consultation.

What's going on here? Is the teacher not focusing her instruction on what she really intends students to learn? Or perhaps this example shows that the Studio Habits of Mind are too narrow or too broad to be useful? Actually, we think all is well, both with the teacher and with the habits. The habits easily make explicit the quick and nuanced moves of an expert artist's thinking. An artist's mind flows dynamically from one way of addressing artistic problems to another, and the teacher's conversational shifts make that visible. Once a teacher makes her tacit expertise explicit, she can work on the elements of it that are of most interest, refining her teaching as she might her artwork.

So, perhaps the artist–teacher comments first on how she sees the work and the referent, focusing momentarily on the disposition to Observe. Next, she considers how she might depict the idea differently (Envision). Then, she may play with the idea a bit (Stretch and Explore), as a way to refine or create new techniques (Develop Craft). Without a pause, she might model different ways to approach the visual problem (Stretch and Explore), thinking aloud as she draws and describing what she sees (Reflect: Question and Explain; Observe), how well it works (Reflect: Evaluate), and how it "reads" to her (Express). All this can occur in under 3 minutes!

While the example above depicts the broad reach of habits as they are taught and learned in a Students-at-Work session, the Studio Habits of Mind are embedded throughout all of the Studio Structures for learning. Teachers addressed each of the habits of mind, individually and in many combinations or "clusters," not only in Students-at-Work sessions, but also in Demonstration–Lectures, Critiques, and Exhibitions. The next four chapters illustrate examples of how teachers emphasize each individual Studio Habit of Mind and how they interweave the Studio Habits of Mind within all of the structures by which studio instruction is organized.

THIRTEEN

Demonstration–Lecture and the Studio Habits of Mind

The Demonstration–Lecture structure is used to introduce ideas, assignments, and the particular Studio Habits of Mind that will be developed in the Students-at-Work and Critique structures in the class (see Chapter 3). As the teacher deliberately models working, seeing, and thinking as an artist, all the Studio Habits of Mind occur naturally. By slowing down the processes of making, perceiving, and reflecting about art and art-making for students in Demonstration–Lectures, teachers foster students' mindful attention to nuances that might otherwise pass by unnoticed.

FOSTERING PARTICULAR STUDIO HABITS OF MIND THROUGH DEMONSTRATION–LECTURES

In what follows, we illustrate how Demonstration–Lectures can promote the development of particular Studio Habits of Mind.

Develop Craft

Often, an assignment either requires or guides students to experiment with specific materials, tools, or procedures. Demonstration–Lectures, therefore, introduce students to particular features that are most likely to come up as opportunities and challenges as they work on Developing Craft.

For example, when Beth Balliro introduced clay to her 9th-grade students in her Sketching in Clay class (see Example 11.1), she showed them the practical realities of working with clay in their studio classroom at the Boston Arts Academy. She showed them where tools and materials were kept, what was available, when they could use them, how they needed to care for them, and even how to clean clay off tables and prewash their hands in a bucket so the sink would not clog with clay. Later in this same class, Beth assigned students the task of making a "chop," a traditional name-stamp used by potters. That provided further opportunities to clarify practical issues, such as the need to mark work for easy identification, to put work in progress and finished work on different shelves, and to treat unfired work delicately. She used the chop assignment as an opportunity to demonstrate the slab-roller, a large tool for flattening clay into slabs for a variety of hand-building and sculptural projects. Such practical, grounded demonstrations greatly ease the inconveniences and minimize the dangers of working in the environments of studio classrooms, with messy materials and sharp tools. Through the demonstrations, students develop clear images of what they need to do and how they need to do it.

Engage and Persist

Watching a skilled craftsperson at work is mesmerizing, and teachers often use Demonstration–Lectures to interest students in the potential of techniques, materials, or tools that they can learn to use at high levels of expertise. For instance, when Jason Green threw spouts "off the hump" (i.e., he stuck a large mound of clay to the wheel, then centered and formed only a small chunk of the top, a technique that facilitates creating many small pieces quickly), the students' focus was palpable as they watched in silent amazement.

In addition to engaging students' interests, teachers use Demonstration–Lectures to model ways to Persist as they demonstrate some of the variety of techniques, tools, and materials that students might employ to address artistic challenges. For instance, Jason also demonstrated how to create spouts by "extruding" (i.e., using a wall-mounted metal pipe with a plunger, called an extruder, that can be fitted with different internal and external shapes, called dies, to make variously shaped tubes of clay), how to make spouts from slabs pressed in the slab-roller by wrapping them around cone-shaped wooden forms, and how to "pull" spouts off wooden dowels (i.e., a technique of repeatedly grasping and sliding a wet hand down a piece of clay to shape it). While no one student would use all of these techniques to create the pouring vessel required by the Ceramic Sets Project (see Examples 12.3 and 13.2 for a more complete description of this assignment), seeing such a broad range of possibilities encouraged persistence in finding and developing techniques that would serve students' particular creative intentions.

Envision

Demonstration–Lectures are a way for teachers to model a range of possibilities inherent in their assignments and help students open their imaginations to what could and might be done within the assignments' constraints. Recall Jason's spring Tile Project (see Examples 6.1 and 7.2), in which students were assigned to create low-relief sculptures of nine mold-pressed tiles. During the Demonstration–Lecture at the beginning of this class, Jason not only demonstrated techniques, but also showed students a wide range of images of tiles from different cultures. Kathleen Marsh did a similar "tour" of possibilities with a slide show of drawn self-portraits to introduce a self-portrait assignment to her seniors (in which students drew themselves wearing hats and vests they created themselves; see Example 14.4). By studying a wide range of examples that satisfy the challenges of an assignment in different ways, students are less likely to hold onto a mistaken belief that there is one "right" way to solve the problem.

In addition to helping students imagine possibilities for pattern, form, and color through multiple examples, teachers also help them envision the *process* of the assigned work. For example, Jason helped them envision making tiles by demonstrating step-by-step how to use tools and materials. He showed students how to build a mold box, how to press clay into it and how to get it out, how to arrange wooden shapes and other objects in the mold to create patterns, and how to consider common problems like direction of forms (e.g., letters come out backwards when they are pressed in this way).

Express

Teachers often gather a range of samples—of works, techniques, materials, tools, or ideas—to guide students' thinking about how to express

personal meanings, feelings, or ideas in their work. Similar to the way Critiques let students see many possible solutions and hear many possible responses from their classmates, Demonstration–Lectures offer a chance to gain a wider view of the field of art, both from the present and the past. Such a broad and varied perspective encourages students to consider reasons for the variations that they observe, to think about what these variations "say," and what they themselves might "say" with a particular material, tool, or technique. For example, Jason often brought in artworks that he owned which were made by professionals (as well as a mud-wasp's nest that he had found in the clay studio and fired). Beth often copied packets of pictures for her students to achieve a similar objective. In Jim's opening class on contour drawing (see Example 15.1), he gathered descriptive words from the students onto a written list to describe the still-life they'd been drawing.

> Just take a look at these words. Take a look at them and think about how this might relate to the way you're drawing. . . . What we do in drawing, we express things by the way that we put lines down, by the way that we draw. These objects don't mean anything. It's just some old junk I piled up here. OK? But, you're already making psychological, making emotional connections, making connections to other things by looking at this. We do this with everything. OK? So, [that's] what makes drawing interesting.

In Demonstration–Lectures, teachers point out characteristics of the works or processes of interest to students because of similarity to something they recently made (e.g., drawings of a still-life, handles, spouts, glazes), or something they were about to use in a new assignment (e.g., expressive marks and lines, lips of a pouring vessel, coils, the mood or idea conveyed by a form or glaze, or the way a group of objects interrelates).

Observe

Demonstration–Lectures help students "see more" by exploiting their already developed interest in observation. Visual arts students are usually adept at learning from looking, and developing the disposition to do so is critical to their continued growth as thinking artists. For example, Guy Michel Telemaque opens his 9th-grade design class session by introducing students to the Viewfinder Project (see Example 9.1). He asked students to use a viewfinder to "see the world in a new way" so that they could begin to stand back from what they *knew* and start to see the world as design.

Often, the processes involved in using and caring for materials and tools, and working with particular techniques, are complex, multistep operations. Showing these steps in the context of preparing to make something is an effective way of giving students a great deal of information in a sort of visual–temporal "outline" form, which they can then use when they need to refine their understanding. In an early drawing class on perspective, for example, Jim followed up on a Students-at-Work session (when students drew still-lifes of boxes) and a Critique of those drawings (when students identified and discussed what "bugged" them about their work), with a quick, efficient demonstration of one- and two-point perspective drawing (see Examples 3.3, 5.3, and 9.2). By showing how to create a horizon line and a vanishing point or points, he could model how to draw boxes from any angle—a task they had just completed without that insight and which they would revisit immediately after the demonstration. Jim could then take the lesson one step further, by showing, through removing the rectangular case of an old film projector, how nongeometric objects could be "seen" through their geometry, so that objects of any shape could be understood through these simple perspective rules. His demonstration simplified to its essence a technique that can be very complex.

Reflect

Question and Explain. Because Demonstration–Lectures are generally brief, teachers often do not dwell here on developing students' disposition to Question and Explain. However, the Question and Explain Studio Habit of Mind is sometimes fostered in Demonstration–Lectures. For example, as the teachers showed works of art, they often modeled the internal conversations that the creators of these works might have had while creating them. And as students become attuned to different features of particular types of work, they have a chance to practice raising questions and suggesting possible explanations for the forms, styles, appearances, or methods that they have noticed in their recent art-making efforts. For example, when examining a collection of vessels for the Ceramic Sets assignment (see Examples 12.3 and 13.2), Jason's students asked about techniques for making different vessel "feet," probably motivated by their efforts to trim the bottoms of vessels just before the Demonstration–Lecture.

They also focused on variations in handles and lips, which had been their recent concern in throwing cups, and on glazes, since they had just gotten their first glazed pieces out of the kiln. Both teachers' "thinking aloud" and students' practicing raising and answering questions help develop the Question and Explain disposition.

Evaluate. Similarly, Evaluation is a more peripheral focus in Demonstration–Lectures, but it is there. This Studio Habit of Mind shows up as teachers point out common challenges and solutions that arise from techniques, as when Jason pointed out how he was using his arm on his leg to build a solid foundation to support his throwing hands while working on the wheel (see Examples 5.4 and 14.1). He sets his own performance as a standard against which students can evaluate their own wheel-throwing. In addition, examining a wide spectrum of examples related to a particular assignment offers chances for appreciation of what works, what individuals like, and what is possible. All contribute to students' understanding of quality and help them develop their habits of evaluation.

Stretch and Explore

Just as the variety of forms, techniques, and materials that teachers use in Demonstration–Lectures allows students to envision more and to consider possibilities for expression, that range of possibilities also reinforces the habit of deliberately stretching beyond a current level of ability and responding to "errors" as opportunities—because that is what is modeled in the objects and processes the teacher shows. For example, in Jason's Repeating Units Project (see Example 11.2), his Demonstration–Lecture kept raising new possibilities for what might count as a unit (a bottle, a brick, a plug of clay, a cell in a wasp's nest), and kept raising "what if" questions about techniques (what if you ripped it with your fingers, cut it with a needle tool or with knotted string, or pressed it with burlap or the bottom of a cup). All of these possibilities helped set students up to explore, push beyond the known, and observe accidents as opportunities and options for creation.

Understand Art Worlds

Domain. Demonstration–Lectures are a prime opportunity for teachers to inform students about the context of the culture of art in which they are working as artists. Jim showed students historical works that drew on the processes he was asking them to try. Guy Michel encouraged browsing through numerous journals and magazines to find examples of design techniques students were exploring, such as fonts, layouts, and color schemes. Beth worked to expand students' attitudes about what counted as "art" by showing students the objects from African and Japanese cultures that they might otherwise see as "only utilitarian." Jason showed students books of tiles from contemporary and ancient Asian and Middle Eastern cultures. In each case, work by other artists (past and present) is used as a way to expand students' thinking about what is possible, what has been done, and what they might try. The learning of *domain* in the art studio occurs in the context of work that students are currently doing, and not as an isolated "style" that they should simply learn "because it's important in art history."

Communities. The teaching in studio classes of art history and contemporary artistic practice sometimes happens through Demonstration–Lectures that focus on grounding students' own work in the contexts of the work of others. When teachers model processes, focus attention on the work of professional artists, or show students characteristics of particular art materials, these methods all emphasize the ways in which artists have worked in their own historical context, which includes the relationships to other artists as well as the relationship to their audience. While we only rarely saw teachers introduce assignments that required students to work in teams (Kathleen's Egg Drop Project is a notable exception; see Example 12.6), we frequently saw teachers remind students in explicit and implicit ways in Demonstration–Lectures that they were artists, and that artists were individuals who worked within various communities.

These communities include the student–teacher pair, peers in a class, visual art students within a school of students, student artists within a local community of artists, and student artists operating within a community of past and contemporary artists whose works form a context for the students' work. For example, when the Boston Arts Academy seniors prepared for their senior show, Kathleen used a Demonstration–Lecture to focus on community by establishing a volunteer group to plan the invitations with a visiting designer. She also set up another group to decide how to allocate space equitably to feature each student's work. We also saw teachers set up assignments that required sharing tools or materials. Recall that Jason's students created a library of molds that they shared in creating textured "skins" for the Coil Sculpture Project (see Examples 3.2, 10.2, and 12.5).

INTEGRATING STUDIO HABITS OF MIND IN THE DEMONSTRATION–LECTURE

The next two examples show how a Demonstration–Lecture integrates several Studio Habits of Mind.

TEACHING THE THEORY AND PRACTICE OF COLOR: INVENTING COLORS PROJECT   (EXAMPLE 13.1)

In Beth Balliro's Inventing Colors Project (see Examples 5.1 and 7.1), which is taught near the midpoint of her second-semester 9th-grade course at the Boston Arts Academy, she uses a 20-minute Demonstration–Lecture to introduce three purposes for the painting unit that students are about to undertake:

- Developing a theoretical appreciation for color (Understand Art Worlds: Domain)
- Understanding how to work (Develop Craft: Technique and Studio Practice)
- Helping students develop the disposition to experiment with materials and take risks in low-stakes "sketch" paintings (Stretch and Explore).

As Beth outlines the basics of color theory with the color wheel she has drawn on the board, the focus is on Understand Art Worlds: Domain. She asks students to copy the wheel into their notebooks and refers to it throughout her short Demonstration–Lecture, which now changes focus to emphasize Develop Craft: Technique. "This is a magical wheel, . . . because you can invent any color you want, if you understand how this wheel works." She explains that color is difficult to mix with acrylic paints, which they will be using (Develop Craft: Technique). When they begin to work, the focus will shift again to Stretch and Explore as students start to create a couple of "sketch" paintings. But, for now, the Demonstration–Lecture focuses on Develop Craft: Technique and Understand Art Worlds: Domain.

Beth uses the wheel to introduce primary colors. "You can't really make them. . . . If you were a cook, that's the first ingredients of your recipe, those colors." As is typical for Demonstration–Lectures, she introduces the information that students will use right away: "So the paints I'm going to have you use today. . . . Can you guess?" [*gesturing toward the board*]. The students respond: "Red, yellow, and blue. Plus white."

Next, Beth introduces secondary colors, again referring to the board so students see their relationship to the primaries—those colors mixed by combining the two primaries on either side (Understand Art Worlds: Domain). She suggests that the hue varies by the ratio of the primaries to each other in the mix and suggests that they experiment with that when they're working. "I want you to play today. You're really playing with mixing" (Stretch and Explore). Then she introduces the complementary colors, with reference to how they stand opposite the primaries on the color wheel and how they contrast with each other, and she closes with the neutrals: "A neutral color happens when you mix a color with its opposite" (Understand Art Worlds: Domain).

As the time to paint approaches, Beth sets the students up to paint experimentally by telling them that the color wheel doesn't work perfectly.

> *My* teacher said, "If you mix red plus blue, you'll get purple." So I took red, like the color of his shirt red [*pointing to a student's shirt*], and I took blue, sort of the color of his shirt blue, and what did I get? Brown. And I thought, "I thought you said . . . ?" What would be the problem there? Well, this red has a little bit of orange in it. So it's not completely true, but it's something to guide you. That's why I'm going to give you two shades of blue, because sometimes blue acts differently [*holding up two cans of blue paint*] (Stretch and Explore).

With the theory taken care of, Beth concludes the Demonstration–Lecture by showing students the materials they need to do the assignment, where to get them, and how to set them up (Develop Craft: Studio Practice). She shows students their palettes (new white Frisbees), paints (fresh tubes of acrylic), and new brushes, which she reminds them to use and clean carefully. She shows students how to set up their palettes with the colors in the order of the color wheel, shows them "gloss medium," to "make colors clearer" or "see-through," and shows them the paper they'll use. The students transition quickly to a Students-at-Work session in which they create two paintings of imaginary settings, one using complementary colors and one using neutral colors.

DESIGN INSPIRED BY OBJECTS: CERAMIC SETS PROJECT (EXAMPLE 13.2)

The Demonstration–Lecture with which Jason introduces his Ceramic Set Project (see Example 12.3), taught in the middle of the first semester of his yearlong ceramics course, emphasizes the relationships among four goals:

- Looking carefully at objects to see how they were made (Observe).
- Planning ceramic design in a variety of ways (Envision).
- Making choices to convey ideas or feelings (Express).
- Synthesizing technical skills learned over the term (Develop Craft: Technique).

During this portion of his Demonstration–Lecture (which occupies 40 minutes), Jason shows students a range of tools, techniques, and processes that they might employ to express meaning in the design and creation of their "sets."

Goal 1: Observe

In this Demonstration–Lecture, Jason shows students several tools and techniques to add to their repertoire of choices for this final assignment of the first term. He shows them new tools (e.g., the clay extruder for pressing spouts, dowels for pulling spouts) and new techniques (e.g., throwing small cups off a hump that, when cut in half vertically, become pitcher spouts). He also shows them new uses for old tools and techniques if they are combined with new ones (e.g., using slabs to roll spouts around dowels).

> You saw the spouts over on those other teapots, which are made in a way very similar to this (Observe, Develop Craft: Technique). We can pull spouts on dowels [*beginning to form clay*]. Very similar to pulling handles (Observe, Develop Craft: Technique). You want to put this through the middle as close as you can get to the middle [*pushing dowel through the clay*] and you want to get water on this [*removing the clay and dampening the dowel*] so it slides and just like you're pulling a handle, you can pull a spout [*beginning to form the spout over the dowel*] (Observe, Develop Craft: Technique).

Goal 2: Envision

As Jason demonstrates the various tools and techniques, he emphasizes how students might think creatively about their use. The interplay between techniques and ideas, therefore, is modeled as seamless. He teaches his students how to make the leap between the concrete materials and tools and the aesthetic purposes to which they aspire.

You can pretty dramatically change the form of something by cutting in . . . and adjusting (Envision). Now all these connections I would score—slip and score—so they would stay together (Develop Craft: Technique) [*beginning to form and shape a spout and attaching the spout to the tube*]. But just to give you the idea, there's the spout (Envision). And ahh, something like this [*using the tube made in the extractor*], you could use [*beginning to cut the form*] and alter . . . in some way to make some weird spout (Develop Craft: Technique, Stretch and Explore, Envision).

Goal 3: Express

In his initial interview, Jason was skeptical about the importance of teaching expression. On probing, it became clear that he worried that art was often trivialized by emphasizing its therapeutic uses as a way of "merely expressing feelings." However, using our expanded definition of Express, which includes the expression of concepts, personal meanings, *and* feelings, we observed Jason including Express as a goal in many classes that might appear on the surface to focus exclusively on skills. Jason shows that craft is necessary in order to express meaning.

As Jason begins to form the spout over the dowel (Observe, Develop Craft: Technique), he explains:

But as you pull, this will get tighter and tighter, so you have to keep adding water on this and making sure that it's loose and sliding. And then you may also put some sort of lines in [*forming lines in the clay*] (Express, Develop Craft: Technique). And you might do something like spin it [*spinning the clay, making a spiral shape*] (Stretch and Explore, Develop Craft: Technique). Then you can slide it off [*removing the clay from the dowel*]. Then if you really want to . . . give it some shape, you might have to turn it on its side and let that get leather-hard and then come back and cut it, the exact shape that you want it (Develop Craft: Technique, Express).

It may be difficult to understand why we label some of these examples as Express. Jason emphasized to us in interviews and to students in class that how artists touch clay leaves impressions that convey different meanings. A glaze applied with splashing "feels" more casual, so the object may feel more informal or convey a reference to the idea of movement, as Zen ceramics often do. A smooth surface feels more worked, so the object may convey more formality. For these reasons, we see Jason's references to different ways to touch or mark the clay as emphasizing "Express."

Goal 4: Develop Craft: Technique

When Jason shows his students how to use a tool or technique, he almost always encourages them to think about the many possible ways they could use it in their own work. Thus, he uses a "cluster" of Observe–Express–Envision–Develop Craft: Technique to make sure that students are not only learning skills, but also understanding the artistic purpose and potential of artistic tools and techniques.

So, now we need to score this with our scoring tool before we put it together (Develop Craft: Technique). I'll score this side [*scoring the clay*] (Observe, Develop Craft: Technique). And we can press this together [*pressing the seam*] (Develop Craft: Technique). And I'm using this part of my hand [*pointing to the part of his hand he is using*] to try not to get too many fingerprints all over it (Observe, Express). And you might leave the seam (Express). If you don't want the seam to show (Express), you can also roll this [*rolling the tube on the table*] and later when it gets a bit harder you can come back with a rubber rib and go over that (Develop Craft: Technique).

With this ceramic sets assignment, Jason has helped his students develop a variety of Studio Habits of Mind. They learn to observe as they look carefully at ceramics; they learn to envision as they plan their designs; they learn to express as they think about conveying some kind of idea or feeling in their set; and all the while they are learning to acquire technical skills required for expertise in ceramics.

This chapter has illustrated the complexities and richness of Demonstration–Lectures and the role that they play in fostering Studio Habits of Mind. In the next chapter, we focus on the Students-at-Work structure, in which the assignments, concepts, processes, approaches, and attitudes introduced and modeled in Demonstration–Lectures are practiced by students as they create artworks under the personalized guidance of their artist–teachers.

FOURTEEN

Students-at-Work and the Studio Habits of Mind

Teachers may emphasize any or all of the Studio Habits of Mind during Students-at-Work sessions. Because Students-at-Work sessions always involve working with art materials, Develop Craft: Technique is a central goal. But as mentioned, this Studio Habit of Mind is rarely taught in isolation. In the individual consults with students, teachers often cluster instruction about a number of Studio Habits of Mind that help students understand the connections among habits and how to integrate them into their working process. Certain clusters of Studio Habits of Mind occur together frequently in a single student–teacher interaction. (For instance, Develop Craft: Technique was often layered with Observe, Envision, and Reflect: Question and Explain, and Evaluate).

STUDIOS HABITS OF MIND ARE TAUGHT IN CLUSTERS

The two examples that follow show how teachers, depending on their goals, emphasize differing clusters of Studio Habits in their interactions with students during a given studio work session.

INTRODUCING THROWING: CENTERING ON THE WHEEL PROJECT (EXAMPLE 14.1)

This example is taken from a Vase Project introduced in mid-October in Jason Green's introductory year-long ceramics course for 9th–12th-graders at Walnut Hill (see also Example 5.4). Looking at Jason's interactions with two students over the course of his centering lesson, we see how even the seemingly narrow technical issue of trimming

a pot can become a vehicle for students to develop the disposition to think with a wide range of Studio Habits of Mind. Two students, one advanced, one a beginner, are having technical problems with trimming. Jason asks questions that help them verbalize their technical difficulties and see what in their working process led to these difficulties. He patiently demonstrates techniques, observes the students, and guides their hands as they try techniques. He looks with them at other finished pieces to get ideas for successfully solving their own problems. When a beginning student is discouraged and wants to destroy the pieces she has built, Jason encourages her not to be too hasty in her evaluation, and to Stretch and Explore in her Envisioning of the possibilities:

> You should save a lot of your stuff even if you think it's not working right now, because since these vases are going to be put together out of different parts, you might be able to use a lot of the parts . . . even if it doesn't come out exactly the way you want it. It might not matter because you might cut it up and use it a whole new way.

Jason thus helps these students Engage and Persist through work they are finding very difficult. He frequently encourages them to keep trying and assures them that they will succeed. When the beginning student complains that she feels so far behind, Jason doesn't dismiss her concern, but responds in a reassuring way:

> Don't worry about that. Just [*laughing*] just don't worry about it, because your skills will catch up. You missed some classes so . . . most everyone in

here is two classes ahead of you, so they've had a lot more hours on the wheel. So it's easy to look around and see that everyone's making really tall things and you're not right now, but don't worry about it. It's still really early in the trimester so just keep practicing, and it'll come along OK.

When an advanced student feels frustrated with her lack of facility to achieve the delicate lip she envisions, he encourages her, saying she just needs to practice and showing her the precise skills necessary. He also makes sure to spend some time with her looking over her other work, pointing out its many strengths, and praising her on her progress so far, thus helping her Engage and Persist.

As these two students wrestle with trimming their vessels, Jason works with them to solve technical problems and thus Develop Craft. He also encourages them to look closely at their work and his demonstrations (Observe), consider their progress (Reflect: Question and Explain, and Evaluate), imagine new possibilities (Envision), move beyond their current capabilities (Stretch and Explore), and stick with it through difficulties (Engage and Persist).

CONNECTING WORLDS: SECRET RITUAL VESSELS PROJECT   (EXAMPLE 14.2)

During her Secret Ritual Vessels Project in the middle of her second-semester course for 9th-graders at the Boston Arts Academy, Beth Balliro's interactions with students focus on yet another cluster of Studio Habits of Mind. An ongoing theme in her 9th-grade class is to build connections between students' art-making and their daily lives. Through a homework assignment for which she asks students to "spy" on how the people they know use various vessels in their daily lives, Beth inspires her students to notice the world around them and connect it to their learning in art. The day's lesson continues this focus on vessels, shifting to their ritual uses. Each student has been assigned a type of vessel to create secretly (an heirloom, something to hold holy water, a cat's water bowl), and they are to make a set of three vessels of this type. The aim of the "secret assignment" is to help students connect with the project (Engage and Persist), think about the function of the objects (Reflect: Question and Explain, and Evaluate), and create symbolic forms that the assigned function suggests (Envision, Express). Also, as is often the case in Beth's classes, her assignment ties into the school's humanities curriculum as she seeks to forge

links between students' own work and artworks produced throughout other times and cultures (see also Examples 3.1 and 12.2). This class builds on earlier field trips to the nearby Museum of Fine Arts. Beth often provides packets of articles, images, and information that explore artists, mythologies, or religious cultures. She wants her students to find links between their works and those of recognized artists.

Beth also wants her students to be able to articulate the thought behind their work—the process they went through in creating the work, the decisions they made, and the relationship of the work to values of subcultures that they understand (Reflect: Question and Explain, and Evaluate). It is not uncommon for students to spend part of the class thinking about a certain type of art, making written and/or drawn notes, and writing in their journals. Articulation is of particular importance to Beth in working with this urban population, and she sees it as a central skill to help these students gain recognition in the broader art world. In this class, the Students-at-Work session is followed by a critique, where students look at each other's vessels set out on tables for display, write their observations about each vessel, and guess the type of "secret assignment" for one vessel.

As the Students-at-Work session starts, Beth directs energy to getting students excited about the project. The prompt of their assigned secret vessel serves to get them interested and focused (Engage and Persist), and to find ways to adapt their own ideas to their assigned form (Express). As students consult with Beth about their ideas, they do a lot of whispering of their ideas to keep their assigned form "top secret."

Early on, Beth consults with students on their ideas (Express), on how to think about their assigned form by imagining and planning possibilities (Envision), and on how to connect it to the idea of ritual (Express, Stretch and Explore, Understand Art Worlds: Communities). For instance, one girl aims to make hers look like a family heirloom wine glass. Beth talks with her about the idea of making it look "old." For students who have a hard time coming up with ideas, Beth asks them questions or helps them consider what the key functional aspects would be. She encourages their thinking of different possible ways to realize the form (Envision) while keeping true to the constraints of the assignment. Beth also reiterates the key idea of functionality in her interactions. For instance, for a student who is to create a vessel that transports something, she suggests thinking about making a lid for it because that would make moving its contents easier. To a student making a very small vessel, she reminds her, "Remember this is for a human, not a mouse. It's so cute. But try to see if you can actually use it, 'cause I'd love for you to have something that you can actually use" (Envision).

As students move further along in the development of their form, Beth works with them to think about what they are making (Reflect: Question and Explain). She talks with them about the strengths and weaknesses of their pieces. For instance, she tells one student, "You've got a solid form and an amazing idea. What I would say now is deal with craftsmanship. Try to make it clean, perfect, beautiful, solid." She also challenges students to think about what their vessel will communicate to others (Express). For a student who is making a water bowl for a cat, Beth asks, "How do we know that this isn't to feed a big cat?" The student thinks and asks if she could write the word "bath" on it. Beth challenges her, "See if you can do it without words" (Stretch and Explore). With this assignment, and in each of these brief interactions, Beth reiterates the challenge to make an object's form express its use, a key artistic concept in ceramics. This project challenges students to move beyond their usual concepts of vessels and their uses (Stretch and Explore, Understand Art Worlds: Domain).

INDIVIDUALIZING DURING STUDENTS-AT-WORK SESSIONS

The examples from Jason and Beth show how teachers' goals for a given class or assignment permeate the casual, impromptu interactions during Students-at-Work sessions. However, another powerful aspect of the Students-at-Work structure is that it allows teachers to differentiate instruction without upsetting the general flow of work for the group. The two examples that follow show different ways in which teachers use the work session to individualize the curriculum.

DIFFERENTIATING FOR STUDENTS OF VARIOUS ABILITY/EXPERIENCE LEVELS: ABSTRACTION PROJECT   (EXAMPLE 14.3)

It's the second semester in Jim Woodside's multi-age drawing class at Walnut Hill. Some of the advanced students are taking this course for the second or even third year. All the students have had at least a full semester of drawing, experimenting with different types of materials and drawing from the figure and from still-life. With this foundation, Jim's students are ready to move on to abstract drawing. Jim creates assignments that engage the wide range of abilities and experiences of his students and then adjusts his instruction to individual needs during the Students-at-Work sessions.

Today Jim has set up a massive tower of twisted paper stretching from ceiling to floor with lighting accentuating the abstract forms present in this still-life. Students have positioned their easels around the structure, and, charcoal in hand, they prepare to draw. As they look at the still-life and begin to set up their compositions, Jim tells the students to think in terms of dark and light shapes on the paper and says, "You can't look at it and get it wrong . . . so feel at ease." Over the next 3 hours, students draw multiple studies on newsprint. Ultimately, each chooses one of his or her sketches to develop into a larger finished drawing.

Over the course of this working session, Jim brings the class together several times for Critiques. He punctuates the Students-at-Work sessions with mini-Demonstration–Lectures about how to observe and draw shapes and the still-life. Jim balances the need to develop less-experienced students' observational skills and techniques with challenging students with stronger backgrounds in drawing to enhance their more developed skills.

Jim has designed a project that will accommodate this wide range of learners. Considering their drawing experiences from the first semester and the technical skills they developed, he now wants to challenge students to explore the concept of abstraction—a concept that Jim recognizes may be difficult for his students. In an interview, he tells us:

Abstract art, to a lot of people, is sort of fringe and something that eccentrics and intellectuals talk about. I mean, these are stereotypes about, caricatures of it. And I'm not saying to them that I understand it all myself, you know. Or that I like it all. . . . But I want them to know that it really grows out of the same stuff that all art grows out of. And they can learn to evaluate it, and they can learn to understand it themselves. And the best way for them to do it is . . . to begin to do it themselves. And that's what I mean. And so . . . what I'm doing here is a little bit artificial and forced, setting up a way for that to happen for them.

The large still-life in the center of the room is not an uncommon set-up in Jim's class. Observing a still-life, choosing compositions from different points in the room, creating multiple sketches with various materials, and working toward a more finished piece over the course of several weeks are all familiar activities by this point in the year. Jim deliberately decided to design an assignment similar in scope and feel to the representational drawing with which students had become comfortable earlier in the semester. He wants students to see the link between representational and abstract drawing. Briefly explaining that abstraction is an important art world concept (students are well aware of this but hesitant nonetheless), Jim gently encourages students to do what they always do when looking at a still-life. "Draw what you see," he tells them. By now this phrase is a familiar mantra in the class, so students can easily prepare for this otherwise novel task of observing and trying to make sense of the crumpled paper still-life. Over the course of the afternoon, students begin to see connections to the drawings they made earlier in the year: They see that they are still working with shapes and lines and value.

Helping students build a bridge between representational drawing and abstraction is the primary goal of the class. However, Jim adjusts how he talks to students according to their individual needs. In what follows, Jim works with two beginning students, one who is struggling with the assignment, and one who has more confidence, excitement, and skills.

At five separate times throughout the working session, Jim consults with a 9th-grader new to the school who has limited English skills. About a half hour into the class, Jim notices that this student's page is sparse and that he looks confused. Jim takes the student aside and spreads another student's work out on the floor. He asks the student to observe the series of sketches and notice how each drawing is different. By looking at the work, the student could see how his peer deliberately changed the way she thought about each drawing, purposely using different lines and patterns each time. During this mini-Critique, Jim not only supports the beginning student in overcoming his initial obstacles with the assignment (Engage and Persist), but also helps him refine his observational habits (Observe). Most important, through the example of a peer's success, Jim encourages the student to move beyond his current abilities and try new ways of seeing the still-life (Stretch and Explore). As Jim explains to us later:

I want him to throw himself into the act of drawing. Have fun with it. He really needs to loosen up and really put forms down and manipulate them on the page, and in a big bold way. So I'm always trying to get him to do that, because he doesn't. He's always watching himself. There are all the other kids in the room. And he doesn't have as much experience. . . . But what I was really doing there was showing him an example of a kid from the previous day who I would say is in a somewhat similar situation. And I think giving him a real clue to how to go about it. That helps artistically for him. And also language, you know, he needs to see something. So I was trying to explain that in as simple terms as I could, but I know he didn't understand the whole of it. So giving him an example I thought helped.

A little later, Jim briefly checks in with the student again and encourages him to use the viewfinder, a tool for designing compositions that Jim has frequently employed and discussed in earlier observational drawing sessions (see Examples 3.3, 5.3, and 9.2). Returning to him later, Jim watches the student working and notices that he is looking at too small an area of the paper still-life and is not attending to the larger shapes that would help him make the bridge between observation and abstraction. He sits at the student's drawing easel and demonstrates looking too closely at the paper and how it keeps him from seeing the structural forms in the twisted paper. By explicitly demonstrating both technical drawing skills and the *process* of observing, Jim encourages the student to develop new habits of looking. By drawing on his sketch and then referring to the still-life, Jim shows the student how to see the large shapes and learn to improve his own technical drawing skills (Observe, Reflect, Develop Craft: Technique).

It's now halfway through the class, and the beginning student has made some progress in identifying and drawing large shapes. In his next consult, Jim encourages him to go even further in pushing the lights and darks by using a kneaded eraser on his drawing, a new technique for the student (Stretch and Explore). Jim demonstrates this process right on the drawing, so the student can see clearly how to juxtapose a white surface with a dark black shading to make the forms on his page look like the crumpled paper he is trying to draw (Develop Craft: Technique, Observe).

In the last few minutes of the class, Jim compliments the student's work (Engage and Persist) and gives him some final bits of technical advice, demonstrating how to use white charcoal to make his contrast even stronger (Develop Craft: Technique, Stretch and Explore).

Jim works quite differently with a more confident beginner. With the first student, Jim needed to help him engage with the assignment, use visual techniques to work around the student's limited English proficiency, develop basic drawing techniques, and start to develop a way of observing the structure of the still-life that would help him eventually bridge to ideas of abstraction. This next student, on the other hand, starts off excitedly, with a clear plan of what he wants to do. For his first study, he has darkened his whole page and is using an eraser to depict where the light falls on the paper. Jim supports this idea but also encourages him to explore more of the central ideas of the abstraction in this phase by doing multiple studies rather than focusing so much on technique:

That's really good. That's a good idea, and it would be good for you, and I don't want to discourage that. But I also don't want in this drawing for you to get too much into refining that technique. I want you to think about how those shapes relate to the four sides of the paper. So on your next one, let your approach be a little more with that in mind (Stretch and Explore).

When Jim next returns to this student, he encourages him to explore abstraction further. He tells him to depart from drawing strictly what he observes and become more logical about what he puts on the paper. "I think you should proceed almost like it's a math problem. Like very logically." He shows him how he can develop a "system" for thinking about which lines should be dark and which should be light (Envision). He gives him some tools to do this. He tells him to develop a plan, such as making all the larger forms darker. When the student seems a bit hesitant ("Outline it?"), Jim explains a core idea of abstraction: "That way there's a purpose for what you're doing. It's not just decorating your drawing. And that logic is really important, especially in an abstract drawing. It gives you a sense of purpose and relationship to what you're doing" (Stretch and Explore, Understand Art Worlds: Domain).

After students have done several studies, Jim breaks up the working session with a Critique in which he discusses each student's work. When he discusses one student's work, he comments that it seems to be the one that has gone furthest to abstraction, where you no longer easily connect it to its original source of the still-life. He uses the student's piece to reiterate a central idea of abstract drawing. "It's a texture on a piece of paper, and it's a way of organizing a piece of paper. That's what abstract art is. You're taking references from the world and you're organizing them into a two-dimensional world of your own." Following this group critique, the second student walks up to Jim and talks with him about his piece, saying that he's not really pleased with how the lines are working, mentioning his ideas for further work. Jim offers suggestions and supports the student's ideas. Jim reiterates the idea that the goal is to explore options, reminding him "this is just a learning process here" (Stretch and Explore).

INDIVIDUALIZING FOR MULTIPLE AGENDAS: CREATING HAT AND VEST PROJECT (EXAMPLE 14.4)

While Jim's example is about individualizing for a range of experience and ability levels, Kathleen Marsh's story in this Students-at-Work session, taught near the beginning of her second-semester class with seniors at the Boston Arts Academy, is one of a teacher multitasking to keep students on track with the assignment at hand and to help individual students with their outside work.

It's the first day of the final semester for Kathleen's 12th-graders. There's a lot going on, and Kathleen must prepare her students for the final push of their high school art careers. They are in the process of applying to colleges and art schools or preparing for jobs upon graduation. Not only do they need to have their professional portfolios in order, they also need to meet their graduation requirements, which include showing and defending their work in a senior exhibition. The students are somewhat distracted by all these outside events and battling a case of spring semester "senioritis."

Kathleen has much to accomplish in this class session. She introduces students to the current assignment of a self-portrait wearing a hat and vest that they have designed and created out of paper. She also introduces them to what they will be doing over the course of the semester, as well as going over what, as seniors, they will be doing outside of the class. She gives an introduction to the course requirements and reviews the syllabus. Kathleen discusses the defense process and her plans for curating the show and taking slides of finished work. Since students are putting together their final portfolios, she reminds them of this by introducing a several-week self-portrait assignment that will result in a finished value drawing that can be a "showcase piece" in their portfolios.

Today is the first installment of this self-portrait assignment. In this class, students create wearable paper hats and vests from oak tag that express something about their identity. In later sessions, they will make charcoal value drawings of themselves wearing the paper clothing. Today's portion of the assignment challenges students to both Envision and Express something about themselves, as they must imagine what the hats and vests they make now will convey about themselves, and how they will look as they wear them for their value drawings. As seniors, the students are accustomed to working independently. However, Kathleen monitors their progress on this assignment, including instructing and getting materials for students who are proceeding ahead of others to the next phase of the assignment.

While students create the hats and vests, Kathleen consults with each student about the progress of his or her portfolio and completion of tasks for the senior exhibition. This is in part an administrative task to make sure the students are on target in their application process, but it can also be a chance to model an important process of evaluation. For instance, Kathleen spends time with one student, looking over each piece of his portfolio, discussing ways of finishing some of the pieces, and identifying which ones he should include in the senior show. She later explained that this is one of the strongest students in the class, but he had initially only selected two pieces to include in the show. Kathleen discussed working over the course of several years with this student on his tendency toward perfectionism and being overly self-critical.

The flexibility of the Students-at-Work session allows Kathleen to keep the group focused on their work, while also adapting to students' varying work paces on a multiphase assignment. In addition, she has many chances to address crucial issues with each student that are not tied explicitly to this class assignment. In a single working session, Kathleen is able to keep the class as a whole engaged in working (Engage and Persist), while connecting with individual students on issues central to their development as artists, such as the preparation of their portfolios (Reflect: Evaluate, Develop Craft: Studio Practice and Technique) and progress in applying to college and/or art school (Understand Art Worlds: Communities).

This chapter has illustrated how teachers use Students-at-Work sessions to keep their art-making goals at the center of the learning process while personalizing instruction to suit a range of student needs. The Studio Habits of Mind emphasized by an assignment sometimes take a back seat to habits of importance to a particular student at a given time. In the Critique structure, described in the chapter that follows, both general and personal goals become the focus.

FIFTEEN

Critique and the Studio Habits of Mind

Critiques, by their very nature, foster the Studio Habit of Mind of Reflect: Question and Explain and, especially, Evaluate—learning how to judge what makes one work better or more effective than another. However, in the Critiques we observed, learning to evaluate works was only one of many goals. In every Critique we analyzed, teachers intended to teach at least five of the Studio Habits of Mind.

TEACHING STUDIO HABITS OF MIND THROUGH CRITIQUE

Develop Craft

Looking at students' work collectively often provides illustrations of how particular techniques can function differently in different works, which can help students expand their ideas about craft. In addition, techniques are often offered as solutions to problems that students identify in works. For instance, in one of Jim Woodside's Critiques, he asked students to identify errors in perspective in their own work, and they worked together to figure out how to correct them.

Engage and Persist

Critiques can be highly motivating. Knowing that everyone is going to look at and comment on their work can spur students to put their full effort into it. In addition, the critique process can engage students by giving them new insights into their work. For instance, Jim often uses Critiques at the early stage of a drawing to help students identify the potential of a piece and to get them excited about its possibilities. Mid-process Critiques can also help students work through difficulties in a piece, either by identifying unrecognized strengths in their work, or by offering specific advice on aspects that they could change. In Critiques, the current piece is treated as an opportunity for deeper commitment to work and learn. For instance, Jason Green tells a student, "The glaze is transparent because you put it on thin. But you can try re-firing that and put the same glaze on thicker."

Envision

As students stand before their work, they are encouraged to think about what would have happened if they had done it another way. For instance, Kathleen Marsh asks a student to think about how much white space he intended to leave in his self-portrait. Jim Woodside asks students to imagine how one student's drawing would look if she had fully drawn the leg rather than leaving it unfinished. Guy Michel Telemaque asks students to think of ways a given photo could heighten its focus on light as the subject. Frequently in Critiques, teachers also specifically ask students to envision how they will finish a piece, or what they envision working on next.

Even without direction, as students look at and discuss each other's work, they envision different possibilities for how the work could look. In a senior Critique session, students' comments frequently involve envisioning their own and other students' pieces differently. For instance, one student notes, "It would just be a really nice photo if that wasn't there and there weren't arms just showing."

Express

Critiques offer an important chance for students to get some distance and recognize some of the global properties conveyed in their work that they might miss while immersed in the process of making. In addition, Critiques offer a chance for students to hear how others interpret their work. One of Guy Michel's design students described finding out that while her intention in a flag design was to celebrate her native Puerto Rico by showing that it was so "hot," other students interpreted it as an image of burning the Puerto Rican flag. Critiques offer a testing ground for finding out how one's work communicates.

Observe

The type of observation most particular to Critiques is that of observing works in comparison to one another. During the process of making works, most of the observation involves students looking carefully at their own work, and in the case of observational drawing, looking at the relationship between the work and the referent. In Critiques, the focus shifts. Generally, observing in Critiques involves looking at your own work in the context of pieces created by other students or in relation to multiple drawings of your own. Teachers often encourage specific observational comparisons, such as when Kathleen asked students to notice what different colors contributed to the skin tones in students' portraits or when Jim asked students to compare the expressive effects of different types of line quality.

Reflect

Question and Explain. More so than at any other time in the studio class, reflecting about student work is highlighted during Critiques. Teachers strive to draw students into a discussion that moves beyond just noting what they like and dislike, and into observing in the context of particular artistic concepts. Critiques are often framed around a set of targeted questions, such as when Guy Michel asked his photography students, "Why is this a photograph about light? All photographs depend on light; how are these [for the light assignment] different from every other photograph?" Another example is when Beth Balliro asked students to guess the intended function of their fellow students' clay vessels and to start thinking about the relationship between the vessels' forms and their ritual functions.

Evaluate. Critiques offer an important chance for students to evaluate their own and peers' work. Critiques often begin with the teacher asking which of the drawings students think work and why, or asking them to comment on what works or doesn't work in their own piece. Sometimes an evaluative process precedes the Critique; students might be asked to choose their best work to put up for critique. Evaluation in Critiques is often analytical. Rather than merely sorting "good" from "bad" work, students learn to identify which aspects of a work are most effective and which may detract from the effect of a piece. As Jason explains, "I really try not to say something's good or bad. I just say this is what it is communicating."

Stretch and Explore

Just seeing the range of work produced by the group may push individual students to expand their thinking about their own work. To foster the Stretch and Explore aspect of Critique, teachers assign projects that are likely to yield diverse results. For example, Jason Green spoke about deliberately choosing glazes that produce widely varying results in order to promote more student exploration. During Critiques, he invited students to analyze the results of their explorations of materials much as they would analyze a scientific experiment. When errors are the focus, they serve as a chance to diagnose and/or as an opportunity for a work to grow in new directions. But the responses that students receive in a Critique generally do not emphasize failures. Rather, Critiques offer suggestions for how to think about what can be seen in the work and how the student artist might explore other possibilities.

Understand Art Worlds

Domain. Teachers draw connections between student art and professional art, and they make allusions to historical and contemporary art references as they point out features in students' work. They may tell students that their work reminds them of a particular artist, sometimes showing them an image or two. This informs students about the larger culture of art and art history, but its greater purpose appears to be to emphasize students' connections to the historical and current community of working artists. For instance, during a Critique, Jim Woodside commented on one student's developing a certain "electric line quality" and use of space in his work:

He's really finding a way to draw, a kind of language that's his own, that will succeed for him as he approaches different kinds of problems. But that's something that he came up with really on his own, playing around with this project [*pointing to self-portrait from previous class*]. And I certainly think it's something that he can take into the way that he draws something like this [*holding up a sketch that the student is currently working on*]. . . . It reminds me of a Dubuffet painting.

In this Critique, Jim identified aspects of a student's emerging style and tied it to the larger art world.

Teachers present Critiques as reflective processes, including evaluation, that happen in professional arts communities, and not merely as isolated elements of an art class. As Beth prepares 9th-graders for a Critique, for example, she explains that Critiques are part of being an artist and that some Critiques are meant to be about evaluation, while others focus more on other aspects of reflection.

Communities. The social aspect of Critique is one of its defining features. Teachers focus on how students learn to value responses from peers and on ways to offer respectful and constructive criticism to their peers. Critiques reinforce the idea that artmaking is a communal process, not only a private activity. Art is made to be shown to others and discussed, and that can be learned through the social process of Critique.

INTEGRATING STUDIO HABITS OF MIND THROUGH CRITIQUE

The eight Studio Habits of Mind fostered by Critiques are usually not discussed separately, but rather are integrated flexibly during Critique sessions. This integration is illustrated by the following examples of Critiques from Jim Woodside's drawing class at Walnut Hill.

COMPARING WORKS:
CONTOUR DRAWING PROJECT   (EXAMPLE 15.1)

While each teacher we observed held a Critique at least once, Jim held multiple Critiques in nearly every class session of his multiage drawing class. These Critiques were not necessarily formal, lengthy discussions; sometimes they lasted only a few minutes. However, Jim's consistent use of Critiques stresses the importance he places on coming together as a group to look at and discuss the work that has been done.

In the first class session of the year in Jim's drawing course, he introduces Critiques as a central but informal part of the routine:

What we'll do is, we'll draw for a while. Then we'll put some drawings up on the wall, and we'll start to look at them and talk about them. And that's something we'll do a lot in this class. Those of you that have had me before, we, we always do that—we draw, put the drawings up, talk about them.

After the students do a few quick drawings of the still-life, some blind contour (in which students do not look at the paper but only at the referent) and some in which students look at both the still-life and the drawing, Jim asks each student to hang a blind and nonblind drawing next to each other. Before beginning the discussion, Jim gives the students a specific thinking task to guide their observation and reflection: "Everybody take a look at their two drawings, and just think in your mind how to compare the two. Just to describe the difference between your two drawings." This task helps students integrate learning how to Observe with learning to Reflect. Jim encourages them to evaluate their works, asking which they preferred and why.

As students make comments, Jim acknowledges and expands on their responses in a positive and encouraging way. For instance, one student says of a blind drawing, "Notice all her details are not . . . it's detailed but it's not." Jim affirms her evaluation and draws this comment into its fuller meaning:

It's detailed but it's not. Yeah, that's really good. I couldn't have said it that well. That's very true. I mean, we have all the information here [*pointing to a section of the drawing*], we know it's there, yet it doesn't seem like it's overly precise, or overly worked.

In this first class session, he wants to ensure that students feel comfortable talking in the group, and his comments help them to Engage and Persist in the Critique process.

While Jim uses this Critique to create a positive social atmosphere, it also works to build students' understanding of key aspects of the assignment.

Through discussion, students come to recognize characteristic differences between blind and non-blind drawings. A few minutes into the Critique, Jim moves a pair of drawings that reflect this distinction well to the center of the wall and asks students to focus on them. Building on students' comments, Jim introduces the idea that while the nonblind drawings may have been more technically accurate, the blind drawings have a more direct expressive quality to them:

> Even though this might, there's a certain accuracy that's stronger here [*pointing to a nonblind drawing*]. These things are placed more in position. But there's a kind of believability here [*pointing to a blind drawing*], and that's a word that I'll use a lot throughout the year, *believability*. What makes drawing interesting is how direct your relationship is to what you're looking at, OK? And here, the relationship is in a way very direct, very honest. . . . There's not other things in the way. Like your perception of how it should look.

While students talk frequently in this Critique, Jim carefully guides the discussion to center on this key point. Thus, through a process involving the Studio Habits of Observe and Reflect (both Question and Explain, and Evaluate), Jim helps students explore a key intended lesson about the relationship between Develop Craft: Technique and Express. Jim also pushes students to see how they could use what they learned in the blind drawings in the rest of their work:

> Now obviously we don't do every drawing in the world covered up and sort of scribbling. But there's a really important lesson here in that—how can you bring some of this state of mind, in a way, to this [*pointing at a nonblind drawing*]? How can you bring this kind of . . . freedom or lack of inhibition into your work?

In this very first Critique of the year, Jim explicitly sets up the expectation that what you learn through Critique of a given assignment should be applied to your work more broadly: Jim challenges students to use the lessons from this assignment and Critique to Stretch and Explore beyond their usual habits of art-making.

As shown, Jim's Critiques help students integrate various Studio Habits of Mind. By encouraging students to Engage and Persist in the Critique, Jim fosters an iterative process in which students practice Observing and Reflecting, while they also explore the relationship between Express and Develop Craft: Technique. In addition, he encourages students to Envision how they might use what they learned to Stretch and Explore beyond their usual drawing habits.

CRITIQUING THROUGHOUT THE PROCESS: FIGURES IN EVOCATIVE SPACE PROJECT   (EXAMPLE 15.2)

Jim often uses Critiques as a way to guide a class and punctuate a working session. In this midsemester figure drawing session, students were meant to focus on the expressive potential of light and of the space between figures (Express, Develop Craft: Technique; see Examples 8.1 and 12.1). Jim has set up dramatic lighting and shows examples of professional artworks (reproductions of paintings by Hopper and Diebenkorn) that have the evocative sense of space and light that he emphasizes in the class assignment. Throughout the 3-hour class, Jim repeatedly holds short Critiques to keep students on track with this focus and also to help them make explicit what they are learning about expression.

Opening Critique

Jim begins the class with a Critique that serves as a transition from one class to the next, by focusing on high-contrast figure drawings from the previous session. Unlike the first class session that centered on getting students to talk, this quick Critique has no student discussion. A key purpose of this Critique is to get students quickly into the mind frame of working and to help them build connections between what they have done in the last session and what they will do today.

Jim notes the effectiveness of all the drawings and comments that he could really see how the students were building on their previous experiences. His praise serves both to encourage students and to reinforce the idea that assignments in the class connect to each other. With a long wooden pointer, Jim draws students' attention to different areas of each drawing as he comments on the high-contrast technique and how it helps students organize space, separate shapes, reduce a complex scene, and maintain the focus on light.

Jim's stated purpose is to get students back in the mind state of working. He tells them, "I want to put you mentally to where you were last week." Jim's comments emphasize the thought process that went into making their drawings: "This shape may have been a lighter gray or toward the lighter end of the spectrum, but you make that decision to go black or white with every gray you see and what you end up with is an abstract composition."

In this, as in all his Critiques, Jim moves beyond discussing technique while simultaneously staying grounded in the work. Here he connects the use of a particular technique (high-contrast drawing) to more expressive properties in one student's drawing:

> It starts to look to me almost like some Native American design, like an Incan blanket. . . . All that is, is a drawing technique, a pretty simple technique of high-contrast drawing, looking at something ordinary in the studio, and you start to move to this whole other realm of all sorts of things that are pretty magical and unusual and really have little to do with the scene we're drawing.

Jim chooses to focus on aspects of the drawings such as expression and light that will be central to the next assignment: He will assign students to do a drawing that focuses on the expressive, evocative properties of the space between two figures. Thus, this Critique, while seemingly a reflection on completed work, prepares students mentally for the coming work session and primes them for key ideas to come.

Critique of Sketches

After students complete a couple of quick sketches of two figures, Jim gathers the class around the array of sketches on the floor for a few minutes. Though he asks students a few questions, Jim is the primary speaker in this Critique, as well. In an interview, Jim explains that the purpose of this Critique was to help students envision their final drawings from the sketches and ensure that they understood the focus of the assignment. "It was to make sure that they had the maps before the journey starts." He also uses the Critique to get students "excited about possibilities of this little assignment by seeing that emotional things are already being said in the pictures."

Jim begins by integrating Observe, Envision, Reflect: Question and Explain, and Evaluate. As he surveys the drawings, he says, "I see plans starting to form in your brains about how you are going to approach this." The group looks at and evaluates the sketches in terms of what they reveal about how students envision the final drawings.

Jim chooses two students' drawings and asks the class to compare their different approaches. One student has exaggerated the distance between the figures and another has made the figures small relative to the space in the room. After talking about the expressive aspects of the piece, Jim asks, "What's different about the choices [Student 1] made and the ones [Student 2] made?" He focuses students' attention on how the drawings treat space differently. This Critique helps students learn to observe their sketches for the purpose of envisioning a more finished drawing. Jim wants them to Reflect: Question and Explain, and to Reflect: Evaluate their sketches for what they are starting to Express, and then to see if they can Envision ways of stretching to heighten this expression.

Final Critique

After the working session, Jim holds a longer Critique that involves more student discussion. In this Critique, each student's work is carefully discussed. This Critique focuses on giving students a chance to Observe and Reflect: Question and Explain, and Evaluate what they have done in their work and to get some practice talking about work (Reflect: Question and Explain). After listening to students' general observations about the works, Jim focuses the questioning on which pieces have the strongest sense of dramatic, evocative light, a central focus of the assignment (Reflect: Evaluate). When students comment on a dramatic piece, Jim often expands on their comments. For instance, he talks about how one piece has the feel of a big movie set in which only a small area is lit up, and that area is where the action is. He ties this to a "pretty strong decision" the student has made in leaving much of the drawing empty. In this way, he models how to connect observations about Express with Develop Craft: Technique. For another student, he holds up a Hopper print for comparison of the dramatic power of light. When students comment that the drawing has an "outside feel" even though it is inside, Jim ties this observation about an expressive property to a more technical idea, showing how this effect results from how the student has highlighted multiple light sources. Again, Jim connects students' learning from practicing to Observe and

Reflect: Evaluate to the central idea of the assignment, which is to link technique and expression (Develop Craft: Technique and Express). His use of the Hopper print is intended to help students begin to connect their own art-making to other artists' work (Understand Art Worlds: Domain).

This Critique proceeds one-by-one through each piece, with students making observations and evaluating their own work and working process, and then listening to comments about it from Jim and the rest of the students. Suggestions for further work involve noticing an interesting aspect nascent in the work (Observe and Reflect: Evaluate) and figuring out ways it could be taken further (Envision and Stretch and Explore). For instance, Jim tells one student that she can work on hers without the models so that she can focus on heightening the contrasts. This suggestion connects to her other recent work (discussed in the opening Critique) that involved building up abstract compositions. Thus, this final Critique integrates all eight Studio Habits of Mind.

These examples of Critiques illustrate that Critiques can have a variety of structures and functions. A key strength is that they aim to help students integrate their learning and development of Studio Habits of Mind. Students are meant to learn how asking questions and explaining ideas can support evaluation of a piece, to connect their work to that produced by others in their class and throughout history, to observe how different techniques can produce different expressive effects, and to stretch beyond their usual habits to envision new possibilities for their work. Teachers can guide Critiques flexibly so that they highlight the integration of different Habits at different times. For instance, in the planning stage of a drawing, Critiques may focus more on tying Observe to Stretch and Explore and Envision. Students are meant to open up and explore a range of possibilities for their work. After the work is complete, the Critique may focus on tying Observe with Reflect: Question and Explain and Evaluate. Students are meant to figure out and describe what aspects of a work function well, which do not, and why.

SIXTEEN

Exhibition and the Studio Habits of Mind

The Exhibition structure is used to display student work publicly and is an "overarching" structure into which the three basic structures—Demonstration–Lecture, Students-at-Work, and Critique—are incorporated. Creating an exhibition can develop any of the Studio Habits of Mind as students and teachers work through the phases and sub-phases of Exhibition described in Chapter 4. Each phase of Exhibition may employ any of the basic Studio Structures, and thus the Studio Habits can be developed within any structure, similar to ways already identified in Chapters 13, 14, and 15. For example, in the Exhibition phase, "Installation: Setting Up the Display," a teacher might do a quick Demonstration–Lecture on a hanging technique, and students would then use that technique in the ensuing Students-at-Work session during which they actually hang work. Critique, too, plays a role in Exhibition: When peers and teachers review the displays, for example, their observations and comments may include some that address how well the hanging technique is used and if it needs to be redone. In what follows, we offer examples of how each Studio Habit might be developed in an Exhibition.

USING EXHIBITION
TO TEACH STUDIO HABITS OF MIND

Develop Craft

Technique. Numerous aspects of Develop Craft: Technique are called for in all four phases of an Exhibition: planning, installing, public, and aftermath. Perhaps the aspect of Technique most uniquely

trained by a traditional gallery Exhibition is the hanging of works. Hanging involves preparing pieces so that attaching them to walls or pedestals doesn't harm them, determining the placement of each work precisely by whatever set of criteria has been agreed upon, leveling each piece exactly, attaching pieces to the wall securely, and making sure that how the work is hung does not distract from the work itself. A wide variety of hand and electric tools needs to be used effectively in hanging, including drills, hammers, pliers, wire-cutters, various attachment hardware, sanders, levels, tape measures, putties, putty knives, paint rollers and brushes, tape for making hard-edge paint lines or covering cords or defining areas, ladders, and upside-down carpet squares and/or dollies for organizing and moving heavy walls and pedestals. Similarly, an online exhibition requires the same attention to the technical requirements of an exhibition space (e.g., protocols for posting material and procedures for testing how the exhibition will be seen in different web browsers and on different size screens).

Studio Practice. During installation, the exhibition space becomes a studio workshop. Therefore Develop Craft: Studio Practice is also called for—arranging the tools so that they can be readily found and shared, keeping everything organized, making sure there are enough pins, that drills are charged, and that the exhibition space is left clean, spackled and re-painted, swept, organized, and ready for the next show. Parallel issues of maintenance arise in online forums as well, such as the need for organization of digital files and coherent naming conventions.

Engage and Persist

Engage. When students are involved in preparing work for public audiences, engagement tends to be high, whether the exhibition is in a physical or virtual space. The gallery or website lends a sense of seriousness and purpose that helps students become fully committed to displaying work so that each piece is honored. Such engaged commitment helps students to sustain the attention to detail required by installation.

Persist. Because an exhibit is a public display, students are motivated to strive for excellence. Corners cannot be cut. Anything that is shown will be read as meaningful; thus fingerprints cannot be on gallery walls unless they are there intentionally, the font on labels must match the style conveyed by the works, labels must be applied straight, and signage or text must be interwoven harmoniously with images. Persistence is critical. Students work long hours on all four phases of an exhibition. For example, at MassArt's Saturday Studios class, after teaching a 2½ hour class ending at noon, the student-teachers install their students' work all Saturday afternoon and into the evening. If they put up the exhibition poorly, they have to take it down and start over. For instance, one student-teacher hung his students' works in the shape of a diamond, but the diamond had nothing to do with the meaning of the work and therefore distracted viewers when looking at the actual works. Once he understood the problem, he hung his works again, undoing and redoing 3 hours of work. This kind of persistence is made possible by engagement.

Envision

Whether planning an exhibition online or in a physical space, a student, a group of students, or students and teachers together must curate, envision a plan, and convey that vision to others. While plans are often altered as installing unfolds, exhibitions typically start with a vision and evolve into a final form. For this reason, it is important that, when displays are installed by multiple people, everyone is present at the same time so that each can respond to one another's emerging decisions.

As an exhibition space is set up, curators have to continuously envision how the exhibit will look to an imagined audience. For a traditional gallery exhibition, should they set up temporary walls or shelving? Where should walls, pedestals, or shelves be? What should viewers see first so that they are drawn into the exhibition space? What works should be close to one another or spaced farther away? Where should the show's title be displayed? How would a piece look if it were hung from the ceiling or across a corner? And where should the signs and labels go so that they complement rather than compete with the displayed works? Similar decisions need to be made for a virtual site: Should a standard theme or template determine the organization, or should the artists design their own website? How should texts and images interrelate? How should the virtual exhibition space be introduced—on the same webpage? In a box at top, bottom, or side? How will the display look on different sizes of screens?

Express

Exhibitions express meaning in ways that are similar to how works of art convey meaning, only on a larger scale through a collection of works—like paragraphs in an article or chapters in a book. Meaning is conveyed by the selection and arrangement of the works, and decisions are guided by the theme and style of the exhibition. Like curators in museums and galleries, students choose work to include in an exhibition and, by doing so, learn to attend closely to the expressive content of work so that each selection contributes to the meaning of the whole. Artist Fred Wilson has applied this approach in his own artwork, which is created by arranging works from a museum's collection into exhibitions that highlight ideas he wishes the audience to ponder. He conveyed the theme of oppression in a 2002 retrospective at Skidmore College's Tang Museum by juxtaposing a reproduction of Picasso's Les Demoiselles d'Avignon, a Cubist painting of female nudes, with a sculpture of four headless and fully-clothed, dark-skinned male mannequins dressed as museum guards. He wanted to highlight attitudes conveyed by museum society about women and African Americans.

The habit of Express is also developed as students learn to curate thematically. When exhibitions are thematically structured, students must select works that, together, express something about the theme. Chapter 4 and the narratives at the end of this chapter offer examples of themes.

Mykael Pushes the Figure

These class and homework drawings by an 11th-grade student at Boston Arts Academy are for a unit on observational drawing. Students closely observed the model and made decisions about how to use value, observation, and composition to translate what they see to paper (Observe, Develop Craft). In consultation with their teacher, students determine their own homework curriculum to prepare for independent work that they will pursue as seniors (Engage and Persist). Kathleen Marsh described homework as "the place where you're required to do your own learning" (Reflect, Envision).

This in-class self-portrait assignment shows Mykael co-developing his mastery of observational drawing (Observe) and facility with drawing tools and techniques (Develop Craft). Placing his mirror at a low angle adds interest to the drawing and adds challenge to the execution (Express, Stretch and Explore, Engage and Persist).

A reclining figured seen from this perspective is a challenge to depict (Express, Develop Craft). The accuracy of this drawing and use of materials—white for highlights, blue paper for midtones (Develop Craft)—shows Mykael applying what he learned in class and homework to his life drawing class (Observe, Express).

Here Mykael took risks (Stretch and Explore). Instead of a full frontal view of the figure, he chose to compose a complex story within a story (Envision, Express): An angled monitor shows a music video of Kayne West and Jay-Z within a larger composition of a room—demonstrating his appreciation that popular culture is a useful resource for subject matter (Understand Art Worlds).

In this homework assignment, Mykael continues to co develop accuracy in observation and ways to use drawing materials to interpret what he sees (Observe, Develop Craft, Express). The student chose to work from a photograph in which Kayne West strikes an expressive pose that he accentuates by using extreme contrasts with black and white in the drawing (Develop Craft, Express, Understand Art Worlds).

Mykael used this homework drawing to explore several colors for modeling the figure with a thin layer of color to create an atmospheric space (Develop Craft, Express, Stretch and Explore). According to Kathleen, Mykael sets goals for himself and likes to carefully plan his work (Envision, Engage and Persist). His classmates appreciate both and often ask him for feedback on their work (Reflect).

Min Develops Her Voice

Min, a senior starting her 3rd year at Walnut Hill, says, "I think I haven't changed much technically, but I am more comfortable and free when I draw than before. I think I'm finding my own style in these drawings. I don't know what it is yet, but I'm starting." Jim Woodside explains that expanding artistic voice (Express) from a base of high-level technical skill (Develop Craft) is one common developmental path for some students at Walnut Hill.

This drawing shows Min's technical skill when she arrived at Walnut Hill. She describes focusing closely on the model (Observe) and her challenge to draw "reversely" using white and color on a black surface, with oil stick, a new material (Stretch and Explore, Develop Craft).

"I wanted to have the feeling of a book and remind you of books" (Express), Min says of her goal for this collage, which was inspired by a still-life of stacked books. Prior to the collage, Min drew a light and shade version of the same still-life on pink paper (Observe) and a collaged drawing on brown cardboard in which she pushed herself to try something new (Engage and Persist, Stretch and Explore): "I started by observing closely. It seemed boring so I did collage on it. I didn't want to put a lot of effort into it. I wanted to do it intuitively" (Envision).

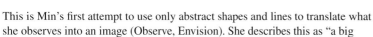

This is Min's first attempt to use only abstract shapes and lines to translate what she observes into an image (Observe, Envision). She describes this as "a big change in my drawing history" (Stretch and Explore). Her teacher also saw it as a leap for her and says: "I think she learned that implying things is often more effective than showing them fully" (Express, Envision, Reflect: Evaluate).

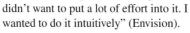

For this observational drawing, students drew on an unfamiliar surface: maps (Observe, Stretch and Explore). Min's drawing creates an abstract mix in which neither figure nor environment dominate. She describes her intent in this way: "This drawing was a big challenge for me (Stretch and Explore). I also tried to imply things (Express, Envision) and merge the figure by using color and shared lines" (Envision, Develop Craft).

Sam's Transformation Over 4 Years

The following images illustrate how an individual student might show growth in the Studio Habits of Mind over time. Over 4 years, we watched Sam progress from minimal engagement in school (Engage and Persist) with limited craft (Develop Craft) except in his graffiti repertoire (Express, Understand Art Worlds), to a student who developed beyond his initial style (Express, Understand Art Worlds, Stretch and Explore) into a reflective (Reflect: Question and Explain; Evaluate; Envision) and engaged artist (Engage and Persist, Express, Observe, Develop Craft, Understand Art Worlds).

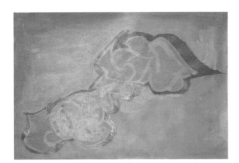

Sam proudly states that he did his familiar graffiti lettering for this 9th-grade logo painting in less than 5 minutes (Low Engage and Persist). He did the minimum, saying: "So I made my name because he wanted us to make a name. . . . And I made up some name . . . just so I could get done with it" (Low Engage and Persist, Low Express). Later in the year, he notes its design flaws: "I kinda used like the wrong colors because it's not really dramatic and you can't really see the outline of the letters" (Reflect and Develop Craft). Looking at it again 2 years later, he's even more blunt: "That is garbage. I don't know what the heck I was thinking. . . . I was just BS-ing" (Observe, Reflect: Evaluate).

By the end of 9th grade, Sam moves beyond doing *only* graffiti: "Say, all right a year ago, I would not be drawing mountains from nothing. I would not be drawing mountains. . . . I don't think I would be doing basically any of the stuff I'm doing now" (Higher Engage and Persist, Higher Express, Some Stretch and Explore). In addition to learning skills of manipulating paint and planning a gray-scale under-painting, Sam analyzes the composition and thinks in terms of the viewer (Observe, Envision, Reflect: Evaluate, Understand Art Worlds: Communities). He says of the turtle: "He's trying to draw the viewer's attention. Like basically the viewer feels like he's in the painting, like he can interact with that figure . . . . like 'look at me, I'm in your face. Like what do you want?'" (Express, Reflect).

In this 3rd-year self-portrait, Sam weaves together the skills he's developing in school with his graffiti style, which he says gives his work "more originality, more flavor" (Reflect: Question and Explain, Express, Develop Craft, Stretch and Explore). He captures a considerable likeness (Observe, Develop Craft) though choosing to draw from a difficult angle so that he could give a sense of the king looking down on the viewer (Develop Craft, Engage and Persist, Express). But he also views the drawing as expressing sorrow and frustration—essentially saying, "I'm king, but I've gotten nowhere" (Express).

Sam's senior exhibition is filled with expressive self-portraits and large-scale layered graffiti landscaped worlds (Express, Develop Craft). This self-portrait reflects his interest in exploring his African heritage through studying African masks (Understand Art Worlds, Express, Observe), a move he says was inspired when he learned about Picasso using African masks (Express, Understand Art Worlds).

A Feast for Your A-MUSE-ment

In Studio Art 3, a junior-level course at the Boston Arts Academy taught in fall 2011 by Mónika Aldarondo, students mounted an exhibition that explored the idea of "muse" (Understand Art Worlds; Express). Through individual and collaborative works installed in the student gallery space outside their classrooms, students created a gallery-as-dining-room "feast" for their artistic muses (Develop Craft, Envision, Express, Understand Art Worlds: Communities, Stretch and Explore).

Students collaboratively generated the exhibition title, A Feast for Your A-MUSE-ment (Express, Understand Art Worlds), and their teacher made and posted a title

sign together with photographs that documented students' learning process as they cooperated to complete all phases of the exhibition (Engage and Persist).

Five "muse" sculptures representing "what inspires you to create your work" (Express, Develop Craft) were created by collaborative groups (Understand Art Worlds: Communities). In this photo, the "Muse for Creative Process and Memory" sits in the exhibition at one end of the dining room table (Envision, Observe). A seat built into the sculpture (Develop Craft) invites audience interaction— viewers sit inside the hooded Creativity Chamber (Stretch and Explore), where fragments of mirrors guide them to reflect on their past experiences to inspire their creative endeavors (Express, Develop Craft, Reflect: Question and Explain).

Students prepared the gallery space by selecting the wall color (Envision, Express, Develop Craft), locating areas for groups of works, specific works, and signage (Envision, Observe), taping edges, and painting a uniform color (Develop Craft) that

conveyed the feeling of a dining room (Express). Students also installed shelves and positioned and secured individual 2D and 3D "mini-muses" and the works they inspired onto shelves, the wall, and the ceiling (Develop Craft, Stretch and Explore).

The "Muse of Mysterious Creatures from Urban Legends" [left front]—"part fish, frog, and octopus, and who now comes out of puddles when it rains" (Reflect: Question and Explain, Stretch and Explore, Express) has joined the other muses for dinner. The table is set with candles, a candelabra, and flowers, all to suggest a formal dining experience (Express), and "what feeds our muses" fills plates and adorns the table (Envision, Express). Foods include the small bright moon suspended on the right, whose "light cast on dark nights feeds the 'Muse of Mythical Characters and Tales'" [right back]. The small white figures on the plate at lower right "whose heads are filled by what's on TV and the Internet so they can't think for themselves" feed a "Muse Against Mass-Media Brainwashing and For Counter-Cultural Voices" [outside the picture frame] (Reflect: Question and Explain, Stretch and Explore, Express).

On the walls of the dining room, students mounted mini-muses that they created weekly during the unit, along with the works that these muses inspired. The works were made in found-frames that each student selected from an assortment provided by their teacher. Students invited peers, families, teachers, administrators, and visiting guests to an opening reception after school from 4 to 6 pm (Understand Art Worlds). The artists "schmoozed" about the work and making the exhibition, and they listened to responses from their guests (Reflect: Question and Explain, Evaluate). Later, students de-installed the show, returned the gallery to its original condition, and discussed strengths and weaknesses of the experience with their teacher and peers (Develop Craft: Technique, Studio Practice, Understand Art Worlds: Communities, Reflect: Question and Explain, Evaluate).

A theme being explored by educators currently is how to display student work to reveal learning—a practice influenced by the Reggio Emilia preschools in Italy, where the art of documenting learning to make it visible has been perfected (Project Zero & Reggio Children, 2001). By selecting works that show change over time and/or including written reflections or transcribed oral comments that speak about the work's development, a display can show the thinking behind the artistic process. Thus exhibitions of learning have a goal different from that of traditional gallery exhibitions. That goal of expressing learning challenges the relative relationship between text and image in customary gallery exhibitions, in which text is subservient to image. In exhibitions of learning, a common error is making text-heavy displays that are difficult to take in as a viewer. Unless teachers attend carefully to the elegance of visual design, text tends to trump aesthetics. Alertness to that potential failing makes it easier to notice when refinements can be made that enhance the display so it is understood by viewers, most of whom do not spend long enough in front of any given display to understand long textual passages.

Observe

The habit of Observe is called upon notably during the planning phase when students select the works that they want to display, whether those works are their own or belong to other artists, and whether the exhibition is physical or virtual. It is helpful to see all the work at the same time—for an exhibition in a gallery space, a common strategy is to lay everything out on the floor, look closely, then choose those works that best represent the artist and the focus of the exhibition. This winnowing requires careful observation: there is no formula. Student curators also must observe works and groupings of works closely enough to be able to choose which works "go together"—either because of their similarity or because together they create a desired meaning or contrast. The entire display must be coherent to the eye as well as the mind, and thus students must keep looking until they deem that all of the parts interrelate. Observe is also required during the installation phase to ensure that works are hung straight and with intended intervals left among them, vertically and horizontally. Similar attention to observation is required for virtual exhibitions. Student curators also need to be alert to anything that may be "off" so they can check it with a level or ruler, by seeking an opinion from someone else, or by checking the formatting on a website.

Reflect

Question and Explain. Whether standing by and talking about their work at a reception, writing artist statements, responding to their own or others' works in online forums, or explaining works to viewers in gallery talks or formal defenses, students need to interpret their works, process, and thinking in words, formally and/or extemporaneously, to public audiences, reviewers, and critics. Because of this, students use and can develop the habit of Question and Explain through mounting or discussing an exhibition, whether online or in a physical space.

Evaluate. When students select the works they want to show, they rely on their disposition to Evaluate. They must look critically at their works and determine which ones are most successful and hence worthy of display. They also need to judge the quality of the exhibit itself, both for each individual work and for the collection. Is work hung straight in a gallery exhibition? Is it re-sized suitably for the web? Are labels or captions error-free and grammatically correct? Are artists' statements and informational texts positioned in ways that make them readable and that enhance rather than distract from the visuals? Does the work cohere and make a strong impression as a whole? Just as rests are critical to musical compositions, so the spaces—between works, between sub-displays, around corners, between captions, signage, or labels and works—are important in an exhibition, whether it is online or in a gallery or hallway. Especially in exhibitions of learning, it is critical to notice when text has overpowered the images so that meaning becomes garbled or lost in the flood of explanatory writing. Using standards from the field of museum exhibition is helpful when judging the success of such exhibitions of learning—looking for balance and for a logical narrative flow. All such judgments are equally important in online and brick-and-mortar contexts.

Stretch and Explore

Exhibitions can be set up formally and traditionally, or they can be set up in experimental ways and forums. When students come up with innovative approaches to showing their work, they are flexing their Stretch and Explore muscles. Professionals in art worlds are continually exploring new definitions of exhibition, stretching them out to the street, onto the web, or, as with artist Jennie Holtzer's work, projected onto the faces of buildings. Artist and MassArt Professor Steve Locke's 2012 show at the Samsøn Gallery in Boston displayed paintings in clusters high and low on walls and on slanted poles at knee, waist, shoulder, and eye-level, so that both the backs and the fronts of the works were visible. In the MassArt Saturday Studios class, students have sometimes expanded the exhibition beyond the gallery—out onto the sidewalk where they chalked ephemeral works or installed inflatable sculptures; or by presenting a fashion show in a nearby hall-way. In an effort to reveal students' learning (as mentioned in Chapter 4), a student-teacher at Mass-Art displayed his students' first drawings of the semester on top of later, more polished drawings. Small signs told the viewers to use the tape handles he had attached on each piece to lift up the early work on top and view the later work, thereby exhibiting change and growth. During another term, a student-teacher took a student's sculpture made on a strand of LED lights and used this string to define the edge of that display in order to frame other students' works. All of these are examples of stretching the boundaries of exhibition formats.

Understand Art Worlds

Domain. Learning how to set up an exhibition requires paying attention to the various ways in which professional artists display their work—by attending professional exhibitions, observing documentation of exhibitions, or participating in online forums. Attention to expert models allows students to learn about setting up a gallery or an outside or web space, using signs or text, spacing works, grouping works (e.g., thematically, by style, by art-ist), and about the ways that fonts, colors, and styles can be used to present a consistent presence to the public. Students can also learn about the exceptional attention to detail that is required by good exhibition practice—such as taping down and/or painting necessary electric cords the same color as the wall so that they disappear. As the exhibition world expands from gallery to street to virtual clouds, students need to continue developing familiarity with the evolving formats used to display artworks.

Communities. An exhibition calls upon and builds communities of makers (the artists) and viewers (the audience). Students installing a gallery or website have to work together as a community, selecting and/or hanging their works at the same time, because they need to see and adjust responsively, for example, to how one work or group of works resonates well or poorly with other works, how the space feels between them, and what unexpected meaning emerges from the juxtapositions. The Exhibition structure also teaches students about the division of labor needed for complex collaborative tasks. Students take on different roles, such as publicity, set-up, or producing labels and signage—all in addition to the central task of hanging their own work. Because Exhibition is the structure in which art is made public, students also need to think about the community that will be an audience for their work. How can they install their work so that the display draws in and speaks to the viewers they anticipate? They need to consider who their audience will be: an adolescent student might choose to show an edgy work in an exhibition to be viewed by her peers, but something less provocative in an exhibition that she expects her grandparents and younger siblings to attend.

INTEGRATING STUDIO HABITS OF MIND IN THE EXHIBITION

Examples from the Boston Arts Academy

Kathleen Marsh Reflects on Exhibition at Boston Arts Academy. Kathleen believes it is important that, by graduation, Boston Arts Academy (BAA) students learn to do the work of mounting a show themselves. For some students, that is part of their training as an artist. But for all of them, it is training to understand the end of the cycle in which artists take their work out of the privacy of the studio and into the public, whoever their "public" may be. It is also a way to develop important dispositions needed to attend to the many dimensions of creating a successful show. To support that goal, the visual art department at BAA now teaches a 4-year series of courses on exhibition.

The introductory course (Exhibitions Zero) focuses on students building and understanding their artist statements and blogs, which are exhibitions in themselves. The course also focuses on how artists interact (BAA calls this "schmoozing") at an opening; how to research art opportunities (concepts, exhibitions, works, and artists); how to plan and take action steps; how to create a web presence; how to photograph, scan, upload, and resize images onto a website; how to critique one's work; how to send email communications about one's work; and how to use Prezi (Powerpoint is now out!).

The sophomore course (Exhibitions 1) teaches students how to begin doing the following: create a wide variety of installations (2D, 3D, and 4D—4D refers to time-based media such as films, animation, or performances), take appropriate risks with their exhibition choices, develop a timeline to prepare and promote the exhibition, and understand the community that will be one's audience. The course also continues the focus on artist statements and reinforces learning how to be a good audience member when responding to others' works in an exhibition.

The junior year course (Exhibitions 2) continues all of these themes and also includes a focus on understanding the exhibition space and on curating skills—that is, students work on selecting and grouping a wide variety of work from their other classes. Students' investigations of space take them to "unconventional" spaces, such as the school cafeteria, closets, ceilings, and the like.

The senior year course (Exhibitions 3) continues again all of these themes but stresses the idea of packaging and branding oneself. Students are expected to work collaboratively and also more autonomously (as a group) than they have in previous years.

Kathleen says, "We haven't figured this all out entirely; we run into problems all the time." It's difficult for students to switch from artist to curator modes. But Kathleen told us that the hallways are always filled with varied artworks from the different classes displayed by students, from inflatable sculpture to performance art, ranging from simplistic to profound. Because they've had many shows, including junior shows where students all work toward one theme, the senior exhibitions have improved steadily over the years.

The next set of examples reveal Studio Habits of Mind within learning experiences centered on understanding Exhibition.

A FRESHMAN SHOW   (EXAMPLE 16.1)

In 2011–2012, BAA 9th-graders collaborated with seniors (Understand Art Worlds: Communities),

who curated the 9th-graders' work in a show focusing on the theme of line (Express). This exhibition combined display with community service (Understand Art Worlds: Communities). The freshman and senior classes were taught by the same teacher, who facilitated coordination between the groups. The work consisted of classic contour line drawings in different colors of markers that were then translated into wire sculpture (Develop Craft: Technique). The senior students wallpapered the school's 3rd-floor hallway, leaving no space between drawings and creating a great wave of color, a ROYGBV spectrum, with the wire pieces layered in front of the drawings and with track lighting used to create shadows on the visual presentation (Develop Craft, Envision, Express). In the description of the show, the seniors wrote that they recalled what it was like to hate your work and be embarrassed by taking risks and trying something new and not wanting to embrace failure (Reflect: Question and Explain; Stretch and Explore). They said to the freshman, "We get it that you won't like it now, because that was us, too. But looking back, we can tell you, this is good work" (Reflect: Evaluate). They affirmed the 9th-graders and pushed them a little bit (Stretch and Explore; Engage and Persist). The message was: "Get tough—the work needs to go up." Kathleen concluded: "Tough love, empathy. It was cool" (Understand Art Worlds).

A SOPHOMORE SHOW   (EXAMPLE 16.2)

In 2011, Exhibitions 1, taught by Guy Michel Telemaque, was offered to Sophomores at BAA for the first time. The course was designed to encourage exploration (Stretch and Explore) and to help students "feel free to experiment." In other classes, they'd gone to MASS MoCA in North Adams, MA (described on their website as "a center . . . [to] present and catalyze the creation of works that chart new creative territory") and to Storm King (the open-air art museum in Mountainville, NY), so they had seen a number of exhibition styles (Understand Art Worlds: Domain; Observe; Reflect: Evaluate). In this course, they visited several local exhibitions—at colleges like MassArt, community galleries, and alternative gallery spaces—in order to observe the "conversation between the form of the space and the artwork" (Understand Art Worlds: Domain; Observe; Reflect: Evaluate; Stretch and Explore). Students completed written reflection sheets about each visit (Observe; Reflect: Question and Explain) before

Guy Michel assigned them the task of transforming one of the exhibitions they had seen, without any constraints—they had limitless (imaginary) money, time, help, even no gravity (Envision; Stretch and Explore). Their designs varied from making minimal adjustments to the existing exhibition to "some very inventive stuff" (Stretch and Explore). Parallel to this introductory work about exhibitions, the students were making artworks about dreams (Express) that they would then exhibit (Envision); they worked collaboratively (Develop Craft; Understand Art Worlds: Communities; Stretch and Explore), which lowered the stakes of the public display by making them feel less personally responsible for each work. After weeks of working collaboratively, Guy Michel announced one day, "Let's make an exhibition" (Develop Craft). The exploratory, collaborative works and the freedom to begin using whatever exhibition skills they already had (which made the display a kind of baseline assessment of exhibition) encouraged students to take an experimental approach (Stretch and Explore). Through group brainstorming, students came up with the idea of a circus: The works were large—24" x 36" or so—and they wanted to hang them like banners in a circus (Envision). As the group played with titles, Cirque du Soleil was mentioned, which led to Circus of Dreams—or, in French, "Cirque du Reve" (Reflect: Question and Explain; Express).

In the first draft of the exhibition, students hung the pieces back to back—so viewers could see both pieces—and from the ceiling in a vertical semi-circle that started up high and gradually got lower (Envision; Stretch and Explore). Once installed, the students and their teacher held a critique in the exhibition (Observe; Reflect: Evaluate) and realized that some of their experiments should not have been shown (Observe; Reflect: Evaluate; Understand Art Worlds: Domain). Students pulled back from experimentation (Stretch and Explore; Reflect: Evaluate; Envision) in the final exhibition, which was a bit more formal (Understand Art Worlds: Domain): four walls of two-dimensional works, with one wall of "bad" dreams and three walls of "good" dreams. The students did choose to cover the windows with colored tissue paper, however, an innovation that changed the quality of light throughout the exhibition to make it softer and more dreamlike, so the experimental stance was not entirely lost (Stretch and Explore; Express).

One student really wanted to work in his comfort zone with plasticine (Engage and Persist). Guy

Michel pushed him to take on a challenge: Can you make a plasticine work that is 15" tall (Stretch and Explore; Develop Craft)? Although the student did not take the advice to build on an armature, he worked hard and made a single piece where his good and bad dreams wrestled with one another (Stretch and Explore; Express). But the work wouldn't stand up when it was exhibited (Develop Craft). Each day, they'd arrive to find it slumped, and they would then try a new solution—sticks inside, leaning for support (Engage and Persist, Stretch and Explore; Develop Craft). But nothing solved the problem permanently, and the student realized that he had exhibited a technical failure (Develop Craft; Reflect: Evaluate). However, his peers really appreciated his work and concept (Understand Arts Worlds: Communities; Express; Reflect: Evaluate). Guy Michel said, "By living through the process of the piece not standing easily, he learned the importance of an armature, which he had resisted initially" (Stretch and Explore; Develop Craft; Reflect: Evaluate). The exhibition motivated him to Develop Craft in his own work and internalize higher standards of quality for his own work (Reflect: Evaluate).

JUNIOR SHOWS (EXAMPLE 16.3)

Every year, the juniors at BAA create a cafeteria show, which lasts only as long as a 45-minute lunch period. Mónika Aldarondo developed this idea, and it has endured (Understand Art Worlds). They made an inflatable sculpture one year—a giant room-sized fort made of plastic and packing tape inflated with fans (Develop Craft; Stretch and Explore). The space had rooms and connecting tunnels that the audience could enter and explore. Another year, a performance art piece used elements of humor and surprise, like certain kinds of contemporary performance art that call attention to things that are usually invisible or unnoticed (Understand Art Worlds). Clay pots with flowers adorned the lunch tables. These were filled with chocolate pudding and mashed oreos that looked like dirt (Develop Craft, Envision, Express). Once the potted plants were on the tables and students sat down to eat their lunches, the visual artists began digging into the "dirt" and eating it. This was of course shocking, and the other students gagged and squealed—the performers had kept the secret and were delighted with themselves (Express). The point? Don't make assumptions—pay attention and you might find something wonderful. Students have all experienced cafeteria shows that were done before them, so the culture builds (Understand Art Worlds). But because the work is displayed for all of their peers in the cafeteria and pushes the limits of conventions in various ways, the students always have to take a leap, a risk (Stretch and Explore). They are never sure how their work will be received—will their audiences think it's cool or ridiculous (Envision, Reflect: Evaluate)?

Kathleen also told us about a recent failure (Stretch and Explore; Reflect: Evaluate). BAA students curated a show with the theme of neighborhood, meant to reveal the qualities of the students' neighborhoods to the upper middle-class viewers at a local farm stand in a well-to-do neighborhood near Boston's Fenway Park (Express; Understand Art Worlds). The students did not do a good job of studying the space and thinking about how the show should look (Envision; Develop Craft; Express). When the work was hung, the space did not feel activated, and the local shoppers at the farm stand did not get a good sense of the kinds of neighborhoods where the students lived. The labels were only half-done, the signage/explanation was inadequate (Reflect: Question and Explain; Develop Craft), and the work seemed to just hang there without a context (Express; Understand Art Worlds). Kathleen told us that while it is really difficult for a teacher to let an exhibition fail because it is so public, it is important to resist the impulse to rush in and fix it. She firmly believes that the work has to stand in all its nakedness in order for students to grow (Stretch and Explore; Understand Art Worlds; Reflect: Evaluate). It's a balancing act—between scaffolding the show so it will succeed vs. the loss of learning that comes from teachers doing the planning that ensures success. On the one hand, if teachers do too much, the students do not experience the value of and need for that planning; but the teacher also has to balance how much failure the students—and the teacher—can tolerate. The conversation about the show is all important in transforming failure into a positive learning experience (Reflect: Question and Explain; Reflect: Evaluate; Stretch and Explore; Understand Art Worlds). It is yet another delicate dance.

MOUNTING A
SENIOR SHOW IN 2002   (EXAMPLE 16.4)

In 2002, near the end of their last-semester course at the Boston Arts Academy, seniors worked on Kathleen Marsh's Mounting the Show Project and prepared their pieces for the end-of-year exhibit in the school's gallery. They each prepared a written artist's statement in which they articulated what they were trying to accomplish in their work (Reflect: Question and Explain; Express). In the classroom, students were matting their pieces (Develop Craft: Technique). Downstairs in the gallery, other students were spackling and painting the gallery walls (Develop Craft: Technique; Studio Practice; Understand Art Worlds: Communities). Student curators in the gallery were planning how to hang the pieces and beginning to do so (Envision; Observe; Understand Art Worlds: Communities; Develop Craft: Technique). Kathleen moved back and forth from gallery to classroom. She spoke to the student curators, "You've already measured the gallery, right, curators? And you've designated how much space each person gets?" (Develop Craft: Technique). She then returned to the classroom, exhorting students to get their pieces chosen and matted (Reflect: Evaluate; Engage and Persist). "I would say you have to put in a minimum of four pieces. . . . So as you mat work, you need to bring it down to the curatorial team." (Develop Craft: Studio Practice; Reflect: Evaluate; Understand Art Worlds: Communities).

MOUNTING A
SENIOR SHOW IN 2012   (EXAMPLE 16.5)

A decade later in 2012, Kathleen told us that students' artists statements are now posted on their school blogs, which students build throughout their 4 years at the school (Reflect: Question and Explain; Understand Art Worlds). These blogs include process work, reflections, images of completed pieces, and written reviews by the student of other artwork and shows that the student has attended (Understand Art Worlds; Reflect: Question and Explain; Reflect: Evaluate). The senior show is mainly as it was in 2002, but now work has to be vetted by the faculty, so there's a review process prior to selecting the work (Reflect: Evaluate; Understand Art Worlds). The faculty realized that this final benchmark needed their stamp of quality in order to meet exit requirements.

Similar to the process from a decade ago, artists and art educators from outside the school are invited to a solo review for each senior (Understand Art Worlds: Communities). In this review, the students give a Demonstration–Lecture about their own work (Reflect: Question and Explain). For each student, three to five reviewers are selected by the faculty for their expertise and understanding of art and their understanding of adolescent artists' development (Reflect: Evaluate; Understand Art Worlds). Reviewers often return, although only some of the 75 or so who are asked come every year. Over time, the collection of reviewers become familiar with the expectations of the BAA faculty for their graduates: Reviewers hold the students to a high, professional standard (Understand Art Worlds; Reflect: Evaluate). Thus students are told what their teachers may already have said repeatedly, but which students hear differently when the Critique is delivered by outsiders (Reflect: Evaluate; Understand Art Worlds). Reviews are held in the gallery, in front of the students' displays. Reviewers have familiarized themselves with the students and their work by looking at the students' blogs before the face-to-face review begins. During reviews, students give a short, prepared presentation to the reviewers that addresses process, formal elements in the works, and context; that is, they place their work on the art history continuum from past to present (Reflect: Question and Explain; Understand Art Worlds). Following that is the Critique, in which reviewers comment, challenge, and raise provocations for the students based on what students have displayed and presented (Reflect: Evaluate; Understand Art Worlds). Reviewers write comments on a standardized form designed to be general enough to embrace the wide diversity of presentations and work while still ensuring that students address the fundamentals for this graduation requirement (Understand Art Worlds; Reflect: Evaluate).

Examples from Walnut Hill

Jim Woodside Reflects on Exhibition at Walnut Hill. Exhibitions are an important part of the culture and rhythm of the Walnut Hill School (WH). Jim describes exhibitions at Walnut Hill as more like a studio visit than a museum show. Exhibitions are a way for students to see their work in relation to the work of others and a way to share their work with the school community. In the community, regular exhibitions contribute to a school culture focused on the arts.

All teachers at Walnut Hill are working artists, and Jim believes that it is important for students to see that their teachers are producing art. Every fall a faculty exhibition of new work is the first exhibition of the year. The faculty show is an opportunity for students to view their teachers' most recent work and a

chance to see examples of formal gallery installations.

Students learn how to create exhibitions themselves by working side-by-side with their teachers to select and mount their own work. Learning is through mentorship rather than through the more explicit course-based model used at BAA, a model Jim describes as "organic," with an emphasis on process that "ties in with the way things are done at the school."

Jim believes that students who are at the school for 3–4 years "learn by seeing." New students quickly catch on: "They just pick it up by experiencing it and by the January show they have a good sense of how the show works. They just know this is something artists do: they exhibit their work."

Teachers initially do the final selection of work for an exhibition and oversee much of the installation. By the time students are seniors they select work to be exhibited, install the exhibit, and handle publicity and the reception. Jim believes students learn by working with someone who knows the process: "Students have to learn what works. It's not a science. We're not at all bashful about telling them we like everything but they really should change that piece. . . . Students learn from their mistakes."

END-OF-TERM EXHIBITIONS   (EXAMPLE 16.6)

Every term at WH there is an exhibition of work created during that term. Jim describes this as an "open house festival." He tells students that the show is an opportunity to show off their work and show off the department: "The show is 100% an extension of what we do during the term and the icing on the cake is a party to celebrate students' achievements." Even if he had a huge gallery space, Jim says, he would not want to make this show more formal.

Student work hangs in the gallery space and throughout all the studios. From 5:00–7:00 PM on the evening of the opening, there is a "huge" reception for the show that is attended by the entire school community and by parents who live locally—all students in the school are required to attend, and the gallery opening is packed with parents and students. Every show is advertised on all school calendars. An art parent organization that raises money during the year arranges for refreshments. Every student is given a card when entering and is required to write something about a piece in the show. As students leave the show they are required to turn in the card. After the opening the cards are distributed to each exhibiting student as feedback on his or her work. Comments vary, ranging from the useful and thoughtful to the cursory "I like it."

The selection process is shared between teacher and students. With each student, Jim goes through the portfolio of their work, and together they choose 5 to 7 pieces from which Jim then chooses final selections for the show. To start the conversation, Jim asks students to choose which pieces are weak and which they really like. He says the 2 or 3 pieces students pick for each usually coincide with what he would pick, but if not, they talk about it and what to do: "Sometimes all it takes is to crop the drawing a bit." As the conversation unfolds, Jim reflects with each student on the quality of individual pieces, the student's progress for the term, and the process of choosing work for exhibition.

Some students may have more work in the show than others. Jim tells students, "This is not a scorecard. Some of you will have more pieces in the show and some fewer." He tries to explain, "This is not only about showing individual pieces. It's showing off the art department as a whole to the community, other departments, and outsiders."

For this show, students in the senior studio class hang their work in the workspace they all share. Each student has a designated "cubby" in which to work. For the end-of-term shows, seniors figure out how to set up their cubby as an open studio showcasing their work. After work is set up, teachers give students feedback on their space and presentation of work.

Installation of the student shows is a time for students to learn more about exhibitions. Teachers direct installation of the show and students help with the physical installation. While installing work, teachers and students talk about what it takes to arrange and hang a show. Jim describes installation as an opportunity for students to learn from their teachers: "Students don't have a good understanding of what this takes, so they learn in the process." Every piece has a label so students all know who did what work. Jim stresses to students that they have to be willing to talk about their work.

Work in the show varies according to what the class worked on during the term. One class might spend much of the term on a few large projects and another class might do many shorter pieces. Teachers often encourage better viewer understanding of the assignment by grouping together work that responds to particular assignments, and sometimes by writing an explanatory paragraph about an assignment. For some assignments this is really important. For example, without a label explaining that the work was from a class in which Jim asked students to draw with markers and crayons, a viewer might think the work was done by young children. In fact, Jim was encouraging students to think back to when they were children and to think of their drawings as play. In this case, then, the grouping was a demonstration of how Jim taught the process of making. For students, grouping also helps reiterate that what they produce is more than the product. The grouping is evidence of what the assignment is designed to teach them, and individual pieces show what students learned.

Jim gave the following summary of the show at the end of each term:

> It's a big, kind of goofy festival and not like going to a museum. It's as close to a performance atmosphere as we can get it. Kids who see it think "Wow! This is great!" and the student artists take pride in their work. It's a good way to complete the semester. . . . It's not about the preciousness of the art work. It's about being able to see everything uncluttered, the work that stands out. The context is conducive to viewing.

A SENIOR SHOW (EXAMPLE 16.7)

Every spring at WH, students in the Senior Studio Class show their work. Each show features 2–3 students, so the number of shows varies depending on the size of the Senior Studio Class. In years when the class is small, there might be four shows. In years when the class has 25 or 30 students, there could be as many as seven or eight shows.

Like the End-of-Term shows, Senior shows are also part of the school culture and an event eagerly awaited on campus. Work is installed in the art building gallery, a setting with pristine white walls and track lighting. Each show has a formal opening attended by large crowds. Jim describes these shows as more like a formal gallery show: "Everyone knows the opening is like a happening. The opening, which includes music, is much more like a gallery opening than are the end-of-term exhibitions."

The work is only up for a short time, typically going up on a Monday or Tuesday and coming down at the end of the week. The students do all the work for their show—they select work, install and de-install it, write labels, create advertising flyers that they hang around campus and in town, and get the information to the office to be included in the calendar. Jim notes that by senior year, teachers have solid relationships with students and students have had a great deal of experience working with their teachers on shows.

KOREAN STUDENT SHOW IN KOREA (EXAMPLE 16.8)

Every spring when they return home for spring break, the many Korean students who attend WH show their work in Korea. One month before the show, Jim ships two to four pieces per student to a framer in Korea. Parents pay for the framing. The show is only for two-dimensional work (to keep shipping expenses down). Choosing work for this show is done in the same way as for the end-of-term student shows—Jim and a student reflect together while looking through the student's portfolio, and they select a group of work from which Jim makes the final selections. However, there is one difference: Jim finds it's sometimes hard to present a variety of work, because students are very concerned about what they want their parents to see.

Like the end-of-term student shows at the school, the Korean show is a big event with a festival-like atmosphere. Both the show and opening draw large crowds of parents, friends, and former graduates. For the Korean community, the show is a celebration of the students and their work.

These examples of Exhibition from Walnut Hill and Boston Arts Academy share many features, yet are also different in a number of important ways. There are certainly many more possible ways to teach Exhibition to students, and each school will develop its own culture around public display of student work. But the examples are meant to catalyze readers' thinking about how Exhibition is an essential component of artistic learning. While Exhibition trains all of the Studio Habits of Mind, each habit is fostered somewhat differently though Exhibition than through other classroom experiences. When students learn about Develop Craft (or any of the other habits) in the context of an Exhibition, they learn something different from what they typically learn in other studio classroom experiences, something that expands their artistic minds. Whether students go on to careers as professional artists or to non-art careers, the Exhibition structure offers a context for understanding more about what art is and is for, what it takes to do it well, and how to convey its meaning effectively to broader publics. When the Exhibition structure is under-taught, as it is in many schools, educators miss an opportunity to teach the rich facets of the Studio Habits of Mind that are developed so well through this structure.

SEVENTEEN

Studio Thinking

A COMMON LANGUAGE FOR PRACTICE, RESEARCH, AND POLICY

In *Smart Schools* (1992), David Perkins describes two components of learning experiences. Teachers must decide *what* students should learn and *how* to teach them. Our analysis of visual arts teaching in studio programs has revealed what we believe to be the real curriculum in arts education. The *what* is a set of studio-centered "thinking dispositions" (Perkins, Jay, & Tishman, 1993) that we call the eight Studio Habits of Mind. We also looked at *how* studio art teachers set up instruction to teach the Studio Habits of Mind, and identified three basic Studio Structures for learning and a newly described overarching structure, Exhibition, that usually extends beyond normal class time and/or space. Together, the eight Studio Habits of Mind and the four Studio Structures for learning make up the Studio Thinking Framework.

In this final chapter, we discuss some of the varied ways the framework has been used in educational contexts. We describe how teachers have used the framework in visual arts, music, theater, dance, and non-arts classes. We also describe how the framework has been used outside of the classroom—in museums, preservice education, research, and policy.

The Studio Thinking Framework is not a recipe for teaching studio classes, but rather is a set of lenses for observing and thinking about teaching and learning in the visual arts and beyond. Since the publication of our first edition, we have witnessed the framework being used in diverse settings—in classes at all grade levels in visual arts, interactive media, dance, theater, and music classes, and also in non-arts classrooms. The response to our work has shown that the framework is adaptable to any subject area. Teachers have reported to us that the Studio Habits of Mind are broad enough to offer guidance for curriculum and teaching in their disciplines, and the Studio Structures for learning foster classroom cultures of thinking and learning across the disciplines by modeling how to organize classroom time and interactions around personalized and collaborative projects. Teachers have used the framework for curriculum planning, for direct instruction (referring to and giving the habits to students), and for assessment. Administrators and researchers have used the framework to guide program evaluation. And the framework has been used in preservice, inservice, and graduate level training in art education. The framework has also stimulated research in arts education.

In classes in any subject, students can be encouraged to Reflect by explaining their working process and evaluating their own and their peers' work, to Stretch and Explore by experimenting, to Engage by finding a project that they can dig into and become passionate about, and to Persist with such projects over long periods of time. They can also be encouraged to Observe by paying close attention to the relevant "data" for their discipline, to Envision what they cannot observe directly, to Express meaning and feeling and personal voice in what they create, and to understand how professionals in the discipline they are studying think, act, and communicate (adapting Understand Art Worlds).

The Studio Structures for learning are just as adaptable. Teachers in any arts or non-arts discipline can create a studio-like environment and use the four structures to promote students' engagement and responsibility for their own learning. By dedicating most classroom time to Students-at-Work (a studio, laboratory, or workshop model), teachers can personalize and differentiate instruction across widely ranging levels of skill as they meet one-on-one with students and provide "just in time" intervention. By inserting into the Students-at-Work structure brief, focused Demonstration–Lectures around processes and information on an as-needed basis, teachers can address those challenges that block students' progress as they occur. These Demonstration–Lectures can be used to highlight how work in a discipline is carried out. Thus, for example, a history teacher might explain the process of searching for primary sources and demonstrate how a particular source could be interpreted. By using a wide variety of in-process, public Critiques throughout the development of students' projects, teachers provide repeated opportunities for students to reflect about their working process. These opportunities allow students to come to understand and internalize quality standards while they create quality products. When they leave the class, the hope is that they take the standards of the discipline with them. Students and teachers in any discipline can create Exhibitions where students display their work to a broader audience (which, for a process of learning exhibition, might also include drafts).

Here we sketch some of the ways in which the framework has been put to use.

USING THE FRAMEWORK: GETTING STARTED

The funny thing is that as I gave the presentation/workshop [on Studio Thinking], all the faculty really enjoyed looking at their own practice through the lens of SHoM.

—Evan Hastings, Consulting
Theatre Teacher, Bangalore, India

The first move we have seen teachers make with the framework is to ask themselves these questions:

- What habits of mind do I tend to emphasize in my own (studio) work and in my classroom?
- What habits are naturally built by particular approaches or assignments I already use ?
- Which habits come up frequently in conversations with particular students and audiences?

After viewing their own work for 6 months or longer through the lens of the habits and naming what they see, teachers begin to use the habits in a variety of other ways. They notice gaps in their practice—some habits that they often neglect—and new opportunities to cluster habits together. Eventually, many begin to consider the Studio Structures for learning and what these offer to their efforts to understand and refine their practices.

The framework provides a language for teachers and students to use when talking about what goes on in classrooms. Teachers have been innovative in developing tools to structure and document conversations about studio thinking. For instance, teachers in Alameda County, California, have begun to use Thinking Walls. Thinking Walls are informal and temporary public documentation panels (developed from documentation practices in the world-famous Reggio Emelia preschools in Northern Italy) that display evidence of learning and serve as places for making connections—individually, in small groups, or in large-group reflection conversations—between what students do and the kinds of learning those experiences are meant to help them develop (Hetland, Cajolet, & Music, 2010). These panels often have examples of students' work or photos of students working, and students and teachers interact with them, writing captions for photos in which a person is featured, or labeling the Studio Habits to which an image is tied. Some teachers post large pie charts with eight wedges labeled for each Studio Habit; students place work, reflections, and photos in the wedges to indicate links to particular Studio Habits. Supported by these visible, collaborative reflection tools, students and teachers are using a common language to talk about learning, shifting the focus from looking only at art products toward a rigor grounded in artworks and artistic process as evidence for thinking.

USING THE FRAMEWORK IN VISUAL ARTS EDUCATION

A Common Language

The Common Core State Standards for English Language Arts and Mathematics have alerted educators across the curriculum to the importance of a dispositional view of learning. The Studio Habits of Mind are in effect the common core in the visual arts, and teachers who have used them can begin to map them onto the core standards developed for English Language Arts and Mathematics. Such work has already begun in Alameda County at the Arts and Humanities Academy at Berkeley High School, as shown in Table 17.1. Louise Music also points out in the Foreword to this Second Edition how the Common Core State Standards initiative aligns with Studio Thinking's dispositional approach.

The Studio Thinking Framework is being used as a shared conceptual language for teachers, students, administrators, parents, and broader communities. Students have been taught ways to use the Studio Habits explicitly for self-assessment, critique, and documentation of learning. Teachers use them to explain to students, parents, colleagues, and administrators what thinking well as an artist requires and how students are developing those capacities. And administrators and policymakers use them similarly at a broader scale, to advocate for appreciation and support of arts programming.

Students Use Studio Habits. Todd Elkin, a visual arts teacher at Washington High School in Freemont, California, introduces his students to the Studio Habits and asks them to paraphrase them in their own words. Engage and Persist, for example, became something like "Find what you want to work on and then work as hard as you can and never stop." He regularly asks students to use these redefined habits to guide ongoing self-assessment as they reflect on their own efforts in sketchbooks and blogs.

Similarly, Lucinda Daily, a photography teacher at Berkeley High in California, noted that the quality of student critiques improved dramatically after she asked students to make notes in the Studio Habit categories when they selected photos to discuss in critiques: "I think that breaking apart the way we see in terms of the language of the Studio Habits of Mind is useful to get the kids to slow down and think about what they are looking at and take more time to really focus."

At the elementary and middle school level, Sharron Cajolet used the Studio Habits with her 3rd- to 8th-grade students at the Lowell Community Charter Public School in Massachusetts. She asked students to reflect on various habits and then archived sample reflections and photographs of work and students-at-work in a classroom binder that the students pored over regularly.

Teachers Communicate with Colleagues. When Arzu Mistry worked as the Integrated Arts teacher at the ASCEND School in Oakland, California, she co-taught one section of arts-integrated content with classroom teachers and then interpreted what the teachers and students had experienced through the lens of the habits. The classroom teacher then taught the second section on her own. In this way, Arzu's

Table 17.1. How Studio Habits Relate to Common Core State Standards

Studio Habits of Mind	English Language Arts Common Core	Math Common Core
Develop Craft	Demonstrate grade-appropriate command of conventions of reading and writing.	Reason abstractly and quantitatively. Use appropriate tools strategically.
Engage and Persist	Read and write routinely. Learn to revise.	Make sense of problems and persevere in solving them.
Envision	Interpret/Analyze. Integrate/Synthesize.	Look for and make use of structure.
Express	Construct arguments—produce clear ideas in writing and speech.	Model with mathematics. Construct viable arguments.
Observe	Listen and comprehend narrative structure. Read written texts closely.	Attend to precision.
Reflect	Respond to texts with self-awareness and awareness of context.	Critique the reasoning of others.
Stretch and Explore	Activate prior knowledge to make hypotheses and generate "what if?" questions.	
Understand Art Worlds	Understand the history and field of literary arts and literature, including popular culture.	Understand the various math disciplines and their real-life applications.

Source: Adapted from Alameda County Office of Education. (2012). Developing Student Habits of Mind for Success Across the Curriculum at the Arts and Humanities Academy at Berkeley High School, Berkeley, California.

non-arts colleagues began to develop a deeper appreciation for what the arts are and can do when used in the context of other subject areas.

Aligning Efforts Across Diverse Communities. In Alameda County, California, Louise Music, then Coordinator of Arts for the county, led the Alliance for Arts Learning Leadership in adopting the Studio Thinking Framework as one of three countywide "analytic lenses" (the other two are *Teaching for Understanding* [Blythe et al., 1998; Wiske, 1998] and *Making Learning Visible* [Project Zero & Reggio Children, 2001]). The frameworks provide a shared conceptual language for teachers, students, administrators, parents, and the community; the language holds together the educational philosophy and practices used throughout the 18-district county. Similarly, under Cleopatra Knight-Wilkins's arts leadership in 2010, the Boston Public Schools adopted the Studio Habits as a common language across the four arts disciplines.

Curriculum Planning

The Studio Thinking Framework has proved useful in curriculum planning. It helps teachers develop and refine goals, tie their goals to mandated standards, troubleshoot curriculum issues, and select targeted resources to enhance units of study.

Developing and Refining Goals. The habits can readily be mapped not only onto the Common Core State Standards in non-arts subjects but also onto state and national standards in visual and performing arts. For example, in the visual arts standards used citywide in Boston in 2011, a standard for 6th–8th graders was the creation of depth on a two-dimensional surface. In addition to the habit of Craft (using art materials to make something), this goal requires attention to Understand Art Worlds (looking at works made by others), Observe (looking closely at the scene to be represented), and Envision (figuring out how to translate a three-dimensional world onto a flat surface and still retain its three-dimensional appearance). The framework also can provide coherence within and across grade levels: While artistic techniques, media, tools, and contexts change from the preschool to postgraduate levels, the same eight habits of mind persist. Using the framework allows teachers to make thoughtful decisions about when to emphasize particular habits.

Teachers often identify clusters of habits emphasized by their curricular goals to clarify what they want students to learn. For instance, Faith Johnson, a preservice teacher in a high school mixed media sculpture course at MassArt, set as one of her goals getting students to talk about their art to others. She thought about this in terms of several of the habits: Reflect (Question and Explain your thinking about art; Evaluate the quality of what you see), Observe (look longer at your work, from many perspectives, to see all that is represented), and Understand Art Worlds (think about how your work is like and different from related works by other artists).

Troubleshooting Curriculum. Jaime Knight, another visual arts teacher at Berkeley High School in Berkeley, California, was teaching a class of about 35 students who were not much interested in being in art class. He was frustrated by their unimaginative choices of subject matter for a linoleum block print—they simply downloaded popular-culture icons such as Tweety Bird and Sponge Bob. Lois Hetland worked with Jaime to use the Studio Habits as a way to diagnose the problem. He realized that he had not made Envision clear to his students, so they skipped it. For the next project, in which students created autobiographical vessels, he built in a number of specific brainstorming experiences to encourage envisioning (e.g., a paper lunch bag with words written outside for the public self and words held inside to describe the private self). The final projects were remarkably different—more diverse, more personal, and much higher in craft. The Studio Habits helped Jaime identify a problem and refine his curriculum so that it aimed directly at a solution to what he felt was going wrong.

Selecting Resources. The framework has also helped teachers to select resources for the teaching of specific Studio Habits. For example, Artist Gwendolyn Huskens's project "Medic Esthetic" uses medical materials such as bandages, plaster, and steel in flesh tones to make designer shoes that resemble orthopedic braces. While teaching a pre-practicum course in Fashion and Fibers at MassArt, Marie Smith decided that using images of this artist's work would help to develop the habits of Stretch and Explore (the materials are novel for shoes), Express (the images convey a social message about women's health), and Understand Art Worlds (the contemporary art world uses humor and juxtaposition to communicate).

Similarly, the rich resource of Art21's films of artists speaking about their work and working processes from within their own studios can be overwhelming to teachers trying to choose samples that align with a particular curricular theme. Viewing the clips through the lenses of the Studio Habits gives teachers ways to see connections across diverse media and practices so that they can curate their classes (a term used by Jessica Hamlin and Joe Fusaro in their Art21 Educators' Program) effectively around a theme and go beyond assignments that mimic an artist's process or material use. Lois Hetland selects Art21 Exclusive videos (1- to 4-minute-long clips targeting a single idea, found on YouTube) to support students in her pre-practicum teaching course in learning important aspects of pedagogy. She posts the videos on her online Moodle site for the students, along with an explanatory narrative, like the one below, identifying where particular habits show:

> This clip is a post-modernist's approach to embroidery. Jessica Rankin addresses meaning (Express) with words as her muse (Reflect: Question and Explain, Envision, and Understand Art Worlds—her art world includes literature and poetry), and embroidery as her medium (Develop Craft: Technique). There's a beautiful view of her open studio with large embroideries-in-process on the walls, showing how she sets up her studio practice (Develop Craft: Studio Practice). Oh, and how about that amazing depiction of engagement? Embroidery is clearly an art form that requires "Engage and Persist." When she talks about capturing the moment, *this very moment*, you can *see* how much that idea means to her, how central it is to what fascinates and perplexes her about language, time, being alive, and being a thinking/feeling being. So this is a great clip for getting a conversation going with students about the importance of engagement in order to persist—it's engagement that causes our drive (inclination) to persist.

Formative Assessment

The framework is a useful tool for formative assessment because it guides teachers' moment-to-moment observations and decisions as they talk with students about their work. For example, a teacher stopping by to talk to a student at work may notice some habits that are clearly demonstrated in this student's work and some that appear underdeveloped. By recognizing and naming strengths and weaknesses in a student's work through the language of the Studio Habits, teachers can focus

the questions and support they offer in a generative manner that helps students internalize how to make decisions that improve their work. For example, instead of saying, "Your colors don't work at all. Stop mixing in white" (Develop Craft) a teacher might say, "Tell me about your vision for the colors in your work. What do you want them to convey (Express) and how do you see them as doing that (Envision and Reflect)?"

Sara Stillman, when she taught at Emeryville High School in Emeryville, California, gave her students the Studio Habits to guide their regular self-assessment. She also used the habits to assess student portfolios when she taught K–5th grades in Oakland, California. Her donated pizza boxes, one per child, lined the hallway like book volumes on shelves. Each box had a grid of the Studio Habits on the inside top. Whenever Sara, students, or parents reviewed the portfolio, they noted connections between what had been made (and what might be remembered that the student said or did in the process of making the work) and particular Studio Habits. Because she dated all works and entries, the grid revealed a narrative portrait in note form for each student's growth over time. Of course, she didn't review every child's portfolio every day or even every week. With well over 100 students, as is common for many art teachers, that would be impossible. But she could review each portfolio two or three times a semester, and that gave her ample documented evidence to communicate trends on report cards.

We have not conducted any systematic surveys to find out where the framework is being used, but people have written to us about a number of other sites (besides those mentioned above) using the framework. While we are aware that there are many more than these, we offer a sample here in Box 17.1. We hope that readers will gain a feeling for the variety of ways in which the framework has been adapted.

USING THE FRAMEWORK IN DANCE, THEATER, AND MUSIC EDUCATION

The Studio Habits can be identified in the teaching of other art forms. In music, for example, one might alter "Observe" to become "Listen and Observe"; in theater, "Observe" might become "Attend" (as suggested by Judith Contrucci, former Coordinator of Visual and Performing Arts for the Cambridge, Massachusetts, public schools). In "Develop Craft," music teachers might shift the subcategory "Studio Practice" to "Rehearsal and Practice." And with

---

Box 17.1. A Sample of Sites Using the Studio Thinking Framework

IN THE CLASSROOM IN THE UNITED STATES AND BEYOND

South Berwyn School District 100 collaborated with the Chicago Teachers' Center at Northeastern Illinois University (http://neiu.edu/~ctc/) on a Department of Education Professional Development for Arts Educators grant from 2008–2011, ARTS Berwyn. Teachers throughout the District continue to use the Studio Thinking Framework as an approach to assessment and reflection across the disciplines. Over 91 arts-integrated units have been analyzed with the Studio Thinking Framework.

Chicago Teachers' Center at Northeastern Illinois University (http://neiu.edu/~ctc/) is using the Framework in collaboration with 50 Chicago Public School K–12 art and content teachers during a 3-year project to connect visual art studio practice with content teaching, built from the foundation of the ARTS Berwyn project. The project connects the Studio Thinking Framework to the Common Core, creating a shared language across schools and with the goal of strengthening critical thinking. Teachers meet face-to-face and on the Studio Thinking blog, everyarteverychild.blogspot.com. In monthly online conversations, the Center is also hosting an international group of educators across disciplines who use the framework. To learn more about their project, visit http://everyarteverychild.org

The San Leandro Public Schools in San Leandro, California, uses the Framework in its elementary and middle schools. Chris Lim, former superintendent of San Leandro, committed her eight elementary schools to a professional development project that paired classroom and art teachers in curriculum design, facilitated by Tana Johnson of the Alameda County Office of Education. The Studio Habits serve as guides for unit goals and assessments, and students learn the language as a means to identify strengths and weaknesses through reflection and motivate sustained investment in learning.

Drishya Kallika Kendra is a school in Bangalore, India, attended by children who live in extreme poverty. Artist-educator Arzu Mistry introduces the framework to her students through an exercise asking them to think about the question "How am I an artist now?", highlighted in the inner circle of a large chart, and "How can I become the artist I want to be?" in the outer circle. Arzu grouped their responses into the Studio Habits and explained the groupings to them. From that time on, the students have used the Habits to guide reflections about the mental processes they use as they work.

---

respect to the Studio Structures for learning, musicians, dancers, and theater artists might add "Performance" or "Ensemble" as overarching learning structures (analogous to Exhibition), since collaborative group contexts are so central in teaching in those domains. With minor alterations to accommodate discipline-specific aims and contexts, the Studio Thinking Framework is being used to guide planning and teaching in other arts disciplines.

Dance

David Alexander, advisor to the Boston Ballet's Center for Dance Education, carried out a 2-year study based on the framework (Alexander, 2007). In 2006, the research team observed 34 intensive ballet classes taught by 11 different teachers, and they interviewed 46 students to understand whether the habits of mind we had described were also being taught in ballet. The students in these classes were involved in dance 8–9 hours per day for 5 weeks. The researchers concluded that young ballet students were being taught all eight habits of mind. While they found that 43% of the content of a class was devoted to craft, they also concluded that the teachers stressed all of the other habits of mind in the service of developing craft. Here are examples of how each habit of mind was taught:

- "Use your muscles to control gravity." (Develop Craft)
- "Don't ever do anything less than what you are capable of . . . in ballet, or life, or anything!" (Engage and Persist)
- "Have you ever watched a cat or dog lick the floor? What they do with their tongue, that's what I want you to do with your foot." (Envision)

Box 17.1. A Sample of Sites Using the Studio Thinking Framework *(continued)*

OUTSIDE OF THE CLASSROOM, IN COMMUNITY CENTERS

The Perpich Center for Arts Education in Minneapolis, MN, http://www.mcae.k12.mn.us/

This community arts center, which serves Minnesota with professional development, an arts high school, research, and an arts library, has facilitated a regional community around Studio Thinking in Minnesota and North and South Dakota. Teachers attend meetings in which they share what they are doing with the framework, discussing what in their practice works, what does not, and what they might do differently.

The Center of Creative Arts (COCA) in St. Louis, MO, http://www.cocastl.org/

This multidisciplinary community arts center uses the framework for faculty development. The teaching artists use the habits when they plan residencies with classroom teachers. The organization has worked on the framework regularly with COCA's teaching-artists in the professional development portion of their faculty meetings. A pie-chart wheel of the Studio Habits is also posted in each studio at COCA, and the director's newsletters for parents often include anecdotes that explicitly highlight which habits are being used in camps and classes. The framework also supports observation of teaching-artists during the center's programs, helping both faculty and administration recognize when the framework is used and how it could be used better.

KID smART in New Orleans, LA, http://www.kidsmart.org/programs.html

KID smART has spent the last several years working with SHoM and the Studio Thinking Framework with teaching artists, exploring Studio Habits as methods of assessment and looking at the framework across artistic disciplines. Studio Thinking has a prominent place in the KID smART logic model. Program outcomes are aligned with Studio Habits to foreground the artistic objectives of the work and support good teaching practice. When Teaching Artists are observed in the classroom, their development and facilitation of Studio Habits with their students is a criterion that becomes a big part of the feedback conversation. Studio Habits give language to correlations among academic learning, college prep habits, and creative habits of mind. The framework has helped classroom teachers and school partners to deepen and shift what they are looking at and seeing in the arts, and including the Studio Habits on the organization's unit planning document guides both teaching artists and classroom teachers in continually thinking about and planning for the development of these habits.

Studio in a School in New York, NY, http://www.studioinaschool.org/

The framework was the evaluation lens in a U.S. Department of Education (DOE) Arts in Education Model Development and Dissemination grant (see the comment from Education Director Aline Hill-Ries, below). Observers learned to assess classrooms and conduct work with reference to the Studio Habits and to examine these reflections over time. Aline wrote to us that

> The NYC DOE, spurred on by the Common Core Standards, has finally come around to a position that should open people's eyes to the critical value of the arts. In New York City's "Instructional Expectations for 2012–13," focus has been placed on developing certain "academic and personal behaviors" that support students' ability to meet higher standards. As you would expect, some of these neatly overlap what you have identified in the original Studio Thinking research as essential learning that happens in the visual arts. The five behaviors they have focused on are: engagement, persistence, organization/ work habits, communication/collaboration, and self-regulation.

The Marwen Center in Chicago, IL, http://www.marwen.org/

Marwen is a free, after-school community center that offers visual art courses, college planning, and career development programs to Chicago's under-served youth in grades 6–12, many of whom travel several hours daily on public transportation to take part. The Center has offered professional development in Studio Thinking as a way to give teaching-artists a common language to learn from one another across media and processes.

- "Have a mind of your own. You have choices/ decisions you can make" (*Note*: this suggests that the teacher is pushing the student to convey personal meaning). (Express)
- "Notice how, with her raised leg engaged, the small inner muscles show up when it's done well." (Observe)
- "Have you noticed your attempts to perfect?" Have you noticed that you have improved? (Reflect)
- "Reach beyond yourself." Do some "experimenting on the job." (Stretch and Explore)
- "In some ways, ballet is about not being human, but being superhuman; about being without limitations, physical or gravitational. Whereas post-modern dance is about what the human can do and not do." (Understand Art Worlds)

In 2007, the research team interviewed dance students about the personal, intellectual, and social (but not physical) qualities needed to succeed in ballet. Students' responses were easily codable into the Studio Habits of Mind, with Engage and Persist, Envision, Reflect, and Observe being the ones most commonly mentioned.

Lois Hetland met Mark Borchelt when he led the dance department at Interlochen Arts Academy in Michigan. In contrast to Western theatrical dance training, which "is typically taught at a rote and ritualized level," Mark "saw immediate application to dance training" in the Studio Thinking Framework.

I have introduced the concepts in dance technique classes as well as dance composition and pedagogy classes with equal success. . . . It is valuable that the dancers learn to evolve past being dependent on external motivation such as out-performing peers or garnering instructor approval, to find a stronger sense of self-motivation that encourages a deeper level of inquiry and curiosity. For example, following a discussion of the concepts of envision and express, students routinely find ways to manipulate the timing and phrasing of an exercise to create a more poignant expression of the movement. . . . By thinking in terms of the Studio Structures, I have been able to organize my classes to more consciously shift between thinking and doing. . . . The studio experience is more positive in tone and focused on unrealized potential rather than a fear of not meeting stated expectations.

The Center of Creative Arts (COCA) in St. Louis (see Box 17.1) uses the framework in dance classes. According to Mark Cross, Director of Interchange at COCA, older ballet students are asked to apply the habits to other careers or professions (e.g., how would they apply it to a sales position), as a way to deepen their understanding of the framework. Younger students are asked to consider the Studio Habits of Mind on a daily basis and to write in a journal where they could see the habits "in action" during their classes. Students learn to watch dance videos the same way—training their ability to observe and critique. Shawna Flanigan, the Director of Education at COCA, uses the Studio Habits of Mind language in her weekly communication email to all of the parents/guardians of summer campers as a way to explain the work of the students in a specific camp. For example, she describes activities in terms of Stretch and Explore, Express, and Develop Craft. The COCA directors also worked with the Board to develop understanding and appreciation of the program by showing them how they were adopting the framework. Board members were given twelve examples of specific COCA classroom activities and then asked to identify the habits of mind taught in each activity.

Theatre

Evan Hastings, a theater teacher who consults internationally, talked to us about his use of the framework at the high school level in schools in Alameda County, California, and with adolescents in the Buena Vista School at the Alameda County Juvenile Justice Center in Hayward, California. He asked students to set their own goals and assess themselves using the framework.

First I would introduce the habits and have the students each select habits that they would like to focus on developing through the course. I asked the students "How will you know if you developed in this habit? What will it look like/ feel like?" Students would create a rubric for assessing their own development of the Habits they selected. Periodically, students would refer back to their goals or reflect on their progress through pair share discussions. As a summative self-evaluation, students would fill out a reflection sheet that had line starters such as "I challenged myself to engage and persist when _____". The student self-evaluations had a heavy influence on the students' final grades.

I also used the SHoM sentence starters to help youth develop artist statements.

Evan has also used the framework with faculty and students at the Srishti School of Art, Design, and Technology, in Bangalore, India. He reported to us that the framework deepened the quality of reflections.

I write each Habit on chart paper and I have them chalk talk (write and draw definitions and associations). Then I place the eight chart sheets on the floor in a circle and I have my students dance around the circle freezing when the music stops, like musical chairs. Whatever Habit they're standing on when the music stops, they have to freeze in a statue that personifies some aspect of this Habit. When the music starts again everyone dances around again. Next when everyone freezes in their statues, I invite them to speak the inner monologues of their statues, further personifying varying aspects of the Habits. This is a fun way to Stretch and Explore our understanding of the Habits.

After the musical habits, then I have the students reflect on their own creative practice and set goals for habits they want to develop. These goals are shared with the whole class and posted on the wall so the students can support and challenge each other toward their self-directed goals.

Music

When the late Maestro Matthew Hazelwood (1954–2012) taught at the Interlochen Arts Academy in Michigan, he developed ways to teach the Studio Habits explicitly to students in his orchestra. In a beautiful example of teaching Envision as he conducted a rehearsal of Tchaikovsky's ballet, Sleeping Beauty, Matt stopped the group after they had played through a section, reached down, and put a pair of ballet toe shoes on his hands. With his hands in the shoes, he "danced" the rhythm of the music on the auditorium floor in a soft, delicate tapping. As he did so, he asked his students to Envision. "Remember, this is a dance. You are in the orchestra pit, and the dancers are on the stage just above you. Let's take it from B." The performance was transformed. The students moved from being tied to the notes in a rote and lifeless rendition to a light expressive flow. This demonstration is a good example of how a conductor can teach students to Envision in order to Express. As he taught, he also stressed Understand Art Worlds. While conducting, he continuously wove in historical anecdotes about the works the students were learning to perform. He told them about how the instruments, acoustics, and audiences differed in past eras so that they could play with a more authentic interpretation. After leaving Interlochen, Mateo (as he was called in Spanish) served as the conductor of the National Youth Orchestra of Colombia and the Music Adviser of Colombia's Batuta Youth Program. With Batuta, he used this Studio Thinking approach in over 100 music centers. Maestro Hazelwood died, tragically and unexpectedly, on May 31, 2012, and we have dedicated this book to him along with Elliot Eisner.

Across Arts Disciplines

One benefit of using the Framework across arts disciplines is that it can help to identify pedagogical patterns that differ across art forms. For example, we learned by observing Mark Borchelt teaching dance at the Interlochen Arts Academy that dance classes tends to be structured with many repetitions of very short structures, such as a 1-minute Demonstration–Lecture, followed by a 2-minute Students-at-Work session and a 30-second Critique. Some music rehearsals at Interlochen were similarly structured, and because conductors demonstrate while students play, the Demonstration–Lecture and Students-at-Work structures often happen simultaneously in ensembles. Perhaps teachers of different art forms can learn more from one another when they have the Framework as a common language. This is particularly important as new forms and fields evolve. For example, learning in the new media arts increasingly demands this shared language as students take on roles of musician, filmmaker, graphic designer, actor, and writer in individual and collaborative media arts projects.

Peter Lutkoski, former chair of the music department and currently middle school assistant principal at the American School of London, used the Studio Thinking Framework as a common language with his music department to refine the department's goals for student learning across the band, choral, and string programs. Pete and Alison Marshall, a theater and dance artist-educator in Phoenix, Arizona, have run annual institutes since 2010 at the American School of London that use the Studio Thinking Framework to support curriculum development in arts and non-arts subjects. They center the work on the theme of "Place" and use London's public spaces and cultural institutions as sites for developing curriculum to build Studio Thinking.

USING THE FRAMEWORK IN NON-ARTS EDUCATION

Non-arts teachers have interpreted the Studio Habits in the language and context of their own disciplines. For example, all disciplines convey meaning (Express), but the ways and forms in which they convey meanings differ. Envision, which is central to the visual arts, is also used in math and science, history, and literature. Understand Art Worlds finds its counterpart when students in biology learn about how scientists at the forefront of genetics have mapped the human genome, when mathematics students learn the history of the Fibonacci sequence, or when students of history compare sources written by historians of different periods.

In what follows we point to a few ways that teachers outside of the arts have used the framework.

Studio Structures for Learning

Too often, arts teachers feel themselves relegated to the remote edge of conversations about reforming teaching and learning. However, with the Studio Structures for learning defined, teachers of other disciplines can consider the benefits of emphasizing the Students-at-Work structure and put the making of disciplinary works at the center of their classes.

The Students-at-Work structure is a natural fit for teachers of any discipline who believe that students need to construct meaning in order to understand. Teachers can observe students while they work and intervene in ways that allow them to differentiate instruction for a widely heterogeneous group of students, depending on specific needs and challenges. The structure allows teachers to emphasize formative assessment, identifying targets of difficulty and offering just-in-time intervention for students as they conduct research, write, or solve problems.

Non-arts teachers may find that, coupled with using Students-at-Work sessions in their classes, Demonstration–Lectures provide just the opportunity they need to model ways that experts in their subject areas conduct disciplinary tasks (e.g., analyzing a primary document, designing an experiment with appropriate controls, finding an intriguing problem in mathematics and systematically working to solve it). Instead of lecturing to students for long periods, teachers can give briefer Demonstration–Lectures (with many visuals illustrating concepts, products, and processes) to introduce ideas useful to ongoing projects that arise as students are working, leaving the majority of class time dedicated to independent project work (Students-at-Work).

At the Centre for Real-World Learning at the University of Winchester, in England, Lucas and Claxton (2010) have argued that all subject areas in school could be taught more like a studio classroom. They suggest teaching English by turning the class into a newspaper office with each student taking on an authentic role; setting up a history class as a research project in which evidence is collected about a particular issue; and giving math students open-ended problems to work on. All of these suggestions put *making* at the center of a classroom, whether this means making a newspaper, an historical argument, or a mathematical solution to a problem whose answers are not in a textbook. Very much in tune with our own thinking, these researchers believe that making—a process that involves all the Studio Habits—can be done with physical tools or symbolic tools (words, numbers). Similar to the example we offered earlier in the Develop Craft chapter about William Kentridge, they argue that when students are involved in making, the habit of Reflection (including evaluation) is practiced because what is made, as well as the process of making it, becomes visible to the maker and the audience, and this invites conversation.

In all of the kinds of examples that these researchers describe, the teacher serves more as a facilitator than a lecturer, the students are self-directed, and the classroom space is organized like a workshop with students in clusters rather than seated facing the teacher. This is just what we have described in the studio structure of Students-at-Work. The Real-World Learning examples all use authentic rather than contrived projects—just like the best projects we describe in this book. These projects extend for long periods of time rather than ending when the bell rings, and they go through numerous cycles of drafting and critique.

Critiques are a logical addition to non-arts classrooms. When teachers make occasions for student work to be viewed and discussed publicly while it is in process, students can learn to function as a community focused on developing understanding as a group. This is what goes on in the Japanese mathematics classrooms described by Stigler and Hiebert in *The Teaching Gap* (1999), in which teachers assign a single problem for a class, groups work to solve that problem, and then the group together discusses not the answer but the processes of problem solving. As teachers identify and define ways to contribute usefully in Critiques, they can reinforce the reflective conversation about learning that happens during Critiques so it is more likely to carry over to times when students return to working individually.

An additional value of the Studio Thinking Framework for non-arts teachers is the assistance it offers for interdisciplinary work. Students usually respond with enthusiasm to arts experiences that are interspersed into instruction in non-arts domains. But often, the non-arts teachers have no idea about what constitutes a genuine arts experience, as opposed to a trivial one. When using arts to invite interest in a non-arts topic, the Studio Habits of Mind can guide teachers to consider artistic values that the activities might foster. This is what upper elementary and middle school teachers, under the leadership of Tana Johnson, Alameda County Office of Education, have been doing since 2008 in the San Leandro Unified School District in California. Elementary classroom teachers partnered with school specialists in visual arts to develop cross-disciplinary projects in reading, writing, and history, while middle school students are proceeding similarly with arts and science integration.

The framework facilitates the development of interdisciplinary units among teachers. Jim Jer-don, Spanish teacher at The Winsor School in Brookline, Massachusetts, reports that middle school teachers in a variety of non-arts disciplines developed a curriculum based on the framework to teach students ways to conduct a rigorous process of research. And Miriam Stahl, arts teacher, and Ray Cagan, history teacher, both at the Arts and Humanities Academy, a small school in the Berkeley Public High School, report using the Studio Habits of Mind as a core structure for planning and assessment across all arts and academic disciplines. Such overlaps are promising areas of exploration for rigorous interdisciplinary research about effectiveness in interdisciplinary curricula.

USING THE FRAMEWORK IN PRESERVICE TEACHER EDUCATION PROGRAMS

Another use of the Studio Thinking Framework is to help beginning teachers understand the purpose and rigor of arts education. The framework is being used regularly in preservice art teacher education at the Massachusetts College of Art and Design, at Pennsylvania State, and at George Mason

University, among a number of others. Dave Donahue (Associate Provost and Professor of Education at Mills College), Jennifer Stuart (art teacher at San Francisco Friends School), and Trena Noval (artist and action researcher who also leads an arts laboratory initiative at Peralta Elementary in Oakland), have modeled ways to use the framework in preservice generalist teacher education at Mills College in Oakland, California.

At George Mason University, the Studio Thinking Framework is used as a tool in the first introductory course for undergraduate BFA students considering becoming art educators. A cornerstone of the course is observation, and as students visit elementary, middle, and high school arts classrooms they use the Studio Thinking Framework to help make sense of what they see. The Framework allows them to discern the structures of studio classes and the learning emphasized therein. In a course on visual thinking, Renee Sandell uses the Framework to help preservice art teachers picture the kinds and range of thinking needed to foster the rich process of visual meaning-making. Faculty have found that the Framework helps shift preservice teachers' thinking from an emphasis on the specific projects, media, and techniques to a more analytic account of what and how students learn through these projects. As students advance in the program, they revisit the Studio Thinking Framework as they read and discuss research in art education, connect arts learning to broader theories of learning and development, and plan curriculum and assessments.

USING THE FRAMEWORK IN MUSEUM AND GALLERY EDUCATION

MassArt's Director of Gallery Education, India Clark (2011), used the Framework to analyze college classes held in the gallery. She identified the Studio Habits and Studio Structures for learning being used and made recommendations to the college faculty for improving their gallery-based classes. Box 17.2 presents a class on Claims and Evidence developed and taught by Ricco Siosocco, a writing teacher in the freshman program at MassArt. Ricco used writing exercises that asked students to investigate images in the Bakalar and Paine Galleries at MassArt. India's analysis revealed that the class cultivated each Studio Habit of Mind. India was initially surprised to see that the Studio Structures were also used in gallery education: There were

Box 17.2. India Clark's Analysis of Ricco Siosocco's Gallery Class: How a Claims and Evidence Exercise Cultivates Studio Habits of Mind

1. Develop Craft by learning knowledge, methods, and forms of the discipline of writing; by using the opportunity to try out crafting their own claims.
2. Engage and Persist by embracing the challenge of the claims exercise and persevering to improve their first attempts; by observing the more polished examples of others, boosting their inclination to further persist.
3. Envision by dreaming up new sentences in claim form from their collected observations and opinions.
4. Express by communicating opinions through writing, the symbol system of the target discipline (written communication)
5. Observe by looking closely at physical art objects; by "looking closely" at one another's examples of written claims.
6. Reflect by presenting claims to the group and critiquing each one, assessing and asserting ideas.
7. Stretch and Explore by experimenting with new and challenging concepts; by learning from error.
8. Understand the Writing World/Art Worlds by introducing knowledge, methods, forms, and purposes related to writing; by further exploring understanding about the art world through exposure to objects in the gallery.

Demonstration–Lectures, Students-at-Work (for example, Ricco's students were asked to experiment with making claims about art works and finding evidence for these claims), and Critique (student groups presented their claims in front of the artworks they had chosen for evidence, and others critiqued their claims).

The Studio Habits Framework is also being used in other museum education programs. One approach used at the National Gallery in Washington, DC, involves looking for the artist's mind in works. Can viewers see evidence that the artist Envisioned? Stretched and Explored? How, for example, do Mark Tansy's paintings (which make clever references to art history) show the artist's perspective on Understand Art Worlds? Similarly, the St. Louis Art Museum, led by former Director of School Services, Mike Murawski (who was recently appointed Director of

Education & Public Programs at the Portland Art Museum in Oregon), uses Studio Thinking as part of their multidimensional gallery experiences that integrate language-based responses to art with nonverbal, creative, and embodied responses. And, at the Columbus Museum of Art, Cindy Meyers Foley, Director of Education, has used Studio Thinking for a decade with the museum's Teaching Artists, saying that they and the education department have found validation, purpose, and distinction within the larger arts community through a Studio Thinking approach to arts education. They use Studio Thinking to help them redefine the boundaries between personal studio practice and teaching practice and work with students as collaborators and co-artists. Teaching Artists often learn new skills alongside students, which blurs the distinctions between expert and novice, changes the dynamic of the lecture-demonstration format of gallery education, and fosters the development of independent, intrinsically motivated, cultural producers.

USING THE FRAMEWORK FOR RESEARCH

Arts Education Research

Since 2003, there have been at least six studies funded by the U.S. Department of Education to support and document how teachers use the framework to plan their curricula and assess student learning. These grants were awarded to the Northeastern Illinois University Teaching Center's Kate Thomas and Matt Dealy for work with the Berwyn School District in Illinois (1 grant), Studio in a School in New York City (1 grant), and the Alameda County Office of Education in California (4 grants). Studio in a School used Studio Thinking as an evaluation tool to check whether student learning developed as a result of artist residencies. And the Alameda Office of Education used the first of four grants for looking at student learning and assessment, the second for building out a systemic structure for what was learned, and the third and fourth to conduct a district-wide initiative partnering classroom and art teachers at the elementary and middle school levels.

New Technologies

Kevin Clark and Kimberly Sheridan have been designing and researching an informal education program in 3-D modeling, animation, and interactive game design for traditionally underserved youth in

Washington, DC since 2007, initially supported for 4 years by the National Science Foundation, with continuing funds provided by Dell, Microsoft, the Entertainment Software Association, and other donors. The researchers have found the Studio Thinking Framework to be a valuable tool in making teaching and learning in this program more open-ended, creative, and student-driven. In the program they designed for their study, the researchers combined the Studio Thinking Framework with a youth mentorship model in what they term a *studio mentorship model*, where more experienced youth act as mentors in the classroom for beginning youth. The research demonstrates how such a model can create transformative technology learning environments in urban areas (Clark & Sheridan, 2010; Khalili, Sheridan, Williams, Clark, & Stegman, 2011; Sheridan, 2011; Sheridan & Clark, 2010; Sheridan, Clark & Williams, 2013).

For instance, Sheridan, Clark, and Williams (2013) describe how the implementation of the studio mentorship model helped a computer programming teacher. He was able to move from his prior approach of teaching precisely designed tasks taught by step-by-step instructions with a focus on skill with programming tools, to posing open-ended computer-design problems where he guided youth mentors to assist beginning students in the use of programming to create interactive games. A comparison of the class in the year before and after implementation of the studio mentorship model is dramatic: The amount of time the teacher spent talking was more than halved, there was more student talk about their work, *and* there was dramatically less "off-task behavior." Students completed more projects and their resulting work was rated by the researchers as more complex and original when taught using the studio approach.

Combining the Studio Thinking Framework with a mentorship model also led to greater openness in youth's conceptions of their own roles, potential, and responsibilities. Before the implementation of a studio approach, youth working in the program took on minor administrative roles. In the more open-ended studio environments, youth mentors not only took on instructing their peers in the moment, but also started proposing and teaching their own class sessions. The program shifted over time from being taught by adult high school teachers to being entirely designed and taught by youth. High-school-aged youth identified new software to teach, developed strategies for teaching it, and presented their work at technology and education conferences (Sheridan, Clark & Williams, 2013).

Transfer of Learning

With Lynn Goldsmith at Education Development Center, Lois Hetland and Ellen Winner are using the framework to guide research on transfer of learning across domains. Supported by a grant from the National Science Foundation, the team has investigated how students learn to envision in art and whether skill in visual art envisioning transfers to envisioning in the discipline of geometry. (Researchers did not try to assess inclination or alertness, which would require observations in a setting that allowed a choice of tasks.) In consultation with artist-teachers, the research team developed a measure of the skill of envisioning in art that consists of a variety of drawing activities: observational drawing, geometric drawing (in which an organic form is reduced to basic geometric forms), drawing a figure from the back when one can only see it from the front, drawing negative space, and imagining and then drawing cast shadows.

The study tracked students' performance on the art envisioning measure as they entered the 9th grade, comparing an art group (visual arts majors at the Boston Arts Academy), a theater group (theater majors at BAA), and a squash group (students in an after-school squash and academic support program at Northeastern University). Students were also tracked in geometry by using a measure the researchers developed from spatial geometry problems released from standardized national and international mathematics tests. The study is still underway, but two preliminary findings are emerging:

- Art majors performed higher than theater and squash students on both the art-envisioning and spatial geometric-reasoning tests.
- Art majors gained more on the spatial geometric-reasoning test than did the other two groups.

But these findings do not conclusively demonstrate transfer, because we could not use an experimental design and randomly assign students to art vs. theater vs. squash. Random assignment would have allowed us to compare art, theater, and squash groups starting from a level playing field—having the same level of spatial reasoning skills in geometry at the beginning of 9th grade. We found that our art group was better on both measures as they entered 9th grade. Thus we cannot claim that their arts experiences caused their spatial geometric-reasoning to improve.

Developing a measure for tracking envisioning in visual art revealed the multifaceted nature of the disposition to Envision. Each section of the art-envisioning test was set up to capture part of this complex habit.

Each habit of mind is probably as complex as Envision. Developing an authentic assessment measure of each habit is going to require that each habit be unpacked so that its components can be understood. And assessing the inclination and alertness of habits in addition to assessing skill will require designing ways to see into the attitudes that shape choices and decisions during the processes of making.

The Studio Thinking Framework could also be used in future research to demonstrate best practices that promote learning. Using this tool, researchers would be able to describe and contrast classroom practices more precisely. Ultimately, research should be able to determine which particular variations result in higher levels of student learning in particular contexts. For now, though, such conclusions are premature. What we present here is a description of the range of patterns that we observed in classrooms. By reflecting on these examples, we believe that teachers can become more aware of and better able to refine their own teaching practices.

USING THE FRAMEWORK IN VISUAL ARTS POLICY

The framework is influencing visual arts education policy in the United States by guiding the development of new state and national standards. For example, in 2008, at a professional development institute for state arts education managers, *Studio Thinking* was read and discussed. The state arts managers are the shapers of arts education policy across the United States. In 2009 the National Art Education Association, the world's largest professional visual arts education association and a leader in educational research, policy, and practice for art education, published *Learning in the Visual Age: The Critical Importance of Visual Arts Education*. This report highlights Studio Thinking as defining what high-quality arts education provides. Also in 2009, according to Karol Gates, content specialist for the Arts at the Colorado Department of Education, our framework guided the development of the new visual arts standards in Colorado and ensured that they focused on dispositions and not just skills. In 1997 they listed

the following five standards, focused on skill and knowledge:

1. Students recognize and use the visual arts as a form of communication.
2. Students know and apply elements of art, principles of design, and sensory and expressive features of visual arts.
3. Students know and apply visual arts materials, tools, techniques, and processes.
4. Students relate the visual arts to various historical and cultural traditions.
5. Students analyze and evaluate the characteristics, merits, and meaning of works of art.

In 2009, the standards became more dispositional. They were reduced to four, three of which bear a remarkable resemblance to our habits:

1. Observe and Learn to Comprehend (Observe)
2. Envision and Critique to Reflect (Envision, Reflect)
3. Invent and Discover to Create (Stretch and Explore)

Most recently, in 2012, the writing group for the new National Visual Arts Standards requested Studio Thinking as one of the resource texts for the new standards currently under development.

The Studio Thinking Framework is a tool to promote professional dialogue across local, district, state, and university contexts and across arts disciplines. In the politically charged atmosphere of accountability and tight budgets, the framework can help explain and justify programs to parents, administrators, and groups who control resource allocation to schools.

As the Studio Thinking Framework is used in more and more ways, we have begun to learn how its value extends even beyond classroom uses. Steve Locke, Associate Professor at MassArt, describes it as the window between his art practice and his teaching that makes the connection between the two apparent. We hope that you, readers of this book, will be alert to any new ways that the Studio Thinking Framework supports your efforts to teach and learn rigorously, both within and beyond the classroom context. When you put the Framework to use, please, let us hear from you!

Project Examples

School and Teacher	Project Name	Example Number
The Boston Arts Academy		
MÓNIKA ALDARONDO	Junior Shows	16.3
	African Pottery	3.1, 12.2
	Imaginary Creatures	8.2, 10.1
BETH BALLIRO	Inventing Colors	5.1, 7.1, 13.1
	Secret Ritual Vessels	14.2
	Sketching in Clay	11.1
	Creating Hat and Vest	14.4
	Egg Drop	12.6
	The Freshman Year	16.1
KATHLEEN MARSH	Making Puppets	6.2
	Mounting the Senior Show in 2002	16.4
	Mounting the Senior Show in 2012	16.5
	Self-Portraits in Colored Pencil	5.2, 10.3
GUY MICHEL TELEMAQUE	A Sophomore Show	16.2
	Using the Viewfinder	9.1
Walnut Hill School		
	Centering on the Wheel	5.4, 14.1
	Ceramic Sets	12.3, 13.2
JASON GREEN	Coil Sculpture	3.2, 10.2, 12.5
	Repeating Units	11.2
	Tile Project	6.1, 7.2
	Abstraction	14.3
	Contour Drawing	15.1
	Cubism	12.4
	End-of-Term Exhibitions	16.1
JIM WOODSIDE	Figures in Evocative Space	8.1, 12.1, 15.2
	Korean Students Show in Korea	16.8
	Light and Boxes	3.3, 5.3, 9.2
	The Senior Show	16.7

Conducting the Research

Research is only as trustworthy as the methods by which it is conducted. This appendix describes the methods we used to develop the Studio Thinking Framework to make transparent the empirical processes we employed in our research design.

SETTINGS AND SUBJECTS

Over the 2001–2002 school year, we filmed 38 classes in five classrooms at two high schools that focus on the arts, the Boston Arts Academy and the Walnut Hill School. Students at the Boston Arts Academy are proportionally representative of the demographic profile of the Boston area in socioeconomic status. Students at Walnut Hill are an international group including local suburban and urban students and students from across the United States and from abroad, with a concentration of Korean students. Students at Walnut Hill are mainly middle or upper-middle class with some students receiving full scholarship. At both schools students are admitted by portfolio review and/or on the basis of admissions tasks and interviews. Students who are admitted showed interest and promise in the visual arts, but few have highly developed levels of technical skills upon admission.

TEACHERS WHO CONTRIBUTED TO THE ORIGINAL RESEARCH

The five teachers who contributed to the original research are all practicing artists. The three teachers at the Boston Arts Academy are licensed by the State of Massachusetts, and all five have Master's degrees in art or art education. We list each teacher below.

Beth Balliro, Boston Arts Academy, Painting and Ceramics

Beth Balliro, an exhibiting artist, began teaching at BAA when it opened in 1998. She is now a faculty member in the Art Education Department at the Massachusetts College of Art and Design.

Jason Green, Walnut Hill, Ceramics and Ceramic Sculpture

Jason Green, an exhibiting artist, began teaching at Walnut Hill in 1998 and is now on the faculty of Alfred University.

Kathleen Marsh, Boston Arts Academy, Sculpture and Drawing

Kathleen Marsh is a founding member of BAA and has been there since 1998. She now serves as Academic Dean for the school.

Guy Michel Telemaque, Boston Arts Academy, Photography and Design

Guy Michel Telemaque, an exhibiting artist, has taught at BAA since 2000 and continues in this position today.

Jim Woodside, Walnut Hill, Drawing

Jim Woodside, an exhibiting artist, has been a teacher and the Director of Visual Art at Walnut Hill since 1988 and continues in this position today.

DATA COLLECTION AND FIRST-LEVEL ANALYSIS

We documented classes that ranged from 1.5 to 3 hours in length; 22 classes at the Boston Arts Academy and 16 classes at Walnut Hill. Nine sessions were 3-hour, 9th-grade classes at the Boston Arts Academy; seven were 1.5-hour 9th-grade classes at the Boston Arts Academy; 16 were 3-hour mixed 9th- through 12th-grade introductory classes at Walnut Hill; and six were 3-hour 12th-grade classes at the Boston Arts Academy. This yielded a total of 103.5 hours of classroom observation. Data included videos with audio shot by our project videographer that focused on the teacher, field notes by a second researcher–observer, and memos written by the observing researcher immediately following each observation. Videos captured teachers talking to students but not conversations between students.

After each filming, we created video clips of events in the classroom that we wanted to learn more about, based on our review of the memo and on debriefing conversations between the videographer and observer. We wrote a standard interview protocol that we revised for each class to suit the particular data, and we followed up with an audiotaped interview of the teacher about a week after the filming. During interviews one researcher viewed clips together with the teacher and probed what was going on. Additional data were collected in the form of photographs of student work and curriculum documents and/or program descriptions.

DATA ANALYSIS

Video and audio recordings of the interviews were transcribed. Analysis triangulated video and audio transcripts, videos, photos of student work and curriculum documents, and field notes and memos. Iteratively, we looked for patterns of interactions and uses of time and space, both within each teacher's classes and across all five teachers. This resulted in identification and then definition of the Studio Structures, which are based on characteristics observed across the teachers.

We then segmented transcripts of the documented classes into categories for each Studio Structure. Next, we reviewed the Students-at-Work segments of four classes we selected randomly as code-development cases, in order to develop categories of what we saw being taught. We looked for patterns in the transcripts and then developed "native" concepts that described how each teacher talked about his or her intentions for student learning. Next, our research team collapsed the teachers' personal concepts into fewer categories, resulting in 11 "codes" for intended learning and a code we called "other." Through iterative comparisons across codes within the four code-development classes, our team of five researchers created a coding manual with examples from the transcripts that we used to guide the next phase of analysis.

At this point, we randomly selected and assigned about 35% of the remaining classes (12) to three members of our research team, two of whom coded each class. During this process, we continued to bring examples that confused us to our meetings to refine our codebook. When analysis of the 12 classes was complete, we tested the reliability across coders and found that it was strong (between 0.7 and 0.9). We then randomly divided the remaining 22 classes among the three coders so that each coder analyzed seven or eight classes.

As we began discussing our preliminary findings with others in the field, we eliminated the "other" category and, in three cases, combined two codes (Technique and Studio Practice were combined into "Develop Craft"; Question and Explain and Evaluate were combined into "Reflect"; and Domain and Collaborate were combined into "Understand Art Worlds: Domain and Communities"). The resulting eight categories of "what" art teachers intend to teach became the eight Studio Habits of Mind presented in the chapters in Part II.

References

Alameda County Office of Education. (2012). Developing student habits of mind for success across the curriculum at the Arts and Humanities Academy at Berkeley High School, Berkeley, California [unpublished document]. Hayward, CA: Author.

Alexander, D. (2010, October). Ballet dance and the development of eight habits of mind. National Dance Education Organization annual conference, Tempe, AZ.

Alexander, D., & Cassell, Y. (2011, October). Researching modern dance and the development of eight habits of mind. National Dance Education Organization annual conference, Minneapolis, MN.

Amabile, T. M. (1996). *Creativity in context*. Boulder, CO: Westview Press.

Baumeister, R. F., & Vohs, K. D. (2007). Self-regulation, ego depletion, and motivation. *Social and Personality Psychology Compass, 1*, 1–14.

Blythe, T., & the researchers and teachers of the Teaching for Understanding Project. (1998). *Teaching for understanding guide*. San Francisco: Jossey-Bass.

Bostrom, M. (2003). *Fulfilling the promise of No Child Left Behind. A meta-analysis of attitudes towards public education*. Public Knowledge LLC. http://www.keepartsinschools.org/Preview/Research/Materials/NoChildLeftBehind-MetaAnalysis.pdf

Burger, K., & Winner, E. (2000). Instruction in visual art: Can it help children learn to read? *Journal of Aesthetic Education, 34*(3–4), 277–294.

Butzlaff, R. (2000). Can music be used to teach reading? *Journal of Aesthetic Education, 34*(3–4), 167–178.

Clark, I. N. (2011). Supporting artists in the gallery: The role of the museum educator at an art college. MALS thesis, Skidmore College, Saratoga Springs, NY.

Clark, K., & Sheridan, K. (2010). Game design through mentoring and collaboration. *Journal of Educational Multimedia and Hypermedia, 19*, 2.

Csikszentmihalyi, M. (1990). *Flow: The psychology of optimal experience*. New York: Harper and Row.

Deasy, R., & Fulbright, H. (2001, January 24). Commentary: The arts impact learning. *Education Week, 20*(19), 34.

Douglas, K., & Jaquith, D. B. (2009). *Engaging learners through artmaking: Choice-based art education in the classroom*. New York: Teachers College.

Dweck, C. S. (2000). *Self-theories: Their role in motivation, personality, and development*. Philadelphia: Psychology Press.

Efland, A. (1976). The school art style: A functional analysis. *Studies in Art Education, 17*(2), 37–44.

Efland, A. (1983). School art and its social origins. *Studies in Art Education, 24*(3), 149–157.

Eisner, E. (2002a). *The arts and the creation of mind*. New Haven, CT: Yale University Press.

Eisner, E. (2002b). What can education learn from the arts about the practice of education? Available at http://www.infed.org/biblio/eisner_arts_and_the_practice_of_education.htm

Ellis, A. (2003, June). *Valuing culture*. Paper presented at conference entitled Valuing Culture, National Theatre Studio, London. Available at http://www.demos.co.uk/catalogue/valuingculturespeeches/

Ericsson, K. A. (Ed.). (1996). *The road to excellence: The acquisition of expert performance in the arts and sciences, sports, and games*. Mahweh, NJ: Erlbaum.

Ericsson, K. A., Nandagopal, K., & Roring, R. W. (2009). Toward a science of exceptional achievement: Attaining superior performance through deliberate practice. *Annals of New York Academy of Science, 1172*, 199–217.

Fiske, E. (Ed.). (1999). *Champions of change: The impact of the arts on learning*. Washington, DC: Arts Education Partnership and President's Committee on the Arts and Humanities.

Getzels, J., & Csikszentmihalyi, M. (1976). *The creative vision: A longitudinal study of problem finding in art*. New York: Wiley.

Gombrich, E. H. (2000). *Art and illusion*. Princeton, NJ: Princeton University Press.

Goodman, N. (1968). *Languages of art: An approach to a theory of symbols*. Indianapolis: Bobbs-Merrill.

Harland, J., Kinder, K., Haynes, J., & Schagen, I. (1998). *The effects and effectiveness of arts education in schools*. Interim Report 1. London: National Foundation for Educational Research.

Hetland, L. (2000a). Listening to music enhances spatial–temporal reasoning: Evidence for the "Mozart effect." *Journal of Aesthetic Education, 34*(3–4), 105–148.

Hetland, L. (2000b). Learning to make music enhances spatial reasoning. *Journal of Aesthetic Education, 34*(3–4), 179–238.

Hetland, L. (2012). Can studio habits help teachers assess arts learning? Case of the King Cobra. In D. Jaquith & N. Hathaway (Eds.), *The learner-directed classroom: Developing creative thinking skills through art* (pp. 123–130). New York: Teachers College Press.

Hetland, L., Cajolet, S., & Music, L. (2010). Documentation in the visual arts: Embedding a common language from research. *Theory Into Practice, 49*(1), 55–63.

Ito, M., et al. (2010). *Hanging out, messing around, and geeking out: Kids living and learning with new media*. Cambridge, MA: MIT Press.

Jaquith, D. B., & Hathaway, N. E. (2012). *The learner directed classroom: Developing creative thinking skills through art*. New York: Teachers College Press.

Jenkins, H., Purushotma, R., Clinton, K., Weigler, M., & Robison, A. (2007). Confronting the challenges of participatory culture: Media education for the 21st century. Available at http://www.newmedialiteracies.org/wp-content/uploads/pdfs/NMLWhitePaper.pdf

Keinanen, M., Hetland, L., & Winner, E. (2000). Teaching cognitive skill through dance: Evidence for near but not far transfer. *Journal of Aesthetic Education, 34* (3–4), 295–306.

Kent, C., & Steward, J. (2008). *Learning by heart: Teachings to free the creative spirit.* New York: Allworth.

Khalili, N., Sheridan, K., Williams, A., Clark, K., & Stegman, M. (2011). Students designing games about immunology: Insights for science learning. *Computers in the Schools, 28*(3), 228–240.

Kimbell, R., Wheeler, T., Miller, S., Bain, J., Wright, R., & Stables, K. (2005). *Assessing design innovation: Final report.* London: Goldsmiths, University of London.

Lampert, M. (2003). *Teaching problems and the problems of teaching.* New Haven, CT: Yale University Press.

Lenhart, A., & Madden, M. (2005). Teen content creators and consumers. Available at http://www.pewinternet.org/Reports/2005/Teen-Content-Creators-and-Consumers.aspx

Lucas, B., & Claxton, G. (2010). *New kinds of smart: How the science of learnable intelligence is changing education.* Maidenhead, England: McGraw Hill, Open University Press.

McCarthy, K., Ondaatje, E. H., Zakaras, L., & Brooks, A. (2004). *Gifts of the muse: Reframing the debate about the benefits of the arts.* Santa Monica, CA: RAND Corporation.

Murfee, E. (1995). *Eloquent evidence: Arts at the core of learning. Report by the President's Committee on the Arts and the Humanities.* Washington, DC: National Assembly of State Arts Agencies.

O'Doherty, B. (2000). *Inside the white cube: The ideology of the gallery space* (Expanded Ed.). Berkeley: University of California Press.

Peppler, K. A. (2010). Media arts: Arts education for a digital age. *Teachers College Record, 112*(8), 2118–2153.

Perkins, D. N. (1992). *Smart schools: From training memories to educating minds.* New York: Free Press.

Perkins, D. (1994). *The intelligent eye: Learning to think by looking at art.* Los Angeles: J. Paul Getty Museum.

Perkins, D. (2001). Embracing Babel: The prospects of instrumental uses of the arts for education. In E. Winner & L. Hetland (Eds.), *Beyond the soundbite: Arts education and academic outcomes* (pp. 117–124). Los Angeles: J. Paul Getty Trust.

Perkins, D. N., Jay, E., & Tishman, S. (1993). Beyond abilities: A dispositional theory of thinking. *Merrill-Palmer Quarterly, 39*(1), 1–21.

Pike, A. W. G., et al. (2012). U-Series dating of Paleolithic art in 11 caves in Spain. *Science, 336,* 1409.

Podlozny, A. (2000). Strengthening verbal skills through the use of classroom drama: A clear link. *Journal of Aesthetic Education, 34*(3–4), 91–104.

Project Zero, & Reggio Children. (2001). *Making learning visible: Children as individual and group learners.* Reggio Emilia, Italy: Reggio Children.

Salomon, G., & Perkins, D. N. (1989). Rocky roads to transfer: Rethinking mechanisms of a neglected phenomenon. *Educational Psychologist, 24*(2), 113–142.

Seidel, S., Tishman, S., Winner, E.., Hetland, L., & Palmer, P. (2009). *The qualities of quality: Understanding excellence in arts education.* Cambridge, MA: Project Zero. Available at http://www.wallacefoundation.org/knowledge-center/arts-education/arts-classroom-instruction/Documents/Understanding-Excellence-in-Arts-Education.pdf

Sheridan, K. M. (2011), Envision and Observe: Using the Studio Thinking Framework for learning and teaching in digital arts. *Mind, Brain, and Education, 5,* 19–26. doi: 10.1111/j.1751-228X.2011.01105.x

Sheridan, K., & Clark, K. (2010). Designing game design studios: Strategies to sustain intrinsic motivation. In *Proceedings of World Conference on Educational Multimedia, Hypermedia and Telecommunications 2010* (pp. 2911–2920). Chesapeake, VA: AACE. Available at http://www.editlib.org/p/35055

Sheridan, K. M., Clark, K., & Williams, A. (2013). Designing games, designing roles: A study of youth agency in an informal education program. *Urban Education.*

Sheridan, K., & Gardner, H. (2012). Artistic development: Three essential spheres. In A. Shimamura & S. Palmer (Eds.), *Aesthetic science: Connecting minds, brains, and experience* (pp. 277–296). Oxford: Oxford University Press.

Solso, R. L. (2001). Brain activities in an expert versus a novice artist: An fMRI study. *Leonardo, 34*(1), 31–34.

Stevenson, H. (1994). *The learning gap: Why our schools are failing and what we can learn from Japanese and Chinese education.* New York: Simon & Schuster.

Stigler, J. W., & Hiebert, J. (1999). *The teaching gap: Best ideas from the world's teachers for improving education in the classroom.* New York: Free Press.

Tishman, S., Jay, E., & Perkins, D. N. (1993). Teaching thinking dispositions: From transmission to enculturation. *Theory Into Practice, 32,* 147–153.

Tishman, S., Perkins, D. N., & Jay, E. (1995). *The thinking classroom: Learning and teaching in a culture of thinking.* Boston: Allyn & Bacon.

Vaughn, K. (2000). Music and mathematics: Modest support for the oft-claimed relationship. *Journal of Aesthetic Education, 34*(3–4), 149–166.

Vaughn, K., & Winner, E. (2000). SAT scores of students who study the arts: What we can and cannot conclude about the association. *Journal of Aesthetic Education, 34*(3–4), 77–89.

Vygotsky, L. (1978). *Mind in society: The development of higher psychological processes.* Cambridge, MA: Harvard University Press.

Vygotsky, L. (1984). *Thought and language.* Cambridge, MA: MIT Press.

Winner. E., & Cooper, M. (2000). Mute those claims: No evidence (yet) for a causal link between arts study and academic achievement. *Journal of Aesthetic Education,* 34(3–4), 11–75.

Winner, E., & Hetland, L. (Eds.). (2000). The arts and academic achievement: What the evidence shows. *Journal of Aesthetic Education, 34*(3–4), 3–307.

Winner, E., & Hetland, L. (2007, Sept. 2). Art for our sake. *Boston Globe,* pp. E1–2. Reprinted in *Arts Education Policy Review, 109*(5), 29–32 (2008, May/June); and in *National Arts Education Association News,* 1 (2007).

Winner, E., & Simmons, S. (Eds.). (1992). *Arts PROPEL: A handbook for visual arts.* Cambridge, MA: Project Zero at the Harvard Graduate School of Education and Educational Testing Service.

Wiske, M. S. (1998). *Teaching for understanding: Linking research with practice.* San Francisco: Jossey-Bass.

Index

About the Authors

Lois Hetland is professor and chair of Art Education at Massachusetts College of Art and Design and senior research affiliate at Project Zero, Harvard Graduate School of Education. She received her Ed.D. from the Harvard Graduate School of Education in 2000. Trained in music and visual arts and formerly an elementary and middle school classroom teacher for 17 years, her work as a developmental psychologist focuses on learning, understanding, and teaching in the arts and other disciplines. Her most recent prior research was a series of meta-analytic reviews for Reviewing Education and the Arts Project (REAP), 1997–2000, including two reviews of music's effects on spatial reasoning. That project's work was published in an invited special issue of the *Journal of Aesthetic Education*, which she co-edited. REAP has been widely discussed in *Beyond the Soundbite: Arts Education and Academic Outcomes* (co-editor, 2001), in a dedicated issue of the *Arts Education Policy Review* (May/June, 2001), in commentary on National Public Radio, and in articles in *The New York Times, Education Week*, and numerous other newspapers and magazines. Lois was co-principal investigator of Project Zero's subcontract to the Alameda County Office of Education's VALUES Project (Visual Arts Learning for Understanding Education in Schools) and of a second subcontract focused on the spread of that pilot, both funded by the United States Department of Education. She was also a co-principal investigator of the Qualities of Quality Project, funded by the Wallace Foundation, served as education chair of Project Zero's annual summer institute from 1996 to 2005, taught online professional development courses for teachers on Harvard's WIDE platform (Widescale Interactive Development for Educators) from 2000 to 2005, and consults nationally and internationally on arts and on teaching and learning for understanding. She authored the staff development guide to Project Zero's video series, *Educating for Understanding*, and co-edited two volumes based on Project Zero's institutes.

Ellen Winner is professor and chair of Psychology at Boston College and a senior research associate at Project Zero, Harvard Graduate School of Education. She received her Ph.D. in developmental psychology from Harvard University in 1978. Her research focuses on learning and cognition in the arts in typical and gifted children. She is the author of more than 100 articles and three books: *Invented Worlds: The Psychology of the Arts*, *The Point of Words: Children's Understanding of Metaphor and Irony*, and *Gifted Children: Myths and Realities*, which has been translated into eight languages and was awarded the Alpha Sigma Nu National Jesuit Book Award in Science. She received the Rudolf Arnheim Award for Outstanding Research by a Senior Scholar in Psychology and the Arts from the American Psychological Association. She is a fellow of the American Psychological Association (Division 10, Psychology and the Arts) and of the International Association of Empirical Aesthetics.

Shirley Veenema is an instructor in visual arts at Phillips Academy, in Andover, Massachusetts, and was a researcher at Harvard Project Zero from 1987 to 2007. She served as project manager and videographer of this project. Originally focused on printmaking and mixed media drawing, much of her current work as an artist is also in media and artist books. Her media work includes five videos for the show, *Dangerous Curves: Art of the Guitar*, at The Museum of Fine Arts, Boston, and a series of interactive documentaries funded by the Cultural Landscape Foundation.

Kimberly M. Sheridan is an assistant professor in the College of Education and Human Development and the College of Visual and Performing Arts at George Mason University. She received her Ed.D. from the Harvard Graduate School of Education in 2006. Trained in the visual arts and developmental psychology, her work in the learning sciences focuses on how contexts and technologies shape learning, with a particular focus on new media and arts learning. From 2007–2011 she was co-principal investigator, with Dr. Kevin Clark, on the National Science Foundation-funded project, *Game Design Through Mentoring and Collaboration*, where traditionally underserved youth in the Washington, DC area learn 3-D modeling, animation, and game design using a studio model informed by the Studio Thinking Framework. Their work has been featured in numerous outlets, including a documentary by the George Lucas Foundation on *Edutopia*. In 2012, she received a National Science Foundation Cyberlearning grant to co-direct, with Dr. Erica Halverson, the study, *Learning in the Making: Studying and Designing Makerspaces*, in which they research learning in informal communal studios that often combine arts and engineering, and collaborate with the Children's Museum of Pittsburgh's *Makeshop* to design and study making learning experiences.